ROYAL HISTORICAL SOCIETY
STUDIES IN HISTORY

LEGAL RECORDS AND THE HISTORIAN

Volumes already published in this series

Copies obtainable on order from
Swift Printers Ltd., 1-7 Albion Place, Britton Street, London EC1M 5RE

LEGAL RECORDS AND THE HISTORIAN

Papers presented to the Cambridge
Legal History Conference, 7-10 July
1975, and in Lincoln's Inn Old Hall
on 3 July 1974

Edited by

J. H. Baker

LONDON
ROYAL HISTORICAL SOCIETY
1978

© J.H. Baker 1978

ISBN 0 901050 41 5

The Society records its gratitude to the following, whose generosity made possible the initiation of this series: The British Academy; The Pilgrim Trust; The Twenty-Seven Foundation; The United States Embassy's Bicentennial funds; The Wolfson Trust; several private donors.

Printed in England
by Swift Printers Ltd
London, E.C.1.

THIS VOLUME IS DEDICATED
TO THE MEMORY OF

George Derek Gordon Hall
died 15 September 1975

and

Cecil Anthony Francis Meekings
died 20 January 1977

CONTENTS

NOTE ON THE CONTRIBUTORS

J.H. Baker

University Lecturer in Law, and fellow of St. Catharine's College, Cambridge.

Thomas G. Barnes

Professor of Law and History, University of California at Berkeley.

P.A. Brand

Lecturer in Law, University College, Dublin. In 1975 Dr. Brand was assistant keeper of public records, London.

C.W. Brooks

Platnauer Junior Research Fellow in Modern History, Brasenose College, Oxford. In 1975 Mr. Brooks was a research student of Linacre College, Oxford.

J.S. Cockburn

Professor of English History, University of Maryland.

DeLloyd J. Guth

Until 1977 Dr. Guth was a Lecturer in History, University of Lancaster.

C.A.F. Meekings

In 1974 Mr. Meekings was an assistant keeper of public records, and Librarian of the Public Record Office. He died on 20 January 1977.

Dorothy M. Owen

Curator in Ecclesiastical Archives, University Library Cambridge, and fellow of Wolfson College, Cambridge.

J.B. Post

Assistant keeper of public records.

W.R. Prest

Senior Lecturer in History, University of Adelaide.

Sue Sheridan Walker

Associate Professor of History, Northeastern University, Chicago.

NOTE ON THE CONFERENCES

The first Legal History Conference in the present series was held at Aberystwyth on 18-21 July 1972, and the proceedings have been published as *Legal History Studies 1972* (Cardiff, 1975). Such was the success of that conference, that those present appointed a Conference Continuation Committee to arrange another. The committee decided to hold the second residential conference in Cambridge, and to arrange a one-day meeting in London in the interim.

The one-day meeting took place on 3 July 1974, by kind permission of the Treasurer and Masters of the Bench of Lincoln's Inn, in Lincoln's Inn Old Hall. The following papers were delivered: 11.15 a.m., Mr. Meekings' paper (printed below, 97-139); 2.15 p.m., Mr. Post's paper (printed below, 150-64); 3.00 p.m., Professor Dafydd Jenkins, 'Two Seventeenth-Century Cases on Limited Liability' (printed under a slightly different title in *Cambridge Law Journal* 34 (1975), 302-21); 4.45 p.m., Professor A.W.B. Simpson, 'Innovation in Nineteenth-Century Contract Law' (Printed in 91 *LQR* (1975), 247-78).

The Cambridge Legal History Conference was held on 7-10 July 1975 at the invitation of the Faculty Board of Law, University of Cambridge, and was accommodated in St. Catharine's College and Sidney Sussex College. The following papers were delivered: Monday, 7 July, 9 p.m., Professor P.G. Stein, 'Vacarius and Roman Law in Twelfth-Century England' (printed in *Church and Government in the Middle Ages*, ed. C.N.L. Brooke and others (Cambridge, 1976), 119-37). Tuesday, 8 July, 9.30 a.m., Professor Barnes's paper (printed below, 7-28); 11.00 a.m., Mr. Brook's paper (printed below, 41-59); 11.30 a.m., Dr. Prest's paper (printed below, 165-84); 12 noon, Professor J.H. Langbein, 'The Privy Council's Use of Torture to Investigate Crime' (a foretaste of a larger work recently published); 5.00 p.m., Dr. M.T. Clanchy, 'Law and Love in Highworth Hundred, Wiltshire, 1275-87'; 6.00 p.m., Dr. Brand's paper (printed below, 29-40); 6.30 p.m., Professor R.B. Pugh, 'The Writ *de Bono et Malo*' (printed in 92 *LQR* (1976), 258-67); 9.00 p.m., Dr. Cockburn's paper (printed below, 60-79). Wednesday, 9 July, 9.30 a.m., Professor W.M. McGovern, 'Why the Tenant for Years was not a Freeholder' (printed in extended form as 'The Historical Conception of a Lease for Years', *U.C.L.A. Law Review* 23 (1976), 501-28); 11.00 a.m., Professor M.S. Arnold, 'Fourteenth-Century Promises' (printed in *Cambridge Law Journal* 35 (1976), 321-34); 11.30 a.m., Professor Walker's paper (printed below,

185-206); 12 noon, Dr. Owen's paper (printed below, 140-9); 4.00 p.m., Dr. D.J. Guth's paper (printed below, 80-96). Thursday, 10 July, 9.30 a.m., Professor Dr. H. Coing, 'English Literature concerning the Civil Law before 1800' (incorporated substantially in 'Das Schriftum der englischen Civilians und die Kontinentale Rechtsliteratur in der Zeit zwischen 1550 und 1800', *Ius Commune* 5 (1975), 1-55).

A third residential conference was held at the University of Edinburgh on 11-14 July 1977, and a fourth is being planned for the University of Birmingham in July 1979. The Conference Continuation Committee in 1975 were: Dr. J.H. Baker, Mr. G.D.G. Hall, Mr. A. Harding, Professor D. Jenkins, Mr. C.A.F. Meekings and Professor S.F.C. Milsom. Invaluable assistance during the week of the conference was given by Mrs. J.H. Baker. The editor acknowledges his gratitude to them all, and also to Professor G.R. Elton for subsequent assistance. Two members of the committee (Mr. Hall and Mr. Meekings) have since died, each a tragic loss to all historians interested in legal records. The sadness of that recollection is relieved by the memory retained by those who saw them for the last time in Cambridge, happy and content, despite full knowledge of their afflictions, to be among friends and colleagues with whom they could share their love of legal history. This volume is, by the common wish of all concerned, dedicated to their memory.

ABBREVIATIONS

Note: in references to record publications in which the entries are separately numbered, the page-number is given first and then (after a colon) the entry-number.

BIHR   *Bulletin of the Institute of Historical Research* (London, 1923-   ).

BNB   *Bracton's Note-Book: A Collection of Cases decided in the King's Courts during the Reign of Henry the Third, annotated by a Lawyer of that Time, seemingly by Henry of Bratton,* ed. F.W. Maitland (London, 1887). Three volumes.

Bod. Lib.   Bodleian Library, Oxford.

Bracton   *Bracton on the Laws and Customs of England,* ed. [G.H. Woodbine and] S.E. Thorne (Cambridge, Mass., 1968-77). Four volumes.

Brit. Lib.   British Library, London.

C   Public Record Office, Chancery series. C 66, Patent Rolls; C 143, Inquisitions *ad quod damnum.*

CCR   *Calendar of the Close Rolls preserved in the Public Record Office* (H.M.S.O., 1892-   ).

CIM   *Calendar of Inquisitions Miscellaneous (Chancery) preserved in the Public Record Office* (H.M.S.O., 1916-   ).

CP   Public Record Office, Common Pleas series. CP 11, Rolls of Attorneys 1730-50; CP 40, De Banco Rolls; CP 43, Recovery Rolls (from 1583); CP 52, Writs (under arrangement, by counties).

CPR   *Calendar of the Patent Rolls preserved in the Public Record Office* (H.M.S.O., 1891-   ).

CR   *Close Rolls of the Reign of Henry III preserved in the Public Record Office* (H.M.S.O., 1902-38). Fourteen volumes. After Henry III, the Close Rolls are calendared: *CCR.*

CRR   *Curia Regis Rolls preserved in the Public Record Office* (H.M.S.O., 1922-   ).

E	Public Record Office, Exchequer series. E 159, King's Remembrancer's Memoranda Rolls; E 215, Papers of the Commission on Fees; E 368, Lord Treasurer's Remembrancer's Memoranda Rolls.
EHR	*English Historical Review* (London, 1886-).
Fitz. N.B.	A. Fitzherbert, *La nouvelle Natura brevium* (1534). References are to the 1635 edition.
Folger Lib.	Folger Shakespeare Library, Washington D.C.
Glanvill	*The Treatise on the Laws and Customs of England commonly called Glanvill,* ed. G.D.G. Hall (London, 1965).
IND	Public Record Office, Index Room series. Included in this series are the Chief Clerks' Docket Rolls of the King's Bench, and the Prothonotaries' Docket Rolls of the Common Pleas.
JUST	Public Record Office, 'Justices Itinerant' series. JUST 1, Eyre Rolls, Assize Rolls, etc.
KB	Public Record Office, King's Bench series. KB 9, Ancient Indictments; KB 26, Curia Regis Rolls; KB 27, Coram Rege Rolls; KB 29, Controlment Rolls; KB 136, Brevia (files); KB 146, Panella (files). See also the tables below, 125-7.
LHS 1972	*Legal History Studies 1972: Papers presented to the Legal History Conference at Aberystwyth, 18-21 July 1972,* ed. Dafydd Jenkins (Cardiff, 1975).
LQR	*Law Quarterly Review* (London, 1885-).
PR	*Patent Rolls of the Reign of Henry III preserved in the Public Record Office* (H.M.S.O., 1901, 1903). Later rolls are calendared: *CPR.*
PRO 12	Public Record Office, Repair Registers.
PRS	*Publications of the Pipe Roll Society* (London, 1884-).
RDK	*Reports of the Deputy Keeper of Public Records* (H.M.S.O., 1840-88).
RP	*Rotuli Parliamentorum; ut et Petitiones, et Placita in Parliamento* [London, 1783]. Six volumes; and index (1832).
RS	'Rolls Series': *Chronicles and Memorials of Great*

	Britain and Ireland during the Middle Ages, published under the Direction of the Master of the Rolls (London, 1858-1911).
SP	Public Record Office, State Papers series.
SR	*Statutes of the Realm* (Record Commission, London, 1810-25). Eleven volumes.
SS	*Publications of the Selden Society* (London, 1887-).
STAC 8	Public Record Office, Star Chamber Proceedings in the Reign of James I.
TRHS	*Transactions of the Royal Historical Society* (London, 1873-).
WARDS 14	Public Record Office, Court of Wards and Liveries series. 'Miscellaneous Pleadings'.

Year books are cited by term, regnal year, folio, and case number, in that order, from the old collected printed editions. There is a full bibliography of the old year books in A.W. Pollard and G.R. Redgrave, *A Short-Title Catalogue of Books printed in England . . . 1475-1640* (London, 1969 ed.), 213-8 (nos 9551-67). There was an inaccurate reprint of the collected editions, in nine large folio volumes, in 1679-80. Earlier year books in modern editions are cited, in similar manner, from *RS* and *SS* series as indicated. For the abbreviations used in citing later law reports, see *A Manual of Legal Citations* (Institute of Advanced Legal Studies, 1959), i, 39-75.

INTRODUCTION

J.H. Baker

The flourishing state of English legal history needs no further demonstration than is afforded by the success of the series of conferences to which the following papers were contributed. The extent of interest in these conferences has exceeded all expectations, and the diversity of current research in legal materials has also been a surprising revelation. It is remarkable, too, how many of the scholars concerned were under the impression that their interests were peculiar to themselves. One of the main objects of the conference-organisers has been to make all students of legal history familiar with other points of view, and in particular to lower the disciplinary barriers which have traditionally existed between legal historians trained in law and those trained first in history. It is easy to see how such barriers erected themselves. When anyone with formal qualifications in one discipline strays into another he is apt to be regarded, and perhaps even to regard himself, as at best a fumbling amateur and at worst an unwelcome interloper. The historian tended to despise the lawyer as a soul lost to true history because of a training which encouraged him to confuse past and present and to revere authority before reality. The lawyer tended to assume that a historian could never grasp the intellectual history of a discipline into whose mysteries he had not been formally initiated, and would perforce seek refuge from the pains of jurisprudence in the minutiae of facts and figures or in empty generalisations about human nature or social behaviour. Most of us do, of course, suffer from partial blindness of the intellect as a result of our differing educational backgrounds; but most of us have specialist insights by way of compensation, and there can no longer be any excuse for such mutual suspicion or indifference as we have just parodied. One of the most pleasing consequences of establishing an international community of scholars interested in English legal history is the pervasive sense of cooperation and consultation between those with different approaches to similar topics. This volume is itself a reflection of the new spirit of comity. The two gatherings from which the papers are selected were both held under the auspices of traditional law schools; yet the contributors have all been students or teachers in history departments, and much of their work is different in kind from the lawyers' legal history as taught in the Cambridge Law School or in Lincoln's Inn. The selection, made by an editor who teaches legal history to lawyers in both places, is not intended as a slight on the papers of his brother lawyers, most of which are available in print elsewhere: it has been made with the more specific purpose of illustrating the variety of ways in which legal records may be used to further historical scholarship.

If there is one need upon which all English legal historians should be expected to agree, it is that of devoting as much effort as possible to the exploitation of the surviving records of the many courts which have existed in this country. Difficulty of access brought to an end the tradition of record scholarship begun by the prothonotaries and avidly pursued by lawyers such as Prynne and Hale in the seventeenth century. Yet, although that difficulty has been removed by the establishment of the Public Record Office, it has taken a whole century for the importance of the records of litigation to be fully and generally appreciated. The early medievalist was thrown upon the rolls by necessity; but only after much pioneering work by year-book editors, by legal historians seeking to augment the evidence of the law reports, and by historians chasing local or personal details or topics little connected with the law, has the realisation begun to dawn that the historical value of legal records is no less — and often substantially greater — for periods from which a wealth of non-record literature is available. It would be unkind to blame writers such as Holdsworth too severely for not reading plea rolls; they had enough to do exploring the vast mass of literary sources, and they have laid a foundation which others may build upon or destroy. It is easier to rewrite history than to introduce it; and it is a pleasure reserved for the present generation to set out on explorations of the records, assisted by plans constructed by painful scholarship, but never knowing whether the plans will point them in the right direction.

The most obvious use of plea rolls is to trace the history of the substantive law, and this will doubtless be the main concern of the legally trained. With respect to the common law, the task calls for an understanding of special pleading and of the technicalities of legal processes; a discussion of the methods will be more timely when a number of exploratory works now in preparation have been published by the Selden Society. The papers in this volume which treat of the substantive law are mostly concerned with legislation. Legislation has traditionally been given more attention by the history schools than has the common law, perhaps because acts of parliament seem more definitive and accessible than decisions of judges, and because the processes of legislation more readily lend themselves to historical analysis. Until recently, however, a great deal of work on the earlier statutes has necessarily, for want of journals or legislative drafts, been limited to textual analysis and exegesis. The papers by Dr. Brand, Dr. Post and Professor Walker show how much the plea rolls can contribute to the study of early legislation. Records of cases preceding legislation may show how statutory remedies had been anticipated by custom or by ex gratia royal intervention, with the result that the legislation must be viewed not as an act of innovation but as a decisive statement or extension of an earlier rule or practice. The records may show that the statute itself arose out of some specific difficulty in the course of litigation, so that parliament is seen to have been acting more as a supreme court of law than as a legislative assembly as now understood. And records of cases decided after the passage of a statute may show how statutes were proved, understood, modified, or even ignored, by the king's courts. Perhaps it is already common learning that legislation was not always the decisive act of law reform which it later became, and that contemporaries did not view law emanating from parliament as fundamentally different from common law. The newer lesson to be learned is that the study of medieval legislation must begin and end, not with the text, but with the plea rolls.

Another obvious use of the records of legal proceedings is as sources of factual information. Since the central courts produced so much written parchment – in the sixteenth century over three miles of it every year – their records are as a rule more likely to yield references to particular people, places or things than any other class of document. There are probably more pedigrees in the plea rolls than in the heraldic visitations, more casual information about manors and churches, peers and peasants, merchants and lawyers, than can regularly be found elsewhere. It is not within the scope of this volume to discuss the range of such uses, since they have little to do with legal history. But the legal historian can save the fact-seeker from the kind of error which could so easily follow from an imperfect understanding of the way the record came to be made. The vast majority of records do not purport to record true facts, but only allegations or presentments. Even when issue was joined and a verdict taken, the verdict cannot necessarily be assumed to support all the details alleged, because the jury might have been directed or have chosen to decide the issue on the substantial merits rather on the truth of every minor allegation. This grave limitation can never be ignored by anyone who wishes to use legal records for historical purposes. Dr. Cockburn's paper affords a cogent demonstration of the danger in relying on even minor details of places and occupations in indictments and recognizances, which are often at variance with each other. Dr. Cockburn's method may be applied to the records of civil suits where the parties litigated the same matter in a diversity of courts: a practice which, as Professor Barnes remarks, was common in the early-modern period. When allegations in a bill in Chancery or Star Chamber are compared with those in common-law pleadings relating to the same subject-matter, the extent to which facts could be distorted or selectively presented becomes strikingly apparent. It is burdensome, without calendars, to trace parallel suits in different courts; but it is now clear that, in order to build anything like a true picture of the nature of a particular dispute — and that, rather than the objective truth, is usually the only practicable goal — such tedious searches cannot safely be avoided. There are other good reasons for studying the records of different courts in parallel, not least of which is widespread uncertainty as to what will be found where. For example, historians investigating the use of bonds, recognizances and penal actions under Henry VII and Henry VIII might reasonably look at the King's Bench and Exchequer rolls; but, if they stopped there, they would miss most of the evidence, because kings and their ministers (contrary to popular belief) used the Common Pleas. Students of crime and disorder who looked only at Crown proceedings would also lose some of the best evidence available, the appeals of felony recorded on the plea-side of the King's Bench. We could all multiply examples from our own experience, while falling into similar errors ourselves. There is no simple way of avoiding the problem, which will only be overcome by the more thorough exploitation of the records, with as much cooperation as possible between those with different interests.

The one subject for which the records of law courts furnish an abundance of accurate evidence is the history of litigation, and social historians are just becoming aware that litigation played such a central part in the life of the nation that it merits study in its own right. Here, too, there are warnings to be issued; and Professor Barnes and Mr. Brooks make some telling points. The layman is sometimes unaware that the vast majority of suits commenced in the courts never reach a conclusion and are probably not intended to: this is as true today as it was in medieval times. The commencement of proceedings may itself be sufficient to secure satisfaction out of court, it may be a means of compelling serious negotiation with a view to compromise, or it may simply be a form of annoyance in a prolonged feud. Any attempt to evaluate the legal system merely in terms of judgments and their enforcement would therefore be quite misguided. Attempts to assess the litigiousness of the people or of particular classes are also fraught with difficulty. Again, it would be absurd to confine attention to any one court, because increases in the business of one court are often offset by — or may even be the direct result of — the decline of others. Even the statistical investigation of the records of one court requires meticulous attention to detail: there may be several entries relating to one case, perhaps in different bundles, or there may be only one; there may sometimes be no entry on the rolls at all, in which case the files come into their own. The use of short-cuts, such as the docket rolls, presents fresh dangers: for instance, part of the increase in King's Bench business shown by the docket rolls is illusory because it represents a shift to bill procedure, and a consequent shift of business from the filazers (none of whose entries were docketed) to the chief clerk (all of whose entries were). Mr. Brooks has grappled with some of these difficulties, and has come to the tentative conclusion that the level of litigiousness may have been more constant than contemporaries imagined.

The social historian will be wise to concern himself not only with litigation, but also with the profession on which it depended. By any reckoning lawyers were an important section of society, as any progress through English country houses or parish churches will immediately demonstrate; and to treat them simply as undifferentiated constituents of the 'gentry' class is to assume far more than is known. If the better class of lawyers has been unduly neglected as a group, the lower branches of the profession have been virtually ignored. Several of the contributions below show that this defect is at last being remedied; and, once more, records have proved more helpful than might have been supposed. Nor is this an 'early-modern' phenomenon: the editor has reason to think that the plea rolls are about to reveal much new information about the medieval legal profession.

Most accounts of legal records find it necessary to conclude on a note of gloom. The existence of the Public Record Office has transformed historical scholarship, but the records of the central courts are still not fully accessible. The bulk of the plea rolls is so great that they will never be indexed, let alone calendared. Yet, without indices, they are for some purposes virtually useless: if it takes a week to search for one case, as it well might, the potential expense for the researcher may exceed the value of the anticipated result and the week will be devoted to some more productive enterprise. For the same reason, Professor Barnes's valuable experiment with the Star Chamber records will not be extended to the common-law courts. Moreover, many common-law plea rolls are still 'unfit for production', and are unlikely to be made available to the present generation, however important their contents; conservation takes priority over historical impatience. Worse still, a large quantity of legal records has not even been sorted, and it is difficult to tell how much useful material will be found. This must be left for a later generation, but Mr. Meekings' achievements with the King's Bench files at least give us hope that something will be done. The story of how the files were recovered and arranged, mostly from a chaotic existence in the sacks into which they were thrown centuries ago, is told below in fascinating detail. The accompanying calendar and descriptions form a useful supplement to the printed guide to the Public Record Office. But, as Mr. Meekings himself explains, it will be a long time before these new classes of records are fully available to the public; and the corresponding Common Pleas files, many of them still in unsorted sacks, are perhaps ten times the bulk of those which occupied near twenty years of Mr. Meekings' career. The chief consolation for this generation is that there is more than enough to be done with the records available now. And the chief hope which our series of conferences has engendered is that the number of those prepared to undertake the work is at last on the increase.

STAR CHAMBER LITIGANTS AND THEIR COUNSEL, 1596 – 1641

Thomas G. Barnes

There is a charming tale of St Louis, Louis IX of France, sitting in judgment, perhaps under the oak at Vincennes or in the courtyard of the Conciergerie, and of the thief who, as sentence of death was passed upon him, moved the king to spare him for just one year so that he might have time to teach the king's horse to talk. St. Louis's incredulity was matched only by that of the old lag's condemned *copain* who growled that nothing could be gained by such a trick. 'Ah,' whispered the thief, 'something might be gained: within a year the king might be dead, I might be dead, the horse might be dead, the horse might talk.' I do not recall where this story comes from; or whether the king did indeed reprieve the thief. No matter. The thief's ingenious plea in stay of execution was a classic example of what much legal pleading has always been about: the try-on. Once used, the try-on could work. Repetition of the device is, though, less likely to succeed unless the try-on makes new law; if St Louis did spare the thief, I am sure he never spared another on that plea! So also with litigation of a very serious and profound nature. Although the individual try-on does not have much future, a system of litigation that permits, indeed encourages, a constant refining of pleading by a process of mutation and variation on a theme raises the try-on from the plane of forensic tactics to the realm of judicial strategy. Add to such procedural openness, vitality, and suppleness a considerable inchoateness in substantive law and the try-on becomes the vehicle for legal change. In the early decades of the seventeenth century, the English system of litigation was a system in which the try-on was an accepted and wholly acceptable device. To all the advantages that the try-on provided within a single jurisdiction were added the multiple opportunities of many jurisdictions, many courts, and this without a means of reconciling conflicting judgments or of giving ultimate conclusion to what could be virtually infinite litigation.

We can, too hastily, conclude that procedural suppleness, inchoate substantive law, and lack of appellate means to reconcile jurisdictional conflicts necessarily produce inordinate multiplicity of suits and interminable litigation. During a six months' leave this year I have worked in the National Archives in Paris studying the *Conseil Privé* under Henri IV, a court which was structurally but not functionally the

French cognate to the Star Chamber.[1] In the *Conseil Privé* there was almost no room whatever for innovative pleading, very little that was not adequately developed in the substantive law, and the *Conseil's* role was almost entirely to resolve conflicts of jurisdiction and to reconcile contradictory judgments on appeal. All very logical. What staggers me is how much litigating was going on in France at the end of the sixteenth and the early part of the seventeenth centuries, and how radically the amount of litigation increased in the first three decades of the latter in the *Conseil Privé* without any apparent diminution of the litigation in the 'sovereign courts'. Indeed, I have tentatively concluded that the assertiveness of the *Conseil Privé's* appellate, reglementary, and cassationary jurisdiction stimulated increased litigation rather than repressed it.

What can explain the marked increase in English litigation between 1540 and 1640? There is almost no agreement on the answer to that question. I have quite definite notions as to the more fundamental socio-economic and legal causes of the phenomenon, but these are not my particular concern here.[2] I want to deal with the more patent cause, the sensate motivator and yet the instrument of the fundamental causes: the litigant. The litigant given, his lawyers cannot be ignored. I must be honest in making clear that I believe that the litigants, not the lawyers, were the real determinant of the substantive law and, to a lesser extent, the procedural law. What the litigants wanted and were prepared to pay for, the lawyers would propose and the courts would dispose.

Thanks to that demanding and yet self-effacing 'assistant', the computer, I have under control for study purposes 8,228 actions brought by information or bill in Star Chamber between 1603 and 1625. All 'hard', quantitative, data in these cases are rendered amenable to systematic study. This affords statistical material which can illuminate some broad themes about the court's litigants and their litigation,

---

1 The relevant *fonds:* Archives Nationales, V61 et seq. (Arrêts from 1579) and V61221-1223 (Minutes de résultats, 1579-1614); see also U945A ('Du Conseil du Roy' by Michel de Marillac). The ongoing calendaring by a modest-sized staff under the direction of Prof. François Dumont, *Inventaire des Arrêts du Conseil Privé (Henri III et Henri IV)*, vol. I and II (3 fascicules) (Paris, 1969-   ) provides some idea of the nature and range of litigation in the *Conseil Privé*, though the individual entries are too often marred by errors and omissions.

2 T.G. Barnes, 'Due Process and Slow Process in the late Elizabethan-early Stuart Star Chamber', *American Journal of Legal History* 6 (1962), 337-8. The historian of the early Tudor Star Chamber, Dr. J.A. Guy, in his just published *The Cardinal's Court, The Impact of Thomas Wolsey in Star Chamber* (Hassocks, 1977), 126, goes into the general causes for increased litigation which are, in most instances, applicable a century later.

as well as providing a data-retrieval method to summon up 'literary' material from the Jacobean Star Chamber proceedings (STAC 8)[1] My apologies, but some statistics are unavoidable at the outset — nothing else can make quite so clear (and persuasively so) the nature of litigants and litigation.

About the plaintiffs. First, and most striking, is how infrequently the king was a plaintiff. Of the nearly 600 informations by the Attorney-General, only fifty-two can be positively identified as 'pro Rege' proceedings in furtherance of the greater interests of Crown and Commonwealth. The rest of the Attorney-General informations are on relation, and with few exceptions are indistinguishable from private-plaintiff bills. There were sixty-seven corporate or impersonal plaintiffs or relators: patentees, urban corporations, collegiate and capitular bodies, livery companies, and some park-keepers, foresters, and so forth, most of them suing on relation by the Attorney-General. A few individual plaintiffs sued on behalf of themselves and others — parishioners, or tenants of a manor — a primitive form of class action. There were numerous multiple-individual plaintiffs, most of them husband and wife (feme covert), and a few brothers, father-and-son, widow-and-children, or business partners.[2] The 375 women plaintiffs suing as feme sole are very interesting. The social status of 175 of them is known and they show a markedly higher percentage of gentry and noble status than do the men. Some were quite intrepid. Elizabeth and Frances, maiden daughters of the late Sir Henry Brunkard, each with a marriage portion of £3,000, took a house in the parish of St Clement Danes in order to follow their law suits. On a summer's evening in 1615 they repelled two unwanted, drunken callers — a young Bachelor of Arts from Oxford and his friend from the Middle Temple — by emptying a chamberpot of urine on their heads. The girls secured the indictment of the 'roaring boyes', and when they fled the justices' warrant filed a bill in Star Chamber in October charging defamation, conspiracy, unlawful assembly, and forcible entry and praying a *ne exeat regno* on the grounds they were likely to flee the

---

1 In the process of compiling *List and Index to the Proceedings in Star Chamber for the Reign of James I (1603-1625) in the Public Record Office, London, Class STAC 8*, 3 vols. (Chicago, 1975), I took the opportunity to complete the conflation of the class on a case-unification method undertaken earlier and familiar to two generations of searchers who have used the typescript list to the class in the Round Room; consequently, there has been a net diminution in the number of cases in STAC 8. References in this article to STAC 8 are to the class as rearranged; the physical order now follows the *List and Index*. The statistics which follow are collated from the computer tapes from which the *List and Index* was printed.

2 E.g. thirteen creditors as plaintiffs in STAC 8/121/3.

country.[1] Not bad for a brace of gentle ladies, violent but inviolable and very full of law! Overall, the social status of all plaintiffs and known relators, male and female, breaks down as shown in Table 1.

TABLE 1

status	percentage
Noble	3
Gentry	51
Professional and clergy	4
Merchants	6
Yeomen	14
Husbandmen, artisans, labourers	6
Corporate and impersonal	1
unknown status	15

Those of unknown status can be presumed to have been of the lower orders.

It is difficult to provide equally hard data as to social status of the defendants. Of the 65,000 defendants, I have noted the names of 35,000 of them, but the social status of 19,000 of these just is not given in the proceedings. This understood, those of gentle status comprise almost 50 per cent of the defendants whose status is known; comparable to the same element among the plaintiffs. Star Chamber litigation was gentlemen's business, first and foremost.

What is somewhat surprising in a court where a bill might easily charge scores of defendants with as many as a score of charges comprising eight distinct offences,[2] is the relatively modest number of defendants on an average. Only five of the extant cases have more than 100 (the largest, 185) defendants;[3] 90 per cent of the cases have between one and seventeen and 54 per cent between one and six defendants. The average number of defendants in a Star Chamber action was just over eight. Not all of the defendants charged in the bill would be served with process to appear. A great many of those served with subpoena *ad comparendum* (especially where, as in a riot, the number was high) would never appear or even be pursued.

Plotting the venues of cases by the counties of England and Wales and

1 STAC 8/62/13.

2 The record for the number of charges in a single bill would appear to have been the 278 charges in *Att.-Gen.* v. *Dr Craddocke* (1627) for extortion: Brit. Lib., Lansdowne MS. 620, f.36.

3 STAC 8/256/17 (102 defendants), 227/4 (115), 207/30 (144), 124/13 (166), 207/24 (185)

the cities of London and Westminster produces the rather surprising result that there are no surprising results. Conventional wisdom held Wales to be most litigious; we might suspect that the activity of the Council of the Marches would in fact markedly diminish Welsh cases in Star Chamber. Neither conclusion is borne out by comparing the venue breakdown against the best contemporary figures as to the relative population and wealth of English and Welsh counties, the second nationwide (1636) writ of shipmoney.[1] That assessment was based on recognized ability to pay the tax, and had a sophisticated and up-to-date factual foundation. The correspondence between the venues of Star Chamber cases and the 1636 assessment is so close as to leave no other conclusion than that Star Chamber suits were fairly evenly distributed in proportion to population and wealth. Some offences demonstrate marked local variations in incidence. For example, hunting cases, a highly specialized (and numerically insignificant) aspect of the court's litigation, were heavily concentrated in the south, the west, the midlands, and some of the home counties, with Wales, the Marches, the south-west, the north, and East Anglia only slightly represented. The areas of concentration were those heavily emparked and enchased, with an established magnate aristocracy: almost one-quarter of all hunting cases were brought by peers.

I would fain spare you more statistics, but those that I am moved to provide now point unambiguously to the nature of Star Chamber litigation. The most significant figure is that four-fifths of all 8,228 cases in the Jacobean proceedings had property at base in the litigation; that is, that the motive behind the suit turned upon either real or personal property or both:

subject-matter	percentage
Realty	20
Personalty (incl. chattels real)	40
Both personalty and realty	20
No property involved	20

Certain crimes as principal crimes indicate significant variations from these overall figures. For instance, forgery and perjury — for reasons that are self-evident — involved realty in 25 per cent (as against 20 per cent overall) of the cases. The high incidence of personalty in the case of rescue (53 per cent as against 40 per cent overall) reflected the high incidence of rescue of parties taken on King's Bench *latitat* principally in personal actions.

1   M.D. Gordon, 'The Collection of Ship-money in the Reign of Charles I', *TRHS* 4 (3rd. ser.), 156-162.

The second most significant statistic is intimately connected to the first. In 4,500 cases (55 per cent of the total) there is *explicit* indication that the parties were already at law either in Star Chamber or in some other court, and that the present action was connected in some manner to the other proceedings (see Table 2).

TABLE 2

other courts	percentage
Star Chamber (cross or shoring)	11
Chancery	14
King's Bench	16
Common Pleas	13
Exchequer	5
Requests	1
Wards and Liveries	2
Duchy of Lancaster	1
Councils of the Marches and of the North	3
Assizes and great sessions	5
'Common Law' courts (otherwise unspecified)	3
Ecclesiastical courts	7
Other courts and courts unspecified	18

Because I allowed space on the card for only one other court, and gave priority among conflicting claims (1) to another Star Chamber action, be it cross or shoring, and (2) to another action most directly related to the case in hand, the boldness of these percentages tends to obscure how often more than one other court was involved. Moreover, on computer-sorting of parties, a good many cases in which another Star Chamber action was not explicitly mentioned proved to be crossing or shoring actions. King's Bench was the clear leader. Among English-bill courts, only the Chancery could vie with the two major common-law courts: the Chancery, King's Bench, and Common Pleas accounted for 43 per cent of the cases. The Exchequer (mostly equity, not plea side), Requests, Wards, Duchy Chamber, and the regional Councils comprise only 12 per cent of the cases. The prominence of the ecclesiastical courts grows from the great many allegedly forged wills in suit in Star Chamber either during or after probate. Combining the English-bill courts — Star Chamber, Chancery, Exchequer, and the rest — produces 37 per cent of the total. The common-law courts comprise another 37 per cent. The remaining 26 per cent are ecclesiastical courts, minor jurisdictions, and unknown courts, including most of the genuinely criminal courts involved collaterally in Star Chamber suits.

If further confirmation is required of the essentially civil ends, albeit in criminal raiment, which the Star Chamber was to serve its litigants, it is provided by the relative incidence of the crimes charged arranged in broad categories.[1] Crimes against the Church, the state, and public policy comprise less than 3 per cent. Conceivably, the 6 per cent of the cases in which official malfeasance is charged might receive the august appellation of crimes against the state, but in fact usually the allegation of official misdeeds was merely aggravatory against an adversary who happened to be an official. Likewise with professional and occupational crimes (under 3 per cent), overwhelmingly levelled at lawyers of all types. Crimes in denigration of status – abduction (really a property offence, because an heir's estate was involved) and defamation – are a negligible 2 per cent, though defamation was a major contribution of the court to the substantive law. A sizeable 12 per cent are crimes against property: forgery, fraud, extortion, embezzlement, hunting. Crimes against justice, principally maintenance, champerty, embracery, perjury, subornation, abuse of legal proceedings, contempt, and rescue amount to almost 25 per cent. Crimes against justice are intimately linked to the litigants' proprietary concerns, because together with forgery and fraud they constituted the chief opportunity for mounting collateral actions touching other courts and impeaching other suits. The largest single category of crime charged (37 per cent) was crimes of violence – with riot, rout, unlawful assembly pre-eminent, and destruction of property and forcible entry as incidental to it. These percentages are calculated as if only one crime was charged, whereas in fact it was a rare bill that did not charge three to six crimes from two or three of these categories. Riot, like conspiracy, almost invariably involved other, more substantial crimes. Riot remained the hardy standby in Star Chamber bills. It smoothed over questions as to the court's ability to take cognizance of the case, and with conspiracy provided the procedural net that drew in the adversary's supporters – especially his witnesses – to scare them, to put them to costs, and to impeach their testimony. Lord Keeper Bishop Williams was profoundly correct when he observed in 1625, 'that whereas in ancient time the records of the court [of Star Chamber] are filled with battayles and ryottes soe outragious whereas now wee here not of one in our age.'[2] 'Riot' in Star Chamber proceedings had become virtually a term of art, an allegation for procedural advantage more often than a substantive charge.

---

1 For a brief treatment of crime in the later Star Chamber, see T.G. Barnes, 'Star Chamber and the Sophistication of the Criminal Law', *Criminal Law Review* [1977], 316-26.
2 Lansdowne MS. 620, f.3v.

We come now to the consideration of the motives behind Star Chamber suits. I propose treating them under three broad, and overlapping, headings: (1) short-term actions for gain; (2) collateral actions for advantage with respect to suits pending or determined elsewhere; (3) Star Chamber actions proper, mounted with intention of winning in Star Chamber. I have no statistics here; but, crudely put, the third category is the least pronounced though not the least important, and the first category if large is of minimal importance in terms of litigation as strategy. The second category, collateral actions, is both the most numerous and the most significant.

Short-term actions for gain need not detain us. There were some interesting variations, but the most common was the suit to extort a composition to cease prosecution. This was the well-recognized business practice of the common informer, though that type received little encouragement in Star Chamber and did not become evident there until after the common informers were driven out of the central common-law courts in the 1620s.[1] Less professional small-fry were responsible for the many hit-and-run bills put into Star Chamber. Labourers, husbandmen, and yeomen, some self-styled 'gent's, sometimes admitted *in forma pauperis* (a real abuse), sometimes suing by the Attorney-General on relation, brought most of those actions which while successfully withstanding special pleading never went beyond pleadings to proof.[2] Composition was readily allowed by the court. Indeed, the court seldom bothered whether a formal licence to compound had been sued out. The most eminent practiser in the court, William Hudson, in a rare case in which a relator compounded and was punished for it, defended easy compounding, and Chief Baron Walter (also formerly one of the most practised counsellors in the court) thought composition at any time before a case was set down for trial was a good thing.[3] Some compositions were very fast — four days after the bill was filed in one case.[4] Composition-actions were too common

---

1 An exceptionally active (probably not wholly successful) common informer was the notorious John Sutton, who had a good run in the later 1620s and early 1630s until the court and the Attorney-General combined to drive him away by scaring him off, Lincoln's Inn, MS. 'Starrchamber', f.109; also Harvard Law School, MS.1128, no.199; Bodl. Lib., Bankes MSS. 44/7-9; Folger Library, MS. V.a.278, sub 'S'.

2 For such relator actions, STAC 8/27/14 is a good example. See 41/11, 41/18, 90/12, and a very vexatious pauper in 114/9. One defendant, a merchant-stranger sued for trade deceit in Rhenish wines, smelt a composition action and quashed it with a demurrer that cited the heaviest authority (not all to the point) in standing upon 'the liberties established by Magna Charta and the lawe of nations': STAC 8/10/7.

3 Lansdowne MS. 620, ff.43v & 31.

4 STAC 8/41/18.

to be repressed by the court, too numerous to be controlled by the court, and they remained a grudgingly tolerated abuse.

The principal function of the Court of Star Chamber for the Jacobean litigant was to mount a collateral attack, either to shore up or to cross an action in another court, in furtherance of a large-scale strategy of litigation with the objective of winning a substantial prize. That prize was some form of property. There *were* pure grudge fights, great imbroglios of rivalry and revenge. Yet even the most vexatious of the court's litigants were engaged principally over substantial property interests: Henry, Earl of Lincoln, and his adversary Sir Edward Dymock;[1] Thomas Bard of Gray's Inn and Lincolnshire and Thomas Best of the Inner Temple and Somerset, the two most litigious barristers;[2] Edward Ewer, gent., of Bicknoll, Oxfordshire, 'a man full of subtiltye and cunninge and one that had gained some experience in the law by reason of his multiplicitye of suites wherin all his life tyme he had byn conversant. . . .'[3] Eternally springing hope for something quite substantial accounts for Ewer's notable career as litigant: seven Jacobean suits by him between 1620 and 1624, five suits (by old adversaries) against him, 1605-21, and nine fines imposed upon him by the court, 1597-1631, totalling £1,760, seven of them *pro falso clamore* or for contempt of court.[4] He knew the Fleet Prison better than did its warden.

With collateral actions real strategy entered in. Timing was of the essence from the plaintiff's point of view. The Star Chamber case must go like clockwork, for that mechanism had to be geared to the principal litigation elsewhere, whether the Star Chamber plaintiff was plaintiff or defendant in the other court or courts. When disaster struck the

---

1 STAC 8/17/17 (*Att.-Gen. pro Rege* v. *Earl of Lincoln*), 123/15 (*Dymocke* v. *Earl of Lincoln*); 91/16 (*Earl of Lincoln* v. *Dymocke*), 91/18 (*same* v. *same*), 91/22 (*same* v. *same*), 91/23 (*same* v. *same*). At one time or another, once on a suit and cross-suit, both these assiduous adversaries were fined by Star Chamber *pro falso clamore*.

2 For Best, STAC 8/48/16, 49/13, 61/27 (Thomas Best, plaintiff), 128/10, 177/6 (Thomas Best, defendant); for Bard, STAC 8/40/23 (Bard accused of maintenance), 52/4, 52/5, 56/1 (Bard, plaintiff), 128/5, 210/11, 210/11 (Bard, defendant).

3 *John Austin* v. *Edward Ewer* (1621) STAC 8/40/17.

4 STAC 8/137/3-8 (*Edward Ewer* v. *William Cope, Bt.*), 134/12 (*Edward Ewer* v. *Thomas Moyle*); suits against Ewer, STAC 8/40/17, 149/13, 149/14, 214/28, 214/29. Ewer fined: E 159/413, Trin. 39 Eliz. 1, 177; 421, Trin. 43 Eliz. 1, 64; 425, Hil. 1 Jac.1, 117 (2 fines); 444, Pas. 11 Jac. 1, 226; 448, Trin. 13 Jac. 1, 145; 468, Hil. 4 Car. 1, 2 (2 fines); 471, Trin. 7 Car. 1, 6. In Mich. 1626, Lord Keeper Coventry was prepared to give Ewer enough due-process rope to hang himself with — he was to answer in Star Chamber as soon as his Chancery case was heard or else be committed without further order, Lansdowne MS. 620, f.28v.

plaintiff it was usually the result of dyssynchronization between the actions. The plaintiff did not necessarily seek to win in Star Chamber; but he could not afford to lose too quickly, and he sought to avoid proceedings that endured so long as to become attritive.

The Star Chamber plaintiff had much going for him to assure a high degree of control over the conduct of his case at least through pleading and proof (pre-trial) proceedings. The procedural rules were sophisticated, relatively clear and precise, and even-handed toward both sides. They were very similar to the Chancery rules, but rather than being applied by a number of Masters in Chancery they were ruled upon by only one, the clerk (or deputy clerk) of the court, with resulting continuity. In practice the procedure was supple. A plaintiff who could retain (at some cost) the Attorney-General to proceed by relation had the added advantage of not being tied to the ordinary course of the court — that prerogative of the King's Attorney explains the popularity of relator-actions. A nimble solicitor, assiduously following the suits in all courts and keeping in close contact with the counsel retained and with the principal, was essential. A plaintiff was wise to retain as counsel one of the specializing practisers in the court; his knowledge of the course of the court and his familiarity with the court's four attorneys went far towards assuring smooth procedural progress.

The defendant's strategy was either a quick win, throwing the plaintiff entirely off-balance, or dilatoriness that put him to escalating charges and upset the synchronization of his suits. He, too, had much going for him: the same even-handed rules, able counsel, etc. Perhaps he benefited most from the ingrained acceptance of the necessity for procedural propriety and distaste for peremptoriness which was a long legacy of the system. Successive Lord Keepers from Egerton to Coventry had at least been concerned with, and in Egerton and Coventry had made strenuous attempts to deal with, dilatoriness.[1] The magnitude of the problem they faced is the most striking fact about the court. Dilatoriness began with defendants sitting-out process to appear. For example, between Easter term 1624 and Michaelmas term 1625, 1,871 subpoenas *ad comparendum* passed the seal; in that same period, 803 process of contempt for non-appearance passed: 43 per cent of the number of original process.[2] After he appeared, even if upon commission of rebellion, the defendant had three principal weapons of dilatoriness. The first was for him to move upon affidavit of his age or ill-health to answer and be examined by commission in the country — readily accorded. The second was to make insufficient answer or

---

1 Barnes, 'Due Process and Slow Process', 344-6.
2 PRO 30/38/21-22, process books, 1624-1627.

respond inadequately to the interrogatories at his examination (in the country, or in the office) thus forcing the plaintiff to obtain process *melior* upon certificate after reference to a law-officer or a judge.[1] Each device gained him at least a term's delay even if ultimately he had to pay costs. A variant of the first device was available at the proof stage: the motion to examine more witnesses. In one case, which had been completed through proofs and day-given by the plaintiff (the Attorney-General no less), upon which the court had ordered cause to be shown, the defendant obtained a commission to examine more witnesses which was not executed until eight months later.[2] But it was the third device which is both the most interesting and the most significant, and the one which afforded not only dilatoriness but the possibility of a quick win for the defendant: special-pleading. The demurrer or plea-in-bar was the tool of the best practisers at the Star Chamber bar, who were all masters of the demurrer and special plea. Hudson was the greatest of them all, and his demurrer for Edward Tawton in 1614 that persuaded the court that it would 'not examine what coloured hens the said Johan Taughton hath bred nor whether she hath bred any nor whether a hen were bred of an egge of her owne proper goodes',[3] was the most brilliant of his career! Overall between 1603 and 1625 there was special-pleading in 22.5 per cent of the cases in Star Chamber. What is arresting is the fact that there was a steady overall increase in the percentage of special-pleading to the number of bills put in, from about 16 per cent to about 30 per cent per annum, 1604-24. I stress percentage as ratio, because in that same period there was a steadily falling-off of the number of bills put in, from something over 400 per annum to about 250 per annum. The sudden falling off of litigation in Star Chamber took place in the 1630s. Yet there was a steady downward trend from at least the early years of James I's reign. There is no doubt in my mind that the relative increase in special-pleading influenced the relative decrease in litigation in Star Chamber. The court was becoming less a 'plaintiff's court' and more, perceptibly more, a 'defendant's court'.

Assuming that the plaintiff vaulted the special plea, assuming that he, his solicitor, and his counsel made shrewd provision for the delays caused by dilatoriness and kept the mechanisms of the suits meshed, he could only look forward to a very long haul to a possible win. From 1603 to 1625, the bulk of Star Chamber actions that went to publication required for the pre-trial segment from eight to twenty-one months

---

1 See a copy-book of certificates of referees, Brit. Lib., Additional MS. 37045 (Mich. 1593- Trin. 1595).

2 Earlier proceedings, *Att.-Gen. ex rel. Richard Cranley* v. *Richard Kingswell* (May 1615), cited in STAC 8/90/16.

3 STAC 8/257/24; demurrer, 7 Nov. 1614.

between filing of the bill and the last depositions of witnesses. Trial could not come sooner than three months after depositions; usually, almost two years would elapse before trial, less perhaps because of crowded cause-lists than because of the parties' utilization of procedural delays. Costs, including counsel's fees and payments to solicitors, as well as court costs, were rising. The marginal plaintiff had to make the hard choice whether the Star Chamber action was worth continuing. This brings us to the matter of the litigant's expectations of the court's value in the strategy of his suits.

The crudest and, because it could be stopped at any time without much harm done to the plaintiff's cause elsewhere, the cheapest Star Chamber collateral action was the nuisance suit. It did not address itself to a justiciable issue relevant to litigation in another court. This action was a cost-multiplier. The more complex the suit, the better. Many charges, many defendants — short of suffering penal costs (a peril but no certainty), the plaintiff for relatively little outlay put his opponent to considerable expense. A tithe dispute will serve to illustrate. *John Bussell* v. *Thomas Clowdesley and thirteen others,* over a rectory and tithes in Norfolk, charged lawyer's malfeasance (Clowdesley was a Common Pleas attorney), conspiracy, riot, destruction of property, forgery (of a warrant), perjury, vexatious litigation, and maintenance and champerty[1] All this was to counter by attrition Clowdesley's suits against Bussell in the Common Pleas and King's Bench for possession of the rectory on the basis of a debt action. The Star Chamber case was not really related to the other actions save for the rather feeble charge of champerty. Most such nuisance cases were highly ephemeral in that they seldom went beyond pleadings and examination of some of the defendants.

The discovery action was a purposeful collateral action. It sought to discover evidence, to expose conspirators, accomplices, or other culprits, to uncover trade practices, or even to discover business and technical secrets by putting the defendant to examination upon oath[2] A variant was, of course, examining witnesses, especially close cross-examination of the adversary's witnesses. This is the realm of 'fishing interrogatories'. They were very common, and if carefully drawn and adequately related to a plausible bill would usually be upheld and the defendant compelled to answer by process *melior* upon certificate of a law-officer or judge

1 STAC 8/61/34.
2 For examples of all such actions, STAC 8/10/13, 18/16, 91/6, 93/6, 41/1, 55/30; 61/44 is particularly interesting, since the attorney-defendant alleges the suit is only to force him to betray his client's cause in revealing a privileged communication.

referee. A number of bills explicitly prayed discovery, and this was the principal basis for the allegation of 'no recourse at common law'; in other words, the absence of certainty as to goods or evidence. How the evidence so obtained was used, the degree to which it was admissible elsewhere, depended upon the other jurisdiction. Apparently English-bill courts, especially the Chancery, were considered more favourably inclined to Star Chamber evidence; common-law courts less so.[1] In any event, what was discovered might be the key to successful evidence-eliciting in another court. It was alleged in two cases that the action had been brought only to supply defects in the plaintiff's pending (already post-publication) Chancery suit.[2] Process *duces tecum* and process directed to clerks of other courts were used frequently to bring in written evidence otherwise withheld from plaintiffs.[3] Once in Star Chamber, such evidence would not readily be used elsewhere, thus effectively arresting proceedings in another court.

A limited area of collateral actions were those brought essentially for interlocutory advantage. The Brunkard girls' prayer for process *ne exeat regno* might well have been to make the two 'roaring boyes' amenable to the criminal jurisdiction in which they had already been indicted. Prayers in bills for injunctions to stay proceedings elsewhere (that is, that the party be so enjoined) were few and at best a forlorn hope.[4] The court was very reluctant to grant such an injunction unless the other action was clearly posterior to the Star Chamber suit and patently wrongful. Injunctions to stay probate of wills in question in Star Chamber for suspicion of forgery were less infrequent but still few. Only in the area of granting possession pending trial was the court generous, and then only if the possession had been gotten by riot and the defendant confessed the riot. By the mid-1620s the court was becoming reluctant to grant possession under any circumstances except by decree after trial.[5]

Witness-impeachment was a major category of collateral actions. The crudest form was to charge the adversary's best witnesses as defendants, especially with perjury.[6] Unless there was substance to the charge, the

---

1 See the certificate of Master Thelwall in *Molineux* v. *Urricke* (24 Nov. 1624) in Chancery: C. Monro, *Acta Cancellaria* (1847) 316-7.

2 STAC 8/119/11, 70/14.

3 Lansdowne MS. 620, f.23v.

4 E.g. STAC 8/5/7, to stop a *quare impedit* action in Common Pleas.

5 Lansdowne MS. 620, f.23v.

6 STAC 8/78/11, wherein the defendants complained that all their witnesses had been made parties to the original suit to destroy their testimony; the original suit is

Star Chamber would sever the defendant-witnesses and even accept their testimony.[1] Unless the charge was prosecuted to conviction in Star Chamber, the value of the evidence of the defendant-witnesses elsewhere was little affected. 'Perplexing'[2] and terrifying witnesses was, however, probably pretty efficacious. A more subtle form of witness-impeachment was to bring two actions in Star Chamber, some time apart, and examine the same witnesses in both with a view to uncovering discrepancies in their testimony.[3]

The largest category of serious collateral actions were those which, for want of a better term, I call verdict-impeachment actions. Pre-eminently, these were suits charging (1) perjury in proceedings elsewhere, (2) forgery of a deed or will, the validity of which was in dispute or had been upheld by adjudication elsewhere, (3) fraud by which advantage had been gained and the advantage was in suit or had been adjudged elsewhere, (4) maintenance of suits and champertous buying of titles in suit elsewhere, and (5) embracery of a jury or of jurors who had given their verdict.[4] This remains the most complex and the cloudiest area of collateral actions, for it is very difficult to determine what effect success in Star Chamber had on proceedings elsewhere. In the matters of perjury and embracery, the Star Chamber adamantly refused to proceed until the judgment allegedly obtained by perjured evidence or upon the verdict of an embraced jury had been rendered by the other court;[5] moreover, the plaintiff could not win in Star Chamber if he had not suffered palpable loss by that judgment. However, the Star Chamber would determine the validity of an alleged forgery even while the instrument was in suit elsewhere.[6] This led to finely-wrought issues as

---

24/2. STAC 8/29/10, a suit to discredit witnesses in a High Commission case. Similarly, STAC 8/103/18. See STAC 8/107/11.

1   STAC 8/88/18. Coventry L.K. took strong exception to the practice of charging witnesses as defendants, Lansdowne MS. 620, f.21-21v.

2   STAC 8/70/14.

3   STAC 8/16/10, which alleges this practice in 267/14 and 275/2; 16/10 is a veritable compendium of witness-impeachment tricks.

4   Such cases are many; good examples are STAC 8/8/2, 10/2, 11/17, 11/19, 13/11, 20/30, 23/15. There are 121 cases in STAC 8 of entire juries charged with 'perjured' verdict, i.e. finding against the evidence because of embracery. One case is very interesting: the plaintiff alleges that the jury at nisi prius was so partial, having been given a 'brief note' of the defendant's title before trial, that the plaintiff on the advice of counsel suffered a verdict to pass against him without offering evidence rather than hazard his title, STAC 8/114/2.

5   William Hudson, 'A Treatise of the Court of Star Chamber', *Collectanea Juridica*, 2, ed. F. Hargrave (London, 1792), 80.

6   STAC 8/61/40.

to which court should have possession of the instrument.[1] In one notable case, Star Chamber damned a deed which had been found good by three juries, even though the forger was not a defendant charged in the Star Chamber bill.[2] Maintenance and champerty suits were brought both before and after judgment had passed elsewhere, but the effect of sentence passed in Star Chamber upon judgment elsewhere is very obscure. All such actions depended upon prosecution in Star Chamber to trial and sentence. Fraudulent conveyances, even failure to give notice of encumbrances to a purchaser, could result in damages in Star Chamber.[3] There is no doubt about the effect of a decree damning a deed or will: the instrument was 'null and void at law', kept in the court's possession or even physically cancelled, or the defendant enjoined not to put it in execution.[4] Serious conflicts questions arose. In *Brakenburie's Case,* both the Star Chamber and the Prerogative Court of Canterbury damned a will, but the latter court found the forged will 'proved sufficientlie' to revoke all previous wills and so the estate was put into intestacy.[5] As to what might be done with a Star Chamber decree impeaching a judgment elsewhere, I would suggest, tentatively, that the decree had value if the successful plaintiff brought a new action at common law or in equity (within the rules permitting the same) and then put the proceedings and decree in evidence at the new trial. As Lord Keeper Coventry put it, in the case of a forged deed, 'the plaintiff in a tryall at the comon lawe. . .may have advantage of all deposicions taken in this court. . . .'[6] It was up to the other court to determine the admissibility of the same.

With collateral actions which must be successfully prosecuted through trial to decree we have come to Star Chamber actions proper. There is really no distinction to be made between collateral and proper actions by the 1620s, because from the second decade of the seventeenth century what the persevering plaintiff in Star Chamber sought was damages. The court very rarely awarded damages before 1600, and then usually pursuant to statute.[7] The critical turning point came in 1614 in a case where both sides argued the range of Star Chamber's powers and

---

1   Lansdowne MS. 620, f.36v, in which Star Chamber on motion allowed a forged deed to be taken out of court for use in evidence in 'matter collaterall' in some English-bill proceedings (whether Star Chamber or another court is not clear).

2   Lansdowne MS. 620, ff. 21v-22v.

3   Ibid. ff. 42-42v.

4   STAC 8/22/5, citing verbatim decree damning the will in suit in 199/14.

5   STAC 8/76/12. See also STAC 8/60/13-14, earlier suits in same matter.

6   Lansdowne MS. 620, f.37.

7   STAC 8/55/17, indicates the modest damages occasionally given c.1600: fine to king of £333.6s.8d., and damages to plaintiff of £50.

particularly whether damages could be awarded by the court and how they would be levied.[1] Henceforth, damages were readily given and that generously. Writing about 1626, Hudson observed: 'For damages to the wronged party this court is the best jury; and when they have justly discerned the wrong, they make the most ample recompence, and requite the wronged person's labour and travel sometimes with all his injury.'[2] Whatever problems a successful plaintiff might have in impeaching the verdict of another court, he could expect damages in Star Chamber that would perhaps offset his loss by the adverse judgment. Moreover, the levying of his damages and costs by Star Chamber process took precedence over the levying of the fine to the king by Exchequer process.[3] In this respect, if in no other, the Star Chamber looked more and more like the King's Bench in 1625.

Having said rather more about litigants than I had intended, I wish to conclude with a look at their lawyers. The Proceedings are rich in information about the litigants' professional aides, and the relationship between litigant and lawyer. Upon the suitor's solicitor fell the task of following the legal campaign in the courts. There has been a tendency to think of solicitors as doing primarily the work in English-bill courts that attorneys-at-law did in the common-law courts. In fact, the solicitor not only handled a client's legal business in English bill but also in writ actions, maintaining contact with both counsel and attorney. There is evidence that a number of solicitors in Star Chamber were also attorneys-at-law.[4] The solicitor's responsibility was tactical; the strategic responsibility rested with the litigant-principal. Indeed, to a remarkable extent, even the barrister's responsibility was also tactical. No one who gets into the routine of litigation can come away with anything but amazed respect for the assiduity, knowledge of the law, and generally sound business-sense of the serious litigant in Star Chamber. The serious litigant — male or female — was a continuous litigant, almost invariably involved in a series of suits and usually involved in more than one suit at any one time, often in different courts for substantially the

1   *Att.-Gen. ex rel. Sir Richard Egerton* v. *Sir Thomas Brereton.* Reported: Folger Lib. MS. V.a.133, ff.32v-39v (Moore's Rep.); Noy 103. Sir Julius Caesar's notes of trial: Alnwick Castle, MS. 10, ff.158-164v. Precedents prepared for court: Huntington Library, Ellesmere MS. 2757; copy of same, Lansdowne MS. 639, ff.22-22v. Proceedings: STAC 8/14/7.

2   Hudson, 'Treatise', 226.

3   To levy damages Star Chamber issued a writ of extent, from the court's own process office, under the Great Seal. This would, perforce, pass the seal before process to levy the fine would go out under the greenwax of the Exchequer; Exchequer could not act until the fine was returned to it from Star Chamber by a *mittimus* under the Great Seal, usually some months after the decree.

4   E.g., Roger Prowse, an attorney, as solicitor for a defendant; STAC 8/141/5.

same matter.[1] He litigated as a matter of business practice, less with the intention of vindicating his rights than to obtain advantage over his opponent, bent upon bringing the adversary party to compromise or ultimately wearing him down to defeat and capitulation. About much of the age's litigation there is a flavour of negotiation, that the suits were vehicles to keep open business discussions that would issue, hopefully, in a settlement acceptable to both parties. The private litigant was, by and large, a 'learned lay client' who not only retained his counsel directly but also instructed him directly. This meant that the litigant knew enough law to know what he wanted from the law, and that the task of counsel was to secure it for him. The barrister was less an adviser than an advocate. I disagree with Wilfrid Prest's conclusion in his excellent book on the inns of court that a gentleman's sojourn of a year or two at an inn was largely non-educative.[2] Moots (in which the non-aspirant gentleman-student did not participate) and readings (which he probably seldom attended) aside, court-watching and routine contact with the profession provided tools and experience and a grasp of both the rhetoric and the taxonomy of the law which later enabled the gentleman-litigant to use the bulky and wide-ranging literature of the law to instruct himself in what he needed to know in order to undertake the serious business of litigation.

It follows, then, that the barrister was primarily the instrument of his client. The barrister's formal training, by mooting and attending readings in his inn of court, was directed towards a thorough command of real property law. We have yet much to learn about the issues put to argument in moot, but the readings appear to have centred mostly on statutes relevant to property law. Mooting was meant to tune forensic skills. The readings were instructive in close analysis of the law and the science of technical rigour in the interpretation of statutes, upon which the practice of the law, especially before the courts, put an increasingly high premium. The barrister's formal training of that age placed less emphasis even than do our law schools on acquiring skill in conducting the factual side of a case. Court-watching — not only in Westminster Hall and the English-bill courts upstairs, but in the Guildhall and at county assizes — served to inculcate such skill by example. Since the development of the modern (and complex) law of evidence was only beginning,

1 Thomas Parry, Esq., of Carmarthen town, was almost archetypal. In 1614 he had at least 16 suits going against his principal adversary, John Lloyd, Esq.: three in Star Chamber, four in Exchequer equity, two in Exchequer plea side, five in King's Bench, one before the Council of the Marches, and one at common law, court unknown: STAC 8/23/16. All were concerned with a rectory and tithes once property of the Priory of Carmarthen.

2 W.R. Prest, *The Inns of Court, 1590-1640*, (London, 1972), 153.

considerable leeway was tolerated in handling factual matters in court. The feature of English-bill procedure in which the proofs were written in response to written interrogatories afforded the novice lawyer comprehensive and systematic training in the factual dimension of trial practice. In the Star Chamber proceedings the counsel signing interrogatories are often different from and more junior than those signing the pleadings in the same case, indicating a degree of specialization and the confiding of the factual side to less skilled practisers, to the juniors' ultimate benefit if perhaps at their clients' immediate expense.

I am inclined to believe that the most important training of the fledgling and novice barrister was informal. Court-watching was of incalculable importance and apparently universal. The many extant manuscript commonplace-books with short notes of cases heard and a number of the manuscript 'reports' were the work of students and very junior utter-barristers. Though a more limited opportunity, service in clerical capacities in the courts, as under-clerks, gave some counsel considerable training. The number of such under-clerkships can be underestimated. The Six Clerks in Chancery were in train to having their 'sixty clerks', and in Star Chamber, 1596-1641, there were as many as twenty-five such under-clerkships to the clerk of the court and the three or four attorneys at one time. Two of the leading counsel practising in Star Chamber in the period had passed a brief sojourn as attorneys in the court; one of these, William Hudson, the author of the most comprehensive treatise on the court, had the largest practice of any barrister in the court's history.[1] 'Court keeping' as stewards of customary courts is already well appreciated as a source of training for novices. We do tend to overlook how active the student-lawyer was as a 'common solicitor of causes' while pursuing his way to the bar at his inn. There were many 'common solicitors' who followed their vocation without any thought of being called to the bar: Walter Powell of Monmouthshire, gent., whose journal survives, is archetypal of them.[2]

---

1 From STAC 8, Hudson between 1606 (when he was called by Gray's Inn) to 1625 signed 388 bills as counsel-sole for private plaintiffs, 110 bills as joint-counsel for private plaintiffs, answers, etc., in 308 cases as counsel sole for defendants privately prosecuted, same in 67 cases, jointly. He attended Star Chamber daily until his death in the mid-1630s. He was sought after by both the Attorney-General and private parties on both sides for his services. He was deferred to by the court, and on every difficult point of law his opinion was solicited at bar. He produced a 'literature' on Star Chamber that went beyond the treatise he wrote. Though called ancient at Gray's Inn (1622) and to the bench as Lent Reader, 1625, he never took the coif — his practice was too limited to one court to warrant his advancement to serjeant and he would have gained no pecuniary advantage from that honour.

2 *Diary of Walter Powell of Llantilio Crossenny, 1603-54,* ed. J.A. Bradney, (Bristol, 1907). Hudson echoed a conventional contempt for solicitors (though he

Yet family muniments of papers concerning litigation point to widespread soliciting of causes by future counsel. Francis Moore, solicitor to Henry Percy, ninth Earl of Northumberland, while a student at the Middle Temple in the 1580s, was not a unique phenomenon. He was destined to be a serjeant, was one of the great real-property lawyers of the age, enjoyed a huge practice, and after call was kept on the earl's staff by a regular retainer for virtually his entire career. When the earl sent his younger brothers to the Temple they were bound with Moore and another ex-solicitor of the earl during their sojourn there.[1] The student-solicitor's client might not be so grand; indeed, might be his own father or a relative, as in the case of Wadham Wyndham (a Restoration judge) when he was a student at Lincoln's Inn in the early 1630s.[2] The following of causes was an invaluable apprenticeship for practice at the bar.

How big was the practising bar? The Star Chamber proceedings indicate it was a great deal bigger than we have guessed. Based largely on appearances noted in the printed reports, H.H. Cooper lists 489 practisers for the reigns of James I and Charles I.[3] This figure is too low by far. The 8,228 extant Star Chamber cases for 1603-25 yield the names of 1,250 counsel who signed pleadings in those cases. From Wilfrid Prest's figures for the number of barristers called between 1580 and 1619 — these men could reasonably have been expected to have appeared in the court between 1603 and 1625 — the bar of the period would have comprised about 1,550 counsel.[4] Apparently, the Star Chamber involved at least once three out of four members of the potential bar. To be sure, less than 5 per cent of the counsel signing pleadings in Star Chamber accounted for about 40 per cent of the cases. These men were the

very well knew how important they were) in writing of them as 'a new sort of people. . .unknown to the records of the law, who, like the grasshoppers of Egypt, devour the whole land. . .': Hudson, 'Treatise', 94.

1 *The Household Papers of Henry Percy Ninth Earl of Northumberland*, ed. G.R. Batho, Camden Soc., 3rd. ser. 93 (1962), 48, 74, 90; *Middle Temple Records*, 1 (London, 1904), 375 (Alan and George Percy admitted, 12 May 1597, and bound with Moore and John Carvile).

2 Somerset Record Office, Wyndham MSS. (DD/WY), passim.

3 Cited in Prest, *Inns of Court*, 53.

4 Ibid., 52. It is reasonable to accept that all but a few of the barristers practising in Star Chamber post-1603 were called no earlier than 1580; it was unlikely that many barristers called after 1619 would have appeared in the court before 1625, notwithstanding the non-enforcement of Elizabethan orders requiring some years' seniority at the bar before practising in Star Chamber. Assuming some pre-1580 survivals and some post-1619 entrants, 1,550 barristers could at most be scaled upwards to 1,650.

fifty-four leaders of the bar in the court. Over half of the barristers signing signed only once. However, the Star Chamber was only one of many courts and one with a highly specialized 'sub-bar' of practisers. Any calculation of practice based on court work alone tells nothing about non-trial activity of counsel, particularly conveyancing and drafting. For all of the nearly 1,250 barristers signing in Star Chamber, even those who appear only once in the proceedings, we are justified in inferring that they practised elsewhere too and performed a professional function in non-trial activity.

So centralized is the English bar today, and so apparently centralized was it in the Tudor-Stuart period — the principal courts in Westminster and the bar organized around six inns (the four inns of court and two Serjeants' Inns) in London — it is perhaps surprising that the client-counsel relationship was overwhelmingly founded on the county or, at its broadest, the region from which *both* client and counsel came. With few exceptions, the non-leading counsel in Star Chamber, 1603-1625, were retained by their neighbours at home. Even among the fifty-four leaders, half of these — men such as Leonard Bawtree and Robert Callis of Lincolnshire, Hugh Pyne of Somerset, David Jenkins of Wales — had practices built principally on the county-regional base of their residence. All four of these men used as illustrations were eminent practisers, ultimately readers and benchers of their inns, and Bawtree and Callis became serjeants. Of the rest, eleven were of the king's counsel learned (King's Serjeants, Attorneys- and Solicitors-General, law officers to the queen and the prince, and such-like) retained by private plaintiffs to add weight to their bills. Another half-dozen were men with large general practices which included the Star Chamber; such eminent counsel as Francis Moore, Ranulph Crewe, Humfrey Davenport, Richard Hutton, Thomas Richardson, and John Walter, all of them serjeants and all save Moore ultimately becoming judges. Six more leaders, William Hudson and Thomas Hughes pre-eminent among them, constituted the leading stars of a 'sub-bar' in Star Chamber, men whose practices were probably largely confined to that court but who were 'leaders' in every sense of the word. The rest of the leaders were principally Gray's Inn barristers, and I suspect their practices in Star Chamber were built in part on the fact that the clerical office of the court was in Gray's Inn and they enjoyed with a casual clientele the advantage of propinquity.

To see the bar we cannot stop at Temple Bar but must look to the counties beyond. In Bristol in 1623 there were eight barristers resident; in Gloucester city in 1608, three.[1] All but a couple of these men signed

---

[1] *Visitation of Somerset, 1623,* ed. F.T. Colby, (11 Harleian Soc., 1876), 145;

pleadings in Star Chamber. Though I have not yet looked, I suspect a
few will be found in every major town. More to the point, we must
look to the country-houses of newly gentle barristers, perhaps seeing
such capital messuages as Montacute House[1] less as monuments to the
ostentatious arrival of parvenu lawyers than as the local 'chambers', with
spectacular capacity for advertising the success brought by skill at the
bar, of county-based practices. We might suppose that the prominence
of barristers on the commission of the peace and their attendance at
quarter sessions was less a matter of them doing good and rather more
the opportunity for them to do well by maintaining an obtrusive
presence in the vicinage of their clientele. The organization of provincial
criminal justice and civil trials in England into six assize circuits creating
regional conglomerations of counties for trial work also offered counsel
a chance to create, preserve, and advance local connections essential to
their practices. The 'circuit bar' was already a reality, even if the grace-
ful conviviality of the 'circuit mess' was two centuries away and the
invasion of the 'circuit bar' by purely London types waited for the
steam engine. Of the forty-six counsel positively identified from the
Western Circuit assize orders, 1629-40, thirty-six were resident in one
of the six counties on that circuit at the time of admission to the Inn.[2]
These men were not mere 'country lawyers': some of them are familiar
from Star Chamber proceedings and they furnished a fair share of
readers and benchers. There is no reason to suppose that an active
counsellor was less the barrister at home in the country than in
chambers in London.

The time has come to return to the litigant. But I fear that, in truth,
we return to St Louis, his horse, and the thief: that is to say, to the
try-on. Admittedly, what I have presented here is drawn almost entirely
from the pleadings and proofs of litigation, not the stuff with which
legal historians feel easiest, because the substantive law — the LAW —
is very sparse indeed in such materials. To some extent, in the absence
of the orders and decrees (long since gone), and given the limitations of
a still extensive literature of reports in manuscript, there is no alternative.
There is a sage French proverb, 'Where the goat is tethered, there must it
graze'. Though our grass is poor and close-cropped it yields a sense of
how the litigant and his professional aides, without a very clear notion

---

The Names and Surnames. . .Gloucester. . .1608. . .compiled by John Smith
(London, 1902), 2-3.

1   This great Somerset mansion was completed about 1599 by Edward Phelipps
(Middle Temple), afterwards serjeant-at-law, king's serjeant, and Master of the
Rolls.

2   ASSI 24/20.

of what the litigation would demand, how far it would lead, or even if the result obtained (given a successful end) would prove useful, was prepared to embark upon and continue the suit. The litigant was knowledgeable enough to will the end but not to see the means. This is where the try-on comes in. Against what a shrewd assessment of probabilities would indicate was a poor investment, innumerable litigants in Star Chamber went forward with unfaltering hope that the try-on might work. Uncertainty is never negligible in the doing of law. But the high degree of uncertainty, especially in a court as marginally useful in civil litigation as was Star Chamber, is a marked characteristic of the period. Only in damages could the court hope to compete on equal terms with the civil jurisdictions. The road to damages was a longer, harder, and more costly one in Star Chamber than in King's Bench. Ultimately, the future of the Star Chamber as a litigant's court depended upon its usefulness in mounting collateral actions. By the 1630s, for a great many reasons — pre-emption of the court by the Attorney-General 'pro Rege' for fiscal actions, the increasing shift from a 'plaintiff's court' to a 'defendant's court' by special pleading, probably because of changing patterns of litigation at large, to jumble together more discrete and more general causes — the Star Chamber's usefulness for collateral actions evaporated. The famous act abolishing the Star Chamber in 1641 was really a *coup de grâce,* more a symbolic than an effectual visitation of death upon an already prostrate form. If this is too grim a note upon which to end, perhaps it can be put this way: by 1641, litigants no longer believed that the Star Chamber could make the horse talk.

THE CONTROL OF MORTMAIN ALIENATION IN ENGLAND, 1200 – 1300

P.A. Brand

My object in this paper is to examine the different methods used during the century between 1200 and 1300 for the control of the alienation of land into mortmain:[1] that is to say, to control the sale or gift of land and other forms of real property[2] by laymen to religious houses (such as abbeys, priories and hospitals) or to the incumbents or holders of ecclesiastical dignities or benefices (such as archbishops, bishops, canons, rectors of parish churches, and chantry priests), when such grants were made to themselves and to their ecclesiastical successors.[3] My concern will be with the different types of control exercised originally by lords, and subsequently jointly by lords and the Crown, over alienations into mortmain which took the form of subinfeudations, grants under which the ecclesiastical grantee became the feudal tenant of the grantor and only a sub-tenant of that grantor's lord: since, although it is clear that it was possible by the early thirteenth century for such an alienation to be by way of sub-stitution rather than subinfeudation, the grantee becoming a tenant of the grantor's lord rather than of the grantor himself, it seems virtually certain that transactions of this nature always required the active co-operation of that lord in order to become effective, and were therefore always under their full and effective control.[4]

1 For previous discussion of this subject see, in particular, F. Pollock and F.W. Maitland, *History of English Law before the reign of Edward I* (2nd ed., Cambridge, 1898), i, 329-49; T.F.T. Plucknett, *Legislation of Edward I* (2nd ed., Oxford, 1962), 94-102; J.M.W. Bean, *The Decline of English Feudalism* (Manchester, 1968), 40-66.

2 E.g. advowsons, rent-charges, or rights of common.

3 Alienation by sale or gift to such secular ecclesiastics in a private capacity – grants to them and their heirs, rather than to them and their successors – were not regarded as alienations in mortmain, since they were indistinguishable in legal consequences from grants to laymen.

4 Alienation by way of substitution was already in use in John's reign, and Bracton specifically states that a lord can be forced to accept the homage and service of such a substituted tenant: Pollock and Maitland, *History of English Law*, i, 345. Later evidence, however, suggests that the lord could not be forced to accept the homage of such a substituted tenant, and could continue to avow for services on his original tenant if he had not accepted homage from the substitute: see *Bissemede* v. *Bordelys* (1277) CP 40/23, m.19d; *Alinchecote* v. *Aumale* (1286) CP 40/63, m.55. Note also the clear statement made in 1256 in the court of the abbot of Ramsey to a tenant who wished to make just such an arrangement: 'quod non potest ita homagium suum et tenementum predictum

It is reasonably clear that in the twelfth century it was a generally accepted customary rule in England that no alienation of real property of any importance (and almost all mortmain alienations would belong to this category) could or should be made without obtaining the consent of the lord of whom that property was held.[1] This may simply reflect the close social relationship which still existed between most lords and their tenants in this period: it was socially, as much as legally, unthinkable for a tenant to act in such a matter without the advice and consent of his lord and also of his fellow tenants, meeting together in the lord's court. It may, however, also reflect a very real fear that without such consent being obtained the lord might decide to disseise both grantee and grantor of the property in question, might even take steps to deprive the grantor of his other lands for an action which had tended to the disinheritance of his lord.[2]

What is much less clear is just how far such customary controls over mortmain alienation were still being exercised at the beginning of the thirteenth century. Certainly when in 1203 the prior of Kenilworth impleaded the abbot of Stoneleigh for 'entering his fee' (that is, acquiring land held of the prior by one of his tenants) without his assent and against his will, he claimed that such an action was 'contrary to the custom of the realm',[3] and in 1212 the king's court was willing to entertain litigation brought by William de la Basoche against the prior of Lincoln Hospital for entering his fee without his assent, as also against Adam d'Iseny for selling land of his fee to

remittere nec alium loco suo ponere ad homagium faciendum nec ad alia facienda que ad dominum abbatem pertinent sine assensu ipsius abbatis' (*Court Rolls of the Abbey of Ramsey and of the Honour of Clare*, ed. W.O. Ault (New Haven, 1928), 34). Although unambiguous evidence on the point seems lacking from earlier in the century, it is significant that there are no known cases of lords being forced to take the homage of substitute tenants; and, indeed, there seems to have been no form of action by which this could have been achieved. There is no tenant's equivalent to the lord's *per quae servicia* for the attornment of services conveyed by a final concord.

1 Pollock and Maitland, *History of English Law*, i, 343. Maitland notes that Anglo-Norman custom seems to have started from 'some such idea as this, that the tenant may lawfully do anything that does not seriously damage the interests of his lord. He may make reasonable gifts, but not unreasonable. The reasonableness of the gift would be a matter for the lord's court'.

2 Glanvill, ix, 1. Glanvill states that any action on the tenant's part tending to the lord's disinheritance could, as of right, lead to the total disinheritance of the tenant. In 1260 a lord described an alienation in mortmain in exactly these terms: *Prior of Alvecote* v. *Basset* (1260) JUST 1/456, m.3, Cf. Glanvill, xii, 15, which suggests that it is doubtful whether a tenant could give lands more freely than he himself held them.

3 3 *CRR* 69 (1203). Cf. 2 *CRR* 282 (1203).

the prior without his assent,[1] as if the customary rule was still generally in force. King John's mandate of 1204 in favour of the bishop of London, ordering sheriffs and other local officials to assist the bishop in ensuring that none enter the fee of himself or of his church without his consent, can also, perhaps, be seen merely as lending royal assistance to an old faithful royal servant for the enforcement of a customary right which was by no means obsolete.[2] These are, however, only isolated pieces of evidence and, in so far as they show lords seeking royal assistance for the enforcement of controls, would tend to indicate that purely seignorial controls were breaking down — something that would fit in with other evidence that one of the by-products of Henry II's legal reforms was a general weakening of the powers exercised by lords and their courts.[3]

Some indication of just how far seignorial control of alienation had in practice been weakened by the end of John's reign is provided by two of the clauses added to Magna Carta at the time of its second reissue in 1217.[4] Clause 39 laid down that in future no man was to alienate so large a portion of his tenement that he was unable to perform the services due for the tenement as a whole from the resources left to him in the portion of the tenement which he retained. This was, of course, particularly but not exclusively aimed at alienations in mortmain, since such grants normally reserved only nominal services to the grantor from the grantee.[5] Clause 43 enacted that in future no man was to alienate land to a religious house on condition that the religious house should then grant it back to him — the point of such a transaction being, apparently, to contrive that the grantor's lord's incidental rights would be exercised solely over a valueless seignory, with the religious house enjoying the valuable

---

1 6 *CRR* 342-3 (1212).

2 *Rotuli Litterarum Patentium*, ed. T.D. Hardy (London, 1835), 47. The prohibition was cited in *Bishop of London* v. *Theodoric, son of Edric of Aldgate, and others* (1219) 8 *CRR* 138-9, though it was found not to be applicable as the defendants had purchased the land in question from a sub-tenant rather than a tenant of the bishop. Cf. *Rotuli Litterarum Clausarum*, ed. T.D. Hardy (London, 1833), i, 467.

3 F.W. Maitland, *Select Pleas in Manorial Courts* (2 *SS* 1888) lii-lx; D.W. Sutherland, *The Assize of Novel Disseisin* (Oxford, 1973), 77-86.

4 *Select Charters*, ed. W. Stubbs (9th ed., Oxford, 1913), 343; J.C. Holt, *Magna Carta* (Cambridge, 1965), 356.

5 This clause was rarely cited in pleading, as far as can be discovered from the surviving records. There was an action explicitly based on it brought in the court *coram rege* in Trinity 1273: *Bigge* v. *Maylord* (1273) KB 27/5, m.10. The clause was misquoted in pleading in *Prior of Bricett* v. *Tateshale and others* (1238/39) 3 *BNB* 263-4: 1248.

incidental rights arising out of the demesne tenancy.[1] Alienations
of both these kinds were clearly transactions which would have
been prevented by any lord who was exercising any real control over his
tenants' alienations, so the fact that legislation was now being
enacted with the avowed purpose of preventing such alienations
clearly indicates that by 1217 there were some lords at least who no
longer possessed the power to control them.

It was in the period between the enactment of these two clauses and
the enactment of the first general legislation on mortmain alienations in
1259 that Bracton was writing his treatise. This contains the most
extreme expression of the movement of judicial opinion favouring
freedom of alienation: of what Maitland described as the tendency
of the king's justices to concede to every tenant the fullest
possible power of dealing with his land.[2] Although in the treatise
Bracton acknowledges[3] the constraints on the tenant's freedom to
alienate that had been introduced in 1217, and the further constraints
introduced by legislation of 1228 prohibiting mortmain alienations by
the king's tenants in chief,[4] these are the only constraints that he does
recognise as valid. The tenant's alienation may, he says, cause his lord
loss but it is not wrongful, not actionable. The condition on which land
is granted to a tenant — the motive for the gift expressed in the charter
of feoffment — is that the tenant shall perform homage and specified
services for the land. As long as these are done the lord has no right to
complain if, as a result of an alienation, the incidents of tenure are less
valuable than they had been when the land was first granted to the
tenant.[5] The treatise does, however, provide indirect evidence that even
at the time Bracton was writing lords were attempting in various ways
to protect their interests against damaging alienations. One such way
was to prevent the alienee from ever taking seisin of the land
he had been granted:[6] a method which, as long as the lord acted
immediately at the time of the attempted transfer of seisin and was
always prepared to return the land to its previous tenant, was in

1 Maitland, however, thought that the point of the transaction was to allow the
tenant in question to claim immunity under the charters of a favoured
religious body from various burdens, not necessarily from services as such:
Pollock and Maitland, *History of English Law,* i, 333, n. 6.

2 Ibid., 344.

3 Bracton, iii, 35, 37 (ff. 168v, 169v).

4 *CR 1227-31,* 88. This legislation is discussed in Bean, *Decline of English
Feudalism,* 58.

5 Bracton, ii, 140-2 (ff. 45v-6). Cf. iii, 274 (f. 263v).

6 Bracton says this is wrongful because the lord has no right to enter the land
(which he must do to prevent the new tenant gaining seisin): ii, 141 (f. 46).

practice recognised as being a valid exercise of seignorial power by the king's courts from 1247 onwards.[1] The other method, for which there is also some, rather later, evidence (from the honour court of Lewes in 1266),[2] was that of summoning the alienee to the lord's court to show why he had entered his fee without his permission and to his damage: a procedure presumably intended to secure, at the least, some pecuniary compensation from the unlicensed alienee.[3] There is also further evidence from this period of the king helping lords to control alienations within their fees. In 1235 Westminster Abbey received a royal charter including a clause prohibiting anyone entering the abbey's fee save with the abbot's assent,[4] and the abbot may have been entitled to the assistance of royal officials in enforcing this. From 1243 onwards there are enrolled on the Close Rolls various prohibitions issued on behalf of favoured religious houses or individuals against all other (or sometimes only named other) religious houses entering their fees without their permission. These specifically authorise sheriffs and other royal officers to assist them in enforcing the prohibition.[5] That such prohibitions could, if necessary, be enforced not only by local executive action but also by litigation in the king's court, is shown by a writ on the Close Rolls in 1256 summoning the prior of Luffield to answer in the court *coram rege* for the breach of such a prohibition in purchasing land held of the Hospital of St John the Baptist, Oxford.[6] This writ is of particular interest not only because it is noted on the roll as having been authorised by, among others, Bracton himself,[7] but also because it appears to refer to general

---

1 See the cases cited by Sutherland, *Assize of Novel Disseisin*, 90-4; and *Prior of Caldwell* v. *Swynheved* (1247) JUST 1/4, m.5 (Bedfordshire eyre).

2 *Records of the Barony and Honour of the Rape of Lewes*, ed. A.J. Taylor (64 Sussex Record Soc., 1939), 25. Cf. ibid., 29, 33. The entry records the attachment of the prior of Sele to answer the lord of the court, Earl Warenne, for having entered the earl's fee without his consent.

3 Bracton, ii, 141-2 (f. 46).

4 *Calendar of Charter Rolls*, i, 209.

5 E.g. *CR 1242-7*, 50-1 (a prohibition in favour of the abbot of Westminster against the abbot of Pershore, 1243); ibid., 377 (a general prohibition on behalf of the abbot of Westminster, 1245); ibid., 404 (a prohibition on behalf of the abbot of Reading against the abbot of Boxley in connection with the abbot's fee at Hoo, Kent, 1246); *CR 1251-3*, 498 (a prohibition on behalf of William FitzHerbert while on the king's service in Gascony, 1253).

6 *CR 1254-6*, 400. The prohibition involved is probably that of 1255 (ibid., 124) which specifically forbade the entry of the prior of Luffield or any other religious into the hospital's fee. It was the last of a series of such prohibitions: *CR 1251-3*, 52, 106, 478.

7 The fact that neither the case nor the principle involved are referred to by Bracton in his treatise is relevant to a consideration of the dating and authorship of that treatise.

legislation already then in existence requiring all mortmain alienations to religious houses to have the consent of the lord of whom the land in question was held.[1] There is, however, no other evidence for this legislation.[2]

Such legislation, if indeed it ever existed, and the other controls exercised by lords, were clearly considered inadequate by those responsible for clause 10 of the Petition of the Barons of 1258, which sought a remedy not against mortmain alienations generally but more specifically against alienations in mortmain to religious houses made without lords' consent and which led to losses of wardships, marriages, reliefs and escheats.[3] That the complaint was limited to mortmain alienations to religious houses is evidence that the objection was not just economic or financial in origin, but was also symptomatic of a more general prejudice against the further accumulation of wealth by the old-established religious houses.[4] This complaint led, in 1259, to the enactment (as clause 14 of the Provisions of Westminster) of legislation requiring that all religious houses[5] in future should have the consent of the lord of whom lands were held before entering their fee — the first general mortmain legislation.[6]

Somewhat surprisingly, perhaps, the legislation seems to have been cited very little during the next three years, the period during which it was nominally in force: it was used once in an action by plaint in the special Warwickshire eyre of 1260,[7] and once cited by the justices in making a judgment in an assize of novel disseisin the same year.[8] Thereafter no use was made of it and it is difficult to resist the conclusion that this was because in practice, for political reasons, it was regarded as of no effect. It was also for political reasons (Henry III's need for the support of the Church) that it alone of the twenty-four clauses of the Provisions of Westminster was dropped when the Provisions were re-enacted by the king, now once again in

---

1 '. . . cum . . . provisum est et communiter statutum in regno nostro quod nullus vir religiosus feodum alicuius ingrediatur sine assensu et voluntate sua'.

2 Bean, *Decline of English Feudalism*, 61, suggests that this is a distorted reference to clause 43 of the 1217 Magna Carta. Alternatively, it might refer to the common usage of the realm rather than to specific legislation.

3 *Select Charters*, ed. Stubbs, 375.

4 Cf. S. Wood, *English Monasteries and their Patrons in the Thirteenth Century* (Oxford, 1955), 80.

5 The phrase 'viris religiosis' is probably intended to exclude secular clergy.

6 *CR 1259-61*, 149.

7 *Clinton* v. *Preceptor of Temple Balsall* (1260) JUST 1/953, m.6d. The legislation is not specifically cited in this case.

8 *Prior of Alvecote* v. *Basset* (1260) JUST 1/456, m.3.

control of the country, in January 1263; and kept it out of the subsequent re-issues of the Provisions, by the king in June 1263,[1] by the Montfortian regime in December 1264,[2] and by the king again in 1267 as part of the Statute of Marlborough.[3]

It is of some interest to note that, although tacitly repealed in 1263, clause 14 of the Provisions of Westminster appears to have enjoyed a vigorous after-life. In November 1264 it was cited by a litigant in an assize of novel disseisin and accepted, both by his opponent and by the justices hearing the case, as still being in force.[4] This was under the Montfortian 'baronialist' regime which ruled England after the battle of Lewes and before the re-issue of the Provisions in December 1264 which omitted this clause: that is, during a period when it would have been quite plausible to have argued that it was the original baronial Provisions of 1259 (which included the relevant clause) that were in force, rather than the revised royalist version of the Provisions as re-issued in 1263 (which omitted it). Much more curiously, there is a case on the Bench plea-roll for Michaelmas 1277,[5] which was brought allegedly under a clause of the Statute of Marlborough whose wording is identical to that of clause 14 of the 1259 Provisions, and the writ used in this case was enrolled the following year on the Close Roll.[6] Nor is this an isolated phenomenon. In a case heard during the course of the Yorkshire eyre of 1279-81, probably in Trinity term 1279, the Abbot of Whitby was summoned to answer one Adam de Levynthorpe for breach of the same rule.[7] However, the writ as enrolled on the plea-roll does not state whether or not the rule is statutory in origin, and the abbot does not demur on the existence of the rule but pleads successfully that he had found his church seised of the land in question on succeeding to the abbacy (and therefore had not *himself* entered the land). In a further case, from the same eyre, and this time certainly heard in Trinity term 1279,[8] the

---

1 1 *SR* 8-11, and footnotes; the two texts were identical.

2 *Registrum Malmesburiense*, ed. J.S. Brewer and C.T. Martin (*RS*, 1879), i, 42-50.

3 1 *SR* 19-25.

4 *Prior of Barnwell* v. *Master of the Templars, and others* (1264) JUST · 1/1191, m.15.

5 CP 40/21, m.58d.

6 *CCR 1272-79*, 500-01. The Close Roll writ alone is noted and discussed by Bean, *Decline of English Feudalism*, 51.

7 JUST 1/1055, m.83. Cf. JUST 1/1062, m.17.

8 JUST 1/1074, m.19d. Because of the length of the eyre, the civil pleas were divided into separate terms. This roll contains only cases heard in Trinity term 1279.

Master of the Templars was summoned to answer Roger d'Eyville for a breach of this rule, the rule being stated on this occasion to have been statutory in origin, though no particular statute is mentioned. Unlike the abbot, the master at once demurred to the writ on the grounds that no such legislation as that cited in the writ had ever been published either by the present king or by his predecessors. The justices answered that similar writs had previously been issued by the Chancery and that the writs, and therefore presumably also the presupposition of the statute's existence, had thereby received royal approval.[1] The defendant persisted in his objections, only shifting his ground slightly to argue that legislation such as that cited in the writ had never been agreed to by the magnates of the realm nor published with their consent. He asked that the judges stay judgment on this objection until the king's will on the matter was known.

It was but a matter of months after the hearing of this last case that, at the Michaelmas parliament of 1279, the Statute of Mortmain was enacted.[2] The statute was published on 14 November 1279[3] by a writ sent to the justices of the Bench and also, almost certainly (although no evidence of this survives), like other thirteenth-century legislation, by writs sent to the sheriffs of every county. It was drastic in scope. All alienations in mortmain were henceforth to cease — not only alienations to religious houses but also all alienations to other ecclesiastical tenants, and any attempt at an infraction of the statute was to be punished by the forfeiture of the land concerned. The lord of whom the land was held was to be given a year within which to claim the land for himself by entering in the event of forfeiture. The statute is, however, unclear about what was to happen if he failed to act: as if two different and mutually irreconcilable schemes had been proposed and the legislators had not been able to make up their minds which to adopt. The statute says that each of the superior lords of the fee was in turn to be given six months to claim the land by entering it, but it also says that as soon as the year had elapsed the king was to be allowed to enter it and enfeoff a new tenant, who was to hold the land

---

1 The justices may have been referring to the fact that this writ was issued while the king himself was in France, 11 May to 19 June 1279.

2 1 SR 51.

3 That the date given in the Close Roll version of the statute (14 November) rather than that given in the Patent Roll (15 November) is the correct one, is indicated by the evidence of a case heard in the Bench in Easter term 1284, in which the court (presumably still in possession of the writ sent to it) said the statute had been published on 14 November: *Prior of the Hospitallers* v. *Pocklington* (1284) CP 40/53, m.20.

of its original lord for the services due, and also to perform additional services directly to himself.[1]

In practice, despite the statute, there was not a complete ban on alienations in mortmain after 1279. Within six months of the passing of the statute the king began to grant licences allowing alienations in mortmain 'notwithstanding the statute'. The earliest of these is dated 26 May 1280.[2] Although the very earliest licences seem to have been granted without any preliminary investigation into the proposed alienation, such preliminary enquiries (through inquisitions *ad quod damnum*) were being made from as early as February 1281.[3] By 1284 at the latest, if not indeed from 1281, such an inquisition seems to have been an essential preliminary to the granting of a licence, since in that year an inquisition was held into a proposed alienation by no less a person than the queen mother.[4] The inquisition *ad quod damnum* was authorised by royal writ which was normally addressed to the relevant sheriff or to some other royal official and sought the verdict of twelve jurors, of the locality where the land to be alienated was situated, on a series of questions: whether the proposed alienation was prejudicial or damaging to the interests of the king or others; of whom the land was held and by what service; and what the land was worth. Additional questions sometimes asked were: how many mesnes there were between the intending alienor and the king; and whether the alienor was retaining enough lands to perform in full the services he owed and to sustain various other specified duties whose dereliction would be prejudicial to his neighbours.[5] The inquisition and authorising writ would then be returned to Chancery, which would, it seems, normally forward them to a session of the king's council for consideration by king and council before a licence was granted. The evidence for this lies not only in the annotations commonly found from 1284 onwards of the council's comments on returned inquisitions, but also in the dating of licences: which are heavily concentrated in the periods during and just after sessions of the Great Council or of Parliament.[6]

---

1 Cf. Bereford C.J.'s suggested solution of this problem in Mich. 6 Edw. 2 (34 *SS*, 1918), 75, pl. 20.

2 C 66/99, m.17 [*CPR 1272-81*, 372].

3 C 143/5/17. This is a transcript of the original writ, preceding the returned inquisition.

4 C 143/7/1.

5 This last question is only found in full from June 1290 onwards, and subsequently becomes a standard feature of the writ.

6 I propose to discuss elsewhere the evidence on which the conclusions in this paragraph are based.

An entry on the Parliament Roll for January 1292 notes, among other things, that henceforth no requests for permission to alienate in mortmain will be considered without evidence of the consent of the lord of whom the land was held being produced.[1] Historians have generally seen this as marking a radical change in the licensing system.[2] There is, however, some evidence from as early as 1281, and plentiful evidence from 1285 onwards (from which date the endorsed annotations on inquisitions *ad quod damnum* frequently require evidence of such consent to be produced before the king's licence is given) which suggests that it had been the usual if not invariable practice even before 1292 to require evidence of the lord's consent before the king's consent was given. The memorandum also requires that the potential donor keep some of his lands, that the returned inquest be accompanied by the authorising original writ, and that the writ itself contain all the articles included in the 'new form' of writ (that is, the writ as altered in June 1290). It is in form neither a petition nor the answer to a petition, and the most plausible explanation is that it is an internal, administrative memorandum, intended simply to ensure that the king and his council are not bothered by having to consider inquisitions *ad quod damnum* which stand no chance of success, by allowing Chancery clerks or others working at a fairly low level of discretion to sift the inquisitions before they ever reached the king's council.

Two views have been put forward in recent years concerning the motives behind the statute. Plucknett[3] suggested that the Statute of Mortmain was a 'very dubious piece of political legislation' to which the lay lords present at the 1279 Parliament had been tricked into assenting by 'the bribe of statutory forfeitures' and the 'soft words of the final clause', the provision safeguarding the lord's right to services and feudal incidents even where the king had entered in the lord's default and enfeoffed a new tenant. It was, however, Edward I's intention by means of the statute to acquire 'by a single stroke . . . the sole prerogative of amortization' and Edward had soon

> revealed his plan by issuing when he saw fit his letters of licence to alienate into mortmain. The implication [was] that the king's consent [was] necessary, and that the king's consent [was] sufficient. The flow of property to the Church continued much as before, but from every gift the king took such toll as he could get.

More recently, Bean[4] has suggested that the motives behind the

1   1 *RP* 83, no. 13.
2   Bean, *Decline of English Feudalism*, 64-5.
3   Plucknett, *Legislation of Edward I*, 98, 99.
4   Bean, *Decline of English Feudalism*, 53, 64.

statute were primarily political, the intention being to employ the statute 'as a threat which would bring the clergy to heel'. The Crown had, he argued, only a marginal financial interest in the control of mortmain alienations in the fees of mesne lords: the reason it consented to legislation in 1279 was that it needed the support of the lay magnates against the Church to force the new Archbishop of Canterbury (Pecham) to withdraw certain decisions of his first provincial council which were considered to be prejudicial to the Crown's authority. The threat implied by the statute proved an immediate success, Pecham being 'forced to agree to [the] royal demands at the very parliament at which the statute of Mortmain was promulgated'. Even after the immediate crisis was over, however, the Crown embarked on a policy of licensing alienations instead of agreeing to a total repeal of the statute, since 'the threat of a future policy whereby the Church would be forbidden to acquire land' was thought 'a useful weapon against the recalcitrant clergy'.

Both these views are, I think, mistaken. Against Plucknett it can be argued that it seems to have been much the same group of lay lords who in practice consented to the issuing of licences as had consented to the original legislation. There was therefore no trick involved in the licensing system; and, far from gaining the sole prerogative of amortization as a result of the legislation, in practice what the king got was a share in the control of amortization with the lord of whom the land to be amortized was held. That the Crown's motives were not merely financial is shown not only by the detailed questions answered in inquisitions *ad quod damnum* and the care taken to improve and expand the list of questions asked — all of which show more concern with the control of alienations in the common good than desire for financial return — but also by the fact that a system of fines for licences to alienate does not seem to have come into operation until as late as 1299, when Edward I and his advisers were desperately seeking new sources of finance.[1]

Against Bean it can be argued that it is difficult to see why, if the statute was merely a threat, Edward I should nonetheless have gone on to publish it on 14 November, when its main object (the withdrawal by Pecham) had been achieved at some date between 9 and 11 November?[2] The threat of the statute once enacted seems in fact to have been ineffective in cowing the clergy, who the following year produced a lengthy catalogue of grievances and in 1281 even re-enacted three

1 W. Ryley, *Placita Parliamentaria* (London, 1661), 478.
2 *Councils and Synods*, ed. F.M. Powicke and C.R. Cheney (Oxford, 1964), II, ii, 832.

of the five canons withdrawn by Pecham in 1279, without any cessation of the granting of licences.[1] Nor was Pecham the man to be cowed into submission by a threat to the Church's ability to acquire more lands. He himself had been a noted proponent of the Franciscan theory of poverty, and only ten years previously had launched a scathing attack on the wealth both of the secular clergy and of the monastic orders.[2]

If we are looking for the motives behind the statute, we need look no further than the statute's own words. Lay lords were worried about the damaging effects of such alienations on their income from feudal incidents. The king was worried about the effect of the transfer of landed wealth from laymen to the Church on the number of knights, the military potential of the kingdom.[3] It is possible that at first a complete prohibition of all further alienations was intended, but even if it was not seen from the start, it must soon have become clear that the interests of both mesne lords and king could be adequately safeguarded by a system of licensing. And if we are to look for what precipitated the legislation, we need look no further than the case involving the Master of the Templars which was heard in the Yorkshire eyre of 1279.[4] The case had involved an important political, even constitutional, point. It also involved an important defendant. What more natural than that the case should have been discussed at the Michaelmas parliament of 1279, particularly as some of the justices from the Yorkshire eyre were present at the parliament?[5] Once the specific point had been raised — whether there did exist legislation against mortmain alienations to religious houses — is it not easy to see how this could have led to a more general discussion of mortmain alienations, and thus to the enactment of the statute? May not the otherwise apparently gratuitous reference to the earlier legislation, which the Statute of Mortmain defiantly insisted and affirmed was still in force, be a clue to the origins of the statute in a discussion about whether such legislation did or did not exist?

---

1 Ibid., 887, 906-7.
2 D.L. Douie, *Archbishop Pecham* (Oxford, 1952), 26-31.
3 I propose to discuss this elsewhere.
4 Above, p. 36.
5 G.O. Sayles, *Select Cases in the Court of King's Bench*, i (55 *SS*, 1936), 51: 39.

LITIGANTS AND ATTORNEYS IN THE KING'S BENCH AND COMMON PLEAS, 1560 – 1640

C. W. Brooks

The late sixteenth and early seventeenth centuries were a great age for lawyers. The most famous members of the profession, Egerton, Coke, Noy, Hakewill, Dodderidge, Whitelocke, played an active role in early Stuart political controversy. King Charles I relied so heavily on the advice of his judiciary that the members of the Long Parliament were as anxious to impeach judges as they were Archbishop Laud. But, while we can appreciate the importance of these lawyer-politicians, we know all too little about the structure of the legal profession, its aims, or the way in which the judicial system it operated touched on the lives of those who used it. In any society, the administration of justice is made up of many components – the litigants, the lawyers, the courts, the bureaucracy, procedural and substantive law – and it is difficult to say very much about any one part without looking at the others. But, in the history of English law during the sixteenth and seventeenth centuries, two particular features stand out. The first is that between 1560 and 1640 there was a great, and probably unprecedented, increase in the amount of litigation entertained by the two main common-law courts at Westminster, the King's Bench and Common Pleas. The second is that the increase in litigation was accompanied by an increase in the number of lawyers. Both of these points have been recognised for a long time, but because the plea rolls are such intractable sources[1] the exact dimensions of the increase – who the clients were, how many lawyers practised – have never been fully explored. The purpose of this paper is to say something about the number of cases entering the two courts, about the social status of the litigants, and, finally, about the lawyers (particularly the attorneys) who served them.[2]

The study is based mainly on two sets of documents from the King's Bench and Common Pleas, the docket rolls and the rolls of warrants of attorney. There is no good source from which the number of actions commenced in the two courts can be derived, but the docket rolls are a satisfactory source from which to discover the number of cases in

---

1 J.H. Baker, 'The Dark Age of Legal History', *LHS 1972*, 2, quotes Maitland's comment that the plea rolls are so unwieldy 'that we can hardly hope that much will ever be known about them'.

2 This paper is based on research conducted for an Oxford D.Phil. thesis, which will deal in more detail with a number of assertions made below.

advanced stages which were in progress during any particular year. Thus, counts of docket-roll entries have been made in order to produce statistics on the number of cases in the King's Bench and Common Pleas for the years 1560, 1580, 1606 and 1640.[1] On the other hand, information about the social status and geographical origins of the litigants, along with the forms of action on which they were suing, has been collected from the rolls of warrants, which are found at the end of the plea rolls of each court. An analysis has been made of litigants in sample terms in 1560, 1606 and 1640.[2] It should be emphasised that both the docket rolls and the rolls of warrants are short-cuts to the plea rolls, which are of course the only authoritative source.[3] Because they are short-cuts, worries about their completeness and accuracy inevitably arise and should be kept in mind. But all major problems can be satisfactorily resolved, and on some crucial points — such as the identification of all litigants who claimed the social rank of gentleman or above — there is every reason to believe that the rolls of warrants are more accurate than most other early-modern documents.

The volume of litigation

Studies by Drs Blatcher, Hastings and Ives show that at the end of the fifteenth century about 2,000 cases in advanced stages were making their way through the King's Bench and Common Pleas each year.[4] Following this period came a decline in the fortunes of the common law, which Dr Ives associates with the transfer of property litigation to

1 The docket rolls used for the Common Pleas are IND 54-6, 157-65, 353-8; for the King's Bench, IND 1336, 1339, 1347, 1356, 1370. The docket rolls of both courts relate only to cases enrolled by the prothonotaries and therefore in advanced stages; that is, either cases in which both parties are in court or in which the plaintiff is about to outlaw a defendant for failing to appear. They do not provide a guide to the actual number of suits commenced.

2 The rolls of warrants used are in CP 40/1187, 1753, 2476; and KB 27/1194, 1395, 1649.

3 The use of these documents has required a detailed study of their history, and the procedures which produced them. The most important point to be made now is that since during this period each King's Bench case received only one entry in the plea rolls (and hence in the docket rolls) there is no chance that the numbers of cases have been inflated by counting the same case twice. However, Common Pleas docket rolls could contain more than one reference to the same case in any one year or term. Studies of sample case-loads of various attorneys suggest that about 80% of the total docket-roll entries represent individual cases, so total counts of Common Pleas entries have been reduced by 20% to allow for duplication.

4 M. Blatcher, 'Touching the Writ of Latitat', *Elizabethan Government and Society*, ed. S.T. Bindoff and others (London, 1961), 201, note 1; E.W. Ives, 'Common Lawyers in pre-Reformation England', 18 *TRHS*, 5th ser. (1968), 167; M. Hastings, *The Court of Common Pleas in Fifteenth Century England* (Ithaca, 1947), 183. The work of Blatcher and Ives suggests that an average of about

Chancery. But, by the opening years of the reign of Elizabeth I, the King's Bench had recovered its position, with 914 suits in 1560. Because there is no complete series of docket rolls for the Common Pleas before 1580, exact estimates of its business in 1560 are difficult: though it is probable that the court had surpassed its late-fifteenth-century volume of about 1,500 suits each year. From 1560, however, litigation in both courts began to soar. By 1580, King's Bench litigation had increased by four times to just over 4,000 suits a year. The 9,300 cases in the Common Pleas at the same date represent an equally remarkable increase. Taken together, the two courts were hearing about six times more cases than they had been at the end of the fifteenth century. The increase continued, though at a milder pace, between 1580 and 1606. Business in the Common Pleas doubled; that of the King's Bench went up by more than 50 per cent. From 1606, there was a steady but much less rapid growth, so that by 1640 a total of just over 29,000 cases were making their way through the courts: 8,500 in the King's Bench and 20,625 in the Common Pleas. By 1640 there was three times more litigation than in 1580, perhaps fifteen times more than there had been in the 1490s.

Table I

Cases in advanced stages in the King's Bench and Common Pleas, 1490 − 1640.

	1490	1560	1580	1606	1640
King's Bench	500	914	4,000	6,945	8,537
Common Pleas	1,600	[not known]	9,300	16,508	20,625
Total	2,100		13,300	23,453	29,162

These estimates of the volume of early-modern litigation can be compared with those for England just before the great law reforms, which were compiled by the Parliamentary Committee on Courts of Justice and reported in 1829. According to this source, between 1823 and 1827 an average of 72,224 actions were commenced in the

400-500 cases a year in the King's Bench is likely for the early 1490s; these figures, which are based on the docket rolls, are comparable with mine. The Common Pleas presents difficulties, mainly because there are no docket rolls for that period. For Michaelmas 1483, Hastings counted 6,000 plea-roll entries, but since about 5,100 of these were related to mesne process, this figure is not comparable with the King's Bench figures; if we multiply the remaining 900 entries by 20/8 (the ratio of return-days in Michaelmas term to the total number in the year: Sutherland, *Assize of Novel Disseisin*, 178) we obtain a total of 2,100 cases a year in advanced stages; if we then make the same 20% allowance for duplication as for the Common Pleas figures, a total estimate of 1,680 emerges.

King's Bench and Common Pleas during each year.[1] In 1606, the same two courts were handling a combined total of about 23,500 cases at stages in which both parties had come into court or in which the plaintiff was about to outlaw the defendant for failing to appear. Thus, if a threefold increase in population between 1606 and the 1820s is allowed for, the raw statistics suggest that the rate of litigation was about the same during the two periods. But suits commenced and suits in advanced stages are not comparable. In any age many more suits are commenced than reach the stage at which both parties are about to appear in court. For example, figures for the numbers of original writs sued out in Chancery between 1569 and 1584, which were compiled by a contemporary, suggest that as many as twice as many suits may have been commenced as reached advanced stages in the Common Pleas.[2] This information implies that there was in fact more litigation per head of population under Elizabeth I and the early Stuarts than there was in the early nineteenth century, and this conclusion is supported by what is known about the volume of litigation in other courts. Perhaps surprisingly, the number of suits commenced in Chancery was much the same during the two periods. It averaged about 1,000 in the late sixteenth century and 1,500 in the ten years from 1800 to 1809.[3] On the other hand, common-law actions started in the Exchequer between 1823 and 1827 averaged about 7,400 a year,[4] probably considerably more than were entertained by that court in the early seventeenth century. But against this must be set the existence of the Star Chamber (abolished in 1641) as a thriving early-modern jurisdiction, and the fact that in this period justice was less confined to the central courts than it was during the reign of George IV. In the late sixteenth and early seventeenth centuries town courts, and even manorial courts, were still quite active, whereas they had fallen into disuse by the beginning of the nineteenth century. Thus, it is very likely that the late sixteenth and early seventeenth centuries were the most litigious periods in English history. If mid-twentieth-century England seems less litigious, it is (at least, according to Abel-Smith and Stevens) not because there are fewer disputes to

1 *First Report of His Majesty's Commissioners [on the] Common Law* (1829), 11.

2 'Mr Jones Plan to Farm the Seals for Original Writs': Brit. Lib., Lansdowne MS. 47, f.122.

3 For the late-Elizabethan estimate, see W.J. Jones, *The Elizabethan Court of Chancery* (Oxford, 1967), 304, note 1. Early nineteenth-century figures for bills in Chancery are given in *Report from the Committee Appointed to enquire into the Causes that retard the Decisions of Suits in the High Court of Chancery* (1811), 956.

4 *First Report on the Common Law*, 11.

settle but because arbitration boards and special tribunals have provided a way to take them out of court. This has meant a corresponding decline in the general influence of lawyers in political life and social planning.[1]

However, comparisons with distant future ages would have meant little to Elizabethan Englishmen, because for them the most striking feature of the administration of justice was the rapidity with which the number of law-suits increased between 1560 and 1640. During the reign of Henry VIII, common lawyers had been worried that empty courts would put them out of business.[2] From the reign of Elizabeth I the concern was rather that there were too many suits. No one welcomed this new 'multiplicity of suits', and explanations of it, along with proposals for remedies, began to proliferate. With a few not entirely insignificant exceptions, the reforms on which everyone agreed in principle failed to amount to anything. But contemporary analyses of the causes of the increase were realistic, and they can help us to understand something about how laymen and lawyers conceived the relationship between law and society. Some explained the increase in litigation in terms of failings within the law itself, in particular its uncertainty.[3] Others talked about changes in society or about failings in human nature.[4] In the late sixteenth century, criticisms of the obscurity and inadequacy of the common law seem to have had the widest currency, and it is in this context that Francis Bacon's celebrated proposals for reform and even codification should be seen. His ideas were not exceptional, but only the clearest expression of the fairly flexible outlook of Elizabethan lawyers.[5] With the reign of James I, however, the use of precedents and legal arguments in constitutional disputes brought more partisan defences of the common law. In a political atmosphere where law was looked to as a constitutional guide, the notion that it was uncertain about men's property could not be entertained.[6] As Elizabethan reliance on reason and natural law gave

1 B. Abel-Smith and R. Stevens, *Lawyers and the Courts* (London, 1967), 1-2.

2 F.W. Maitland, *English Law and the Renaissance* (Cambridge, 1901), 22, 82-3.

3 There are many examples. The Lansdowne MSS contain a number of projects for law reform. SP 12/107/95 is a draft parliamentary bill (dated 1576) proposing a code of law and de-centralisation of justice. For more, see C. Brooks and K. Sharpe, 'Debate, History, English Law and the Renaissance', *Past and Present* 72 (August, 1976), 135.

4 These are usually the products of the early seventeenth century. See the works of Coke and Davies, cited below.

5 Brooks and Sharpe, 'History, English Law and the Renaissance', 134-5. Bacon's scheme to reform the statutes was supported by some of the most important lawyers of the day: James Whitelocke, William Noy, Thomas Hedley, William Hakewill, Henry Hobart and Henry Finch.

6 Ibid., 141.

way to the more certain — but in the long run more inhibiting — historical myths of Sir Edward Coke, sociological interpretations of the increase in litigation became more popular.

In terms of general explanations of the sudden increase in common-law litigation, it is difficult to add to the views of Egerton, Bacon, Davies and Coke. What we can do is follow the leads they give us. There is, for example, evidence that some aspects of the substantive law were as uncertain as contemporaries claimed. The rules about important concepts such as the equity of redemption or perpetuities were undergoing change throughout the period. But knowledge of substantive law during this period is all too limited[1] so we must leave this aspect of the problem to those better able to deal with it.

The idea that the influx of litigation was caused by social change has found wide acceptance among social historians in the twentieth century. In the seventeenth century, two very concise statements of this point of view came from Sir John Davies and Sir Edward Coke. Davies claimed that there were more suits, not because the law was imperfect, but because, 'the commodities of the earth being more improved, there is more wealth and consequently there are more contracts reall and personall in the world, which breedeth unthrifts, banckruptes, and bad debtors, more covetousness, and more malice. . .'[2] To this Coke added that the general causes of litigation were the advent of peace and plenty, and the dissolution of the monasteries into many hands.[3] With these views in mind we can now turn to the people who were bringing this vastly increased volume of litigation into the King's Bench and Common Pleas.

The litigants

The social composition of litigants changed relatively little between 1560, the starting-point of the influx of suits, and 1640. Throughout the period, men styled either 'gentleman' or above made up about 30 per cent of all Common Pleas and 20 per cent of all King's Bench litigants. Thus, between 70 and 80 per cent (a considerable majority) of those who utilised these courts were not members of what, for the sake of convenience, is generally called the landed gentry. The non-gentry litigants included in roughly equal proportions men who owned land and those who did not. One-third of all Common Pleas cases arose from the yeomanry, and in the King's Bench these small landowners

1   See Baker, 'The Dark Age of Legal History', 2.
2   J. Davies, 'A Discourse of Law and Lawyers' (1615) in *The Complete Works of Sir John Davies,* ed. A.B. Grosart (London, 1869-76) iii, 266.
3   Bod. Lib., Ashmole MS. 1159, f.78.

accounted for about 15 or 20 per cent of all litigants. But another 25 per cent of the litigants in the Common Pleas, and 35 to 40 per cent of those in the King's Bench, were from the commercial and other classes who either owned no land or for whom it did not serve as a principal source of income. This group of litigants represents a wide range of wealth and occupations. Most were merchants, provincial tailors, grocers, chapmen, bakers or inn-keepers; but carpenters, bricklayers, miners, labourers, and a few university dons, are included. The remainder of the litigants in both courts (about 10 per cent) were lawyers (mainly attorneys), clergymen, and widows who were involved in suits relating to the estates of deceased husbands.[1]

The distribution of litigation in the Common Pleas, and to a lesser extent in the King's Bench, appears to reflect fairly accurately the distribution of wealth in the nation as a whole. It has been estimated that the gentry classes probably owned about 30 per cent of the national wealth, and, as we have seen, they appear as about the same percentage of all litigants in the courts.[2] As in most legal tribunals, wealth was the most important factor in determining how much any particular group used the courts. On the other hand, although it must be true that very few of the litigants below the rank of gentleman came from that part of the population (perhaps 33 per cent) which lived on or below the edge of subsistence, it is clear that provincial farmers, merchants, tailors, miners, and occasionally even labourers, could find legal representation and use the courts. Certainly, these groups were better represented in the King's Bench and Common Pleas than they were at the inns of court, where comparable statistics indicate that only about 10 per cent of the entrants were below the rank of gentleman.[3] Moreover, though the gentry make up about 25 to 30 per cent of the litigants in both courts, the King's Bench does present an even lower percentage of clients from these groups. And in the Common Pleas, if there is any trend at all during these years, it is towards the commercial and lower agricultural classes. If we consider only the status of plaintiffs, the gentry presence in the Common Pleas declines between 1560 and 1640 from 30 per cent to 26 per cent; and the change may be more substantial than the raw data suggest, since about 5 per cent of those plaintiffs listed in the commerical grouping

1 In the rolls of warrants all litigants above the rank of gentleman are styled. Below the rank of gentleman, defendants are described more precisely than plaintiffs, and so the detailed statistics for those below that rank are based on the status of defendants only.

2 G.E. Aylmer, *The King's Servants* (2nd ed., London, 1974), 326-31.

3 W.R. Prest, *The Inns of Court under Elizabeth I and the early Stuarts 1590-1640* (London, 1972), 30.

in 1560 were large London merchants, some of whom were above the rank of gentleman and many of whom were undoubtedly quite wealthy. On this point exact quantitative evidence is not available, but it appears from the plea rolls that these large merchants make up a much more significant proportion of total litigants in 1560 than they do in later years. Thus there is some reason to believe that the status of plaintiffs was undergoing a slight decline. This was complemented by an increase in the number of defendants who were from the groups of gentleman and above. In the Common Pleas between 1560 and 1640 the number of gentry defendants increases by 14 per cent, in the King's Bench by about 7 per cent. The implication of these changes must be that a larger percentage of men above the rank of gentleman were being sued by their social inferiors.

How does this picture of King's Bench and Common Pleas litigants compare with what little we know about social change during the period? It is likely that the reigns of Elizabeth I and the early Stuarts saw an increase in the national wealth. For those with some wealth, even if it were that of the village yeoman, it seems to have been a time of inflation and greater material prosperity.[1] Thus Sir John Davies' explanation of the increase in litigation on this basis seems plausible. Whether or not the national wealth was being re-distributed in any meaningful way is more difficult to say. In one case, that of the attorneys, where we can be reasonably sure that there was an increase in the size and wealth of the group, this seems to be reflected in their presence in the courts. The number of Common Pleas attorneys grew at least three-fold during the period, and they appear as litigants just about that much more often in 1640 than in 1560. But from the vantage point of the Common Pleas, if it is true that the non-landed classes gained an increased share of the national pie, it appears to have made relatively little impact. These groups may have been slightly more liable to sue in 1640 than in 1560, but their overall presence in the courts stays more or less the same. In the King's Bench the status of litigants was even lower than in the Common Pleas; but, once more, there was very little real change over the period. The evidence of both courts suggests than in general we need to be cautious when talking about changes in the status of litigants as a major factor in the legal development of the period.

It is impossible to know exactly how wealthy the non-gentry litigants in the King's Bench and Common Pleas were, but some estimate of the possible range of their wealth can be hazarded. The

1   W.G. Hoskins, *Essays in Leicestershire History* (Liverpool, 1950), 135.

average Exeter merchant may have earned around £100 a year in the early seventeenth century. In medium and smaller sized towns, merchant income was probably (on a liberal estimate) no more than £50 a year,[1] and this is also about the right figure for the average yeoman farmer. Husbandmen and artisans were worth even less. If these figures are right, the implication is that litigation was not nearly so expensive as has usually been thought, and this is verified by the evidence which remains about the costs of suits. The account-book of the Hitchin attorney George Draper contains the charges for hundreds of cases. Very few seem to have cost more than £5, almost none more than £10.[2] My own calculations for the cost of a suit for a £100 debt in the King's Bench and Common Pleas come to between £6 and £8. Indeed, the very large number of litigants from the less wealthy classes suggests that the early-modern courts were surprisingly accessible. It was in the eighteenth and especially the late nineteenth centuries that complaints were heard that high costs were driving clients out of court.[3]

The reasons why men went to law varied from case to case, but some general idea of the issues involved can be gathered from the forms of action on which they sued. By 1560 the old real actions at common law had virtually disappeared.[4] In their place as ways of trying rights to land came first various types of actions of trespass and then *ejectio firmae*, which by the early seventeenth century covered disputes about title to both freehold and copyhold land. Thus, some of the actions of trespass in Table 2[5] involved questions about land, but it also lay for chasing cattle, knocking down hedges, breaking a close and mowing grass, breaking doors and windows, or digging in another man's mine.[6] These cases, like those brought in the Court of Chancery to determine manorial customs, often involved long-standing disputes of considerable personal or social

1 For some estimates of merchant wealth, see R. Grassby, 'The Personal Wealth of the Business Community in 17th Century England', *Economic History Review*, 2nd ser., 23 (1970), 231-2.

2 'The Account Book of George Draper'. I am grateful to Messrs Hawkins and Co., Portmill Lane, Hitchin, Hertfordshire, for allowing me to consult this manuscript in their possession.

3 R. Boote, *Historical Treatise of an Action or Suit at Law* (2nd ed., London, 1781), iii; Abel-Smith and Stevens, *Lawyers and the Courts*, 87.

4 Sutherland, *Assize of Novel Disseisin*, ch. 5; J.H. Baker, *An Introduction to English Legal History* (London, 1971), 167.

5 Based on the rolls of warrants cited in note 2 on p. 42. The total numbers of cases in each year for each court are: Common Pleas, 923, 1,934, 1,229; King's Bench, 82, 1,411, 679.

6 [Anon.], *The Practick Part of the Law: Shewing the Office of a Complete Attorney* (1658), 102-4; Fitz. N.B. 85-92.

Table 2
Actions in the King's Bench and Common Pleas, 1560 – 1640.

| | 1560 | | 1606 | | 1640 | |
	C.P.[a]	K.B.	C.P.	K.B.	C.P.	K.B.
	%	%	%	%	%	%
Debt	67	19	80	46	88	80
Trespass	16	55	6	23	3	5
Actions on the case	2	19	2	19	5	13
Ejectment	1	–	2	8	1	2½
Miscellaneous[b]	14	7	10	5	3	–
Total	100	100	100	100	100	100

a Common recoveries – collusive actions for the breaking of entails – which accounted for 79 (or 9%) of Common Pleas actions in the 1560 sample, have not been included in these figures. After 25 Elizabeth I, recoveries were moved from the plea rolls to a new series of recovery rolls (CP 43), so they do not figure elsewhere in the table. From sample recovery rolls in later years (CP 43/3 and CP 43/91) it is clear that recoveries continued to be an important source of business.

b The miscellaneous actions include detinue, covenant, breaches of statutes, waste (Common Pleas only) and writs of error (King's Bench only).

consequence. They also reflect an agrarian society where force and violence still played a large part in men's affairs. For example, disputes over enclosures could result in actions of trespass, and the great chronicler of lawsuits, John Smith of Nibley, explains how the breaking of closes and forcible entry were commonplace tactics in the property disputes of his master, Lord Berkeley.[1] Throughout the period under discussion, actions of trespass and ejectment continued to make up an important part of the business of the courts; but, as Table 2 shows, the percentage of litigation they constituted (though probably not their absolute numbers) had declined dramatically by 1640. For, in both the King's Bench and Common Pleas, the forms of action which grew most in frequency during this period were debt and actions on the case. In 1560, 67 per cent of cases in the Common Pleas and 19 per cent of those in the King's Bench were based on debt. By 1640, over 80 per cent of all the cases in both courts involved actions of debt, mostly debt on contracts. The second most prevalent kinds of suit were actions on the case, which in 1640 made up 13 per cent of King's Bench litigation and 5 per cent of that in the Common Pleas.

1 John Smith [of Nibley], *The Lives of the Berkeleys* (Gloucester, 1883-95), ii, 296, 302-3.

To some extent, jurisdictional changes may have been responsible for the relative growth of actions of debt in the King's Bench and Common Pleas. The spectacular increase in the percentage of debt cases in the King's Bench is certainly a product of the steady rise in popularity of the bill procedure, which gave the court competence to hear such cases. Moreover, the relative decline of trespass might be accounted for by a movement of cases which would have fallen into that category away from the common-law courts into Star Chamber or Chancery, or even their reincarnation as actions on the case. But if we allow for changes in jurisdiction, we have also to allow for the fact that, even in 1640, the Star Chamber and Chancery handled many times less business than the King's Bench and Common Pleas. On balance, then, it appears that the increase in the amount of litigation in the central courts was accompanied by a significant change in its nature.

The extent to which these changes in the frequency of the various forms of action may reflect changes in society is difficult to assess. There can be little doubt that the legal disputes of the sixteenth and seventeenth centuries often involved more than a man seeking a remedy for a simple wrong done to him. England in these times was a close-knit society and, as in some primitive cultures, law-suits probably involved long-standing animosity between neighbours more frequently than they do today.[1] The vexatious litigant, the man who sued on the slightest chance for gain or merely to annoy an old rival, is a familiar player on the Elizabethan and early Stuart scene.[2] The local connections of rival litigants made the fear of partisan juries widespread.[3] Violence could erupt as a consequence of a long-standing dispute. John Smith writes of how two of Lord Berkeley's followers became overheated and 'multiplied suits against Sir Thomas like the heads of Hidra, soe farr forth suffering their passions to transport them that instead of rakes and sheafpikes to gather tithe to harvest . . . they carried their workfolks out of Berkeley town armed with swords and bucklers, halberds and such like weapons'.[4] Professor Barnes's work on the Star Chamber suggests that the court was the ideal place for the rich man who was willing to try anything in order to win a feud. Barnes also suggests that, since so many of the gentry of the age went to the inns of court, many of them must have been able to direct their

1 M. Gluckman, 'The Judicial Process among the Barotse of Northern Rhodesia', *The Sociology of Law*, ed. V. Aubert (London, 1969), 167.

2 Jones, *Elizabethan Court of Chancery*, 315.

3 A.H. Smith, *County and Court: Government and Politics in Norfolk, 1558-1603* (Oxford, 1974), 150.

4 Smith, *Lives of the Berkeleys*, ii, 313.

own suits.[1] Knowledge of the law rather than of martial arms was the Elizabethan way to vanquish an enemy.[2]

Nevertheless, though the vexatious and learned litigant may have been notorious, the status of the people who sued in the King's Bench and Common Pleas suggests that he was far from typical. It is clear that between 1560 and 1640 the majority of litigants (70 per cent) were not necessarily very rich. Nor could they have been very learned in the law. As we have seen, most were from social groups below those which can be associated with the inns of court. These were by any definition the typical litigants, though they were not the spectacular ones. They were dependent on the legal profession for advice, and in turn the legal profession (especially the attorneys) were dependent on them for the bulk of their business. As Table 2 indicates, by 1640 the vast majority of these litigants were in court on actions of debt or actions on the case. With the important exception of some kinds of action on the case (such as slander), these suits were more likely to have been the result of business dealings than of vindictiveness or ancient disputes between neighbours. On the other hand, actions of trespass — at least, according to seventeenth-century writers — arose from wrongs accompanied by 'a kinde, or at least with a colour of violence'.[3] Although the level of violence represented by these actions can be exaggerated, they do clearly indicate incidents in which men acted first and only afterwards went to law. As cases of debt grew and those of trespass declined, it is possible to see a society in which the rule of law was replacing individual action. The courts were becoming more important as sources of particular remedies than as arenas for personal feuds.

The lawyers

Consideration of the increase in litigation and of the kinds of people involved in it leads to a number of other problems. Questions about the relationship between the King's Bench and Common Pleas, and their relationship with other courts, are obvious. For example, how important were the costs of various courts in determining their availability? From the point of view of professional legal assistance, and perhaps of procedure in general, I suspect that the two common-law courts were cheaper than either the Star Chamber or

1 Above, p.23. For the 'learned lay clients' see also his review of Prest, *Inns of Court 1590-1640*, in *American Historical Review* 78 (1973), 1055.

2 L. Stone, *The Crisis of the Aristocracy* (Oxford, 1966), 240-2.

3 W. Sheppard, *The Faithful Councellor: or, the Marrow of the Law in English* (London, 1653), 280.

Chancery.[1] At this date many suits could go a long way in the King's Bench and Common Pleas without much assistance from barristers or serjeants, who were more expensive than attorneys.[2] One of the most important consequences of the increase in litigation was the changes it brought in the judicial bureaucracy. It is significant that the most severe attacks on the Chancery and Common Pleas during the investigations of Charles I's commissions on fees came from the attorneys.[3] But to conclude, I would like to look at yet another contemporary opinion about the causes of the increase in litigation — the notion that swarms of attorneys were creating a multitude of suits.

Initially, we can turn for help to some facts about the number of attorneys. In 1560 there were about 150 attorneys acting in both the King's Bench and Common Pleas; in 1606 there were 1,000; and in 1640 a minimum of 1,400.[4] This verifies contemporary notions about the numbers of attorneys, but until 1606 their rise follows closely that of the number of suits. In general, this trend continues until 1640, but at that date there is some evidence of overcrowding. In Warwickshire, there were 45 attorneys in 1640, and there were still 45 Common Pleas men in 1732 when the increase in population and the prosperity of Birmingham must have made for more work.[5] More important, although the possibility of death or financial disaster as the result of the civil wars needs to be taken into account, it seems that many of the Warwickshire attorneys who were not well established in 1640 failed to flourish thereafter. The number of attorneys increased so quickly during the reign of Elizabeth I that it is difficult to see where they all came from, how they were trained, or whether they were trained at all. The answers to these questions probably lie in the inns of court and chancery. Dr Prest's figures for inns of court admissions suggest that there was a steep rise in the number of entrants between 1550 and 1570.[6] This was the critical period in terms of the increase in litigation; and it is likely that some of the non-legal factors operative

1 Chancery and Star Chamber suits may have been more costly simply because the procedure of taking evidence in written depositions required much time and effort. Certainly Archbishop Williams, Lord Keeper 1621-25, believed that poor men praised the common law because it was cheaper than equity: G.W. Thomas, 'Archbishop John Williams: Politics and Prerogative Law' (Oxford D.Phil. thesis, 1974), 37.

2 A short tract in the Bedford County Record Office, L28/47 ('A Problem whence it comes to passe that the Courte of Chancery of late . . . is so frequented'), suggests that barristers were rarely needed in the Common Pleas or King's Bench except in difficult cases.

3 The commissioners' papers are in class E 215.

4 The sources for the numbers of attorneys are those cited in notes 1 and 2 on p. 42, above.

5 'Roll of Attorneys 1732' : CP 11/2.

6 For inns of court admissions, see Prest, *Inns of Court 1590-1640,* 5-7.

in the growing interest in higher education during the English Renaissance produced lawyers and attorneys who made litigation more available than it ever had been before. But the close relationship between the increase in the size of the profession and the increase in litigation makes it difficult to break into the circle of cause and effect.

There are, however, a few other pieces of information which might shed more light on the problem. First, contemporary opinion should not be ignored. Secondly, as we have seen, the sorts of people who used the King's Bench and Common Pleas were the sorts of people who must have depended heavily on legal advice. Lastly, we must try to see what the raw figures for numbers of attorneys at various dates really meant in the context of specific communities within the population. In 1560 there were very few attorneys in England. There were, of course, even fewer barristers, but the lower branch is the main concern here. In 1560 there was one attorney for every 20,000 people (taking population as 3,500,000). In 1606 there was one for every 4,000; in 1640 one for every 2,500; and in 1732 one for every 1,500 people in the country. In 1560 this meant that, in some parts of England, access to legal services can hardly have been easy. There were only three attorneys handling cases for Warwickshire at that date, and it seems unlikely that more than one of these lived in the county. Similarly, in Berkshire and Oxfordshire an attorney named John Grove handled most cases, but his practice was spread over both the vast Western and Oxford circuits; probate evidence suggests that he lived in Somerset. Naturally, more prosperous counties had more attorneys. There were five or six reasonably busy members of the lower branch in Gloucestershire at the beginning of the reign. Norfolk, long known for the litigiousness of its population, and accounting for 13 per cent of all Common Pleas litigation in 1560, had fifteen Common Pleas attorneys.[1] Further research is needed on the legal profession of this litigious county, but fifteen attorneys probably meant that the legal profession was beginning to be important in the various administrative posts which existed in town and county government. In Warwickshire, however, and presumably in other less litigious counties, it was not until the seventeenth century that attorneys moved into posts such as town clerk or took over as manorial stewards. By the time of James I, the profession was beginning to make a significant impact on local government. More important, by 1580 and certainly by 1600, there were enough attorneys in most parts of England to be readily available to litigants who wanted them. It must be true that the increased

1 Percentage of cases from the rolls of warrants of attorney, cited in note 2 on p. 42, above.

availability of lawyers made litigation possible for more members of the population, even if it did not directly cause it.

An illustration of this point is the slowness with which the King's Bench came to rival the Common Pleas in volume of litigation. Even in 1640, in spite of its evident procedural advantages, the King's Bench handled only about one-third as many cases as the Common Pleas. The best explanation of why this was so is simply that the King's Bench had fewer attorneys. From about 1570, the attorneys, once operative in both courts, became segregated into one or the other of them. In the King's Bench this process went even further, so that by 1606 the vast majority of the 240 attorneys in the court were also clerks of the chief clerk (prothonotary), and this innovation evidently kept down the number of attorneys.[1] In 1640 the Common Pleas had over 1,000, but the King's Bench only 300 attorneys. Since there were fewer attorneys in the latter, it was more difficult for cases to reach it.

The increase in the amount of litigation in the central courts, the trend for the courts to become more open to non-gentry elements in society, and the increase in the number of lawyers, might therefore have been seen in a postive light as the spread of valuable remedies to greater numbers of people. However, most contemporaries did not think of it that way. To them the multiplicity of suits was a disaster, and the attorneys who brought the cases into the courts a group of dishonest tricksters who were a cancer in the body of the commonwealth. Allegations that the attorneys stirred up suits were accompanied by charges of corruption, and this picture of the profession has come down into the writings of recent historians. Dishonest attorneys did of course exist, but it is fairly easy to show that these were no more typical of the profession as a whole then than they are in the second half of the twentieth-century. For example, relative to the number of practitioners there were very few cases in the papers of the early Stuart commissioners of fees against the attorneys.[2] More lawyers certainly meant more who were corrupt; more lawyers also made regulation of them a more important issue. But, in general, the quality and nature of the lower branch of the legal profession have changed less between 1600 and 1975 than the attitudes of society towards them.

There were several reasons for the distrust and dislike of attorneys. They were almost always of lower social status than their critics; and the economic thinking of the day held that lawyers, instead of adding

1 Percentage of cases from the rolls of warrants of attorney, cited in note 2 on p. 42, above.
2 E 215.

to the national wealth, siphoned their income from those farmers, merchants and tradesmen who did. The author of *Britannia Languens* thought that, as men's estates crumbled, the lawyers made profits just as 'doubtless did some bricklayers get estates by the burning of the city'.[1] These social and economic views of the profession were combined in the caricatures of lawyers which found their way onto the Jacobean stage, in plays such as Jonson's *Staple of the News*.

But what men thought about lawyers was also closely connected with what they thought about law-suits, and, ultimately, with what they thought about the functions of law. In modern capitalist societies, law is often described as a means of resolving conflicts between individuals.[2] In the sixteenth and seventeenth centuries, its role was much more comprehensive. Writers from Sir John Fortescue in the late fifteenth century to Sir Henry Finch in the early seventeenth century thought that the law was the means by which society was held together. Fortescue wrote that the laws were the sinews which extended through the kingdom and held together the body of the people. Finch described law as a means of well ordering civil society. His contemporary, William Fulbecke, believed that without law, 'which I interpret to be an order established by authority, nether house, nor city, nor nation, nor mankind, nor nature, nor world can be'.[3] The idea that law functioned as a remedy, or that increased wealth and trade made more suits inevitable, did exist; but in theory, and in the minds of laymen, law was more than a mere arbiter; it was a reflection of God's will about the way the world should be, a set of precepts which enabled men to tell right from wrong.

These notions about the functions of law implied that law-suits were a potential breach of the social order, more the product of the ill will of men than the result of business-dealings or personal accident. An Elizabethan parliamentary bill for law reform mentions 'the multitude of contentions which for lack of charity rise upon the smallest occasions betwene neighbours'.[4] The Jesuit, Robert Parsons, thought

---

1 'Britannia Languens, or a Discourse of Trade' (1680) in *A Select Collection of Early English Tracts on Commerce,* ed. J.R. McCullock (Cambridge, 1970), 302, 375.

2 See, e.g., H.G. Bredemeier, 'Law as an Integrative Mechanism' in *Sociology of Law,* ed. Aubert, 53.

3 Sir John Fortescue, *De Laudibus Legum Anglie,* ed. S.B. Chrimes (Cambridge, 1942), 31; H. Finch, *Law or a Discourse thereof in Foure Bookes* (London, 1627), 1; W. Fulbecke, *A Direction or Preparative to the Study of Law* (London, 1603), 2.

4 'Reformacyons proposed in Parliament' (1576): SP 12/107/96.

that covetousness caused the multitude of suits.[1] Bread Ryce compared vain men who spent money on law-suits with those who spent it on extravagant clothing.[2] The lawyers, too, were ambivalent about the reasons for going to law. The early seventeenth-century Recorder of London, Sir Anthony Benn, thought that suits were connected mostly with the fact that men said to themselves 'what is thine is mine' as well as 'what is mine is mine'.[3] Sir John Davies cynically observed that, if only all men lived according to the law of nature, there would be no need for law-suits.[4]

Since law-suits were seen as a social evil, it was only natural that, in an age when their number was increasing rapidly, lawyers should have been discredited. The ideal lawyer ought to have been an agent of reconciliation; instead, the multiplicity of suits seemed to reflect a legal profession which encouraged contention between neighbours. Consequently, many men appear to have agreed with the lesson which Robert Burton learned from Plato: that it was a 'great sign of an intemprete and corrupt common wealth where lawyers and physicians did abound'.[5]

Attitudes towards litigation and hence towards lawyers may also have contained a political element. In 1640 one in every eighty Englishmen was using the king's courts, and using these courts implied recognition of the king's rule, often at the expense of the powerful local magnate or lord of the manor. During the late sixteenth century, the common lawyers completely undermined the authority of manorial jurisdictions by recognising the right of copyholders to sue in the central courts.[6] Most lawyers probably agreed with Roger Wilbraham that 'it is every subject's natural birthright to enjoy the benefit of the prince's lawes'.[7] Coke claimed in public that if 'Justice [was] withheld, only the poorer sort are those that smart for it',[8] presumably because they would then be swamped by their richer neighbours.

1 R. Parsons, 'A Memorial of the Reformation of England' in *The Jesuits' Memorial,* ed. E. Gee (London, 1690), 244.

2 *Opinion Diefied. Discovering the Ingins, Traps, and Traynes that are Set in this Age, Whereby to Catch Opinion. By B[read] R[yce] gent. servant to the King* (London, 1613), 21.

3 'Essayes written by Anthony Benn, knight, Recorder of London': Bedford County Record Office, L28/46, f.17v.

4 Davies, 'A Discourse of Law and Lawyers', 267.

5 R. Burton, *The Anatomy of Melancholy* (London, 1813 ed.), ii, 86.

6 See, generally, C. Calthrope, *The Relation Between the Lord of a Manor and the Copy-Holder His Tenant* (London, 1635).

7 Sir Roger Wilbraham's diary and commonplace books (1593-1646): Folger Lib., MS. Mb.42 (microfilm of typescript copy).

8 *The Lord Coke His Speech and Charge* (London, 1607), sig. Civ.

That some of the better sort objected to the increase in litigation because it implied giving ordinary people more access to remedies through law is suggested by one of the few contemporary comments which argued in favour of the increase in litigation and which spoke sympathetically of the attorneys. Its author was a lawyer (probably an attorney) named William Barlee. Barlee was something of a crank, but he was a thoughtful one, and the attorneys have their say too rarely for his evidence not to be useful. During the 1570s he was writing a 'concordance of all written lawes concerning lords of manors',[1] the aim of which was to make the law known to lords of manors and their tenants. But, because the 'Concordance' was designed to disseminate legal knowledge, Barlee feared that the judges might oppose it on the grounds that

> Many suits have arisen in the comen courts, amongst subjects . . .
> since our statute lawes were published in the English tongue to
> the common sort of people. And for this only cause, some . . .
> would have the knowledge of our common laws obscurely hedd
> from the common sort of people, as they are now.

Against this position, Barlee argued that the same reasons had been set forth for the withholding of English scriptures, but had been defeated by natural reason and the express word of God. He concluded by mentioning that counsellors were often helped by learned attorneys, and chastised 'those lawyers who forgett how by juste suits wrongfull dealings are quitely suppressed'.[2] Standing alone, the views of Barlee may not have strength enough to carry convincingly an argument in favour of the increase in litigation. But it must be remembered that the arguments against the increase and against the attorneys came largely from the legal and social establishment. Barlee's ideas suggest how an alternative position could be formulated, and their existence should cause us to wonder why the increase in litigation and lawyers was usually deplored.

The point to be made here is not that, as a group, the attorneys can be seen as in any way especially committed to upholding the rights of the common sort of people. Lawyers are always likely to be found on both sides of a dispute. Barlee himself was concerned that his work, which touched on the thorny question of the rights of copyholders, should not get into the hands of 'rash headed fellows, lest they tare you

1 W. Barlee, *A Concordance of All Written Lawes Concerning Lords of Mannours, Theire Free Tenentes, and Copieholders* (Manorial Society, 1911).
2 Letter from Barlee to William Lord Burghley, dated November 1578: Brit. Lib., Lansdowne MS. 99, f.134.

or your friends in pieces. I mean lest they vexe [lords of manors]'.¹ But he did appreciate that the poor as well as the rich could benefit from litigation; and attorneys, whether or not they intended it, made it possible for more of the lower sort to sue. Despite perpetual complaints about increased fees, law in the seventeenth century was not prohibitively expensive, and the courts opened relatively quickly to a large section of the population. In an age of rising prices, the rights of landowners became crucial, and enough examples of the struggles between landlords and tenants exist to make it clear that recourse to the law was important to both sides. Legality also came into the relationship between urban corporations and the central government. In both cases men who were unlearned in the law could benefit from the increased availability of lawyers. The fact that there were more lawyers than ever before may have forced the law into the position of arbiter. What is more clear is that more lawyers made the law a weapon which could be put into the hands of ordinary men. An example of the exaggerated reaction this development brought from some of the ruling classes in the sixteenth and seventeenth centuries is contained in a petition to the House of Commons just after the Restoration. It accused the attorneys of stirring up suits, and attacked them for using the style of 'gentleman'. But it went on to say that 'they are bold impudent fellows that scarce allow any priviledges, noe not to the very best of his Majestie's subjects'. One of them, claimed the petitioner, had been instrumental in drawing up the indictment of the late martyr, King Charles I. ²

1 Barlee, *Concordance*, 1.
2 'Attorneys in parte Anatomized . . . By a Christian Hand': Bod. Lib., Ashmole MS. 15371, ff.2-12.

TRIAL BY THE BOOK ?
FACT AND THEORY IN THE CRIMINAL PROCESS
1558 – 1625

J.S. Cockburn

There are two fundamentally different approaches to the study of law in action. Many lawyers incline to an essentially theoretical concept, which assumes that a legal system conforms to abstract rules enshrined, by and large, in statutes and legal authorities. Sociologists, on the other hand, are committed to descriptions based on factual observation; they tend therefore to minimize the lawyers' theoretical reasoning and to prefer an explanation which rests on recorded events. This may create an illusion of conflict. But it does not in fact follow that the two approaches are necessarily incompatible, since any full description of a legal system must consider both theory and practice. We hardly need reminding that every game of football is not necessarily played, for the full ninety minutes, in scrupulous conformity with the rules; nor that the laws of most games are applied inconsistently at different times and in different places and are periodically modified to meet changing circumstances or new demands. However, the growing interest shown by sociologists in a field long dominated by essentially theoretical accounts of both law and procedure[1] suggests that a reminder of the gulf between theory and application, in the context of the criminal law, may be opportune.

In the belief that a meaningful history of English criminal justice will emerge only from an effective combination of the theoretical and practical approaches, I have been examining – in the context both of actual trials and of the theoretical guidelines set out by the legal authorities – some 5000 indictments tried at Home Circuit assizes during the period 1558-1625.[2] This exercise is still far from complete: indictments are, as

1 Recent manifestations of this sociological interest include J. Samaha, *Law and Order in Historical Perspective: The Case of Elizabethan Essex* (New York, 1974); J.M. Beattie, 'The Pattern of Crime in England 1660-1800', *Past and Present*, 62 (1974), 47-95; J. Walter and K. Wrightson, 'Dearth and The Social Order in Early Modern England', ibid., 71 (1976), 22-42; and several of the essays in *Crime in England 1550-1800*, ed. J.S. Cockburn (London and Princeton, 1977).

2 In this period the Home Circuit comprised the counties of Essex, Hertfordshire, Kent, Surrey and Sussex. The contents of all the surviving Home Circuit 'indictment' files for the reigns of Elizabeth I and James I are being published in calendar form by Her Majesty's Stationery Office. The first four volumes in this series, containing Herts and Sussex material, appeared in 1975-6; they are here referred to as *Herts*, I, *Herts*, II, *Sussex*, I, and *Sussex*, II, respectively. A further three volumes forthcoming are cited as *Essex*, I, *Kent*, I and *Surrey*, I, respectively. The references, which are to entries not pages, are given in square brackets after the

Sir James Stephen ruefully observed, 'like a slate the greater part of the writing on which has been half rubbed out';[1] and I must apologize for my failure, in some cases, to explain what is written, and, in others, to supply what is not. Nevertheless, the survey has already confirmed a suspicion that the superficial monotony of routine criminal indictments conceals information of great value to our understanding of the thinking behind the law and practice of criminal trials. This essay is intended to demonstrate not only that this record evidence can shed new light upon hitherto dark areas of criminal process, but also that it suggests the need for some modifications in our approach to the history of criminal justice.

A convenient starting-point for any examination of criminal process is the form of the indictment itself.[2] By the middle of the sixteenth century the law governing the form of criminal indictments had been settled for almost 150 years. Every authority on criminal actions — from Marrow at the very end of the fifteenth century[3] to Dalton in the seventeenth[4] — agreed that to sustain an indictment at law the elements of precision and certainty were absolutely essential. Pulton echoed Staunford: 'An indictment which is uncertain is not good'.[5] By 1558 an accurate recital of the accused's name and 'addition' (as defined by the Statute of Additions, 1413)[6] and of the essential facts of the case were universally recognized as imperative to a good indictment. A host of King's Bench decisions during this period, more than thirty reported by Croke and Dyer alone, buttressed the general proposition that 'indictments ought to be precise and certain in every point'.[7] Case law also reiterated the necessity to observe minute variations in drafting — 'dainty and nice differences', as Lambard[8] termed them — stipulating,

Public Record Office call-numbers. Since this essay was written I have examined a further 4,000 indictments. While raising several additional problems, this new material in general reinforces the arguments advanced here.

1 J.F. Stephen, *A History of the Criminal Law of England* (London, 1883), I, 286.

2 A fuller examination of the indictment evidence, with illustrations, appears in J.S. Cockburn, 'Early-modern assize records as historical evidence', *Journal of the Society of Archivists*, 5 (1975), 215-31.

3 T. Marowe, *De Pace Terre et Ecclesie* (a reading on Westminster I, c.1, Inner Temple, 1503), ed. B.H. Putnam in *Early Treatises on the Practice of the Justice of the Peace* (Oxford, 1924), 289, at 383-94.

4 M. Dalton, *The Countrey Justice* (1618), 361.

5 W. Staunford, *Les Plees del Coron* (London, 1577), 95; F. Pulton, *De Pace Regis et Regni* (London, 1609), 175.

6 1 Hen.5, c.5.

7 *R. v. Fitz-Williams* (1604) Cro. Jac. 19, at 20, *per* Gawdy and Yelverton JJ.

8 W. Lambard, *Eirenarcha* (London, 1592), 473.

for example, that the form for valuing inanimate objects in the plural should be 'ad valenciam', that for single inanimate objects and all animate objects, 'precii'.[1] Legal theory was quite clear: failure to observe such formal requirements to the letter rendered the indictment void.

In practice, however, the law, as reflected in assize trials, settled for less stringent standards of drafting. Legal authorities insisted, for instance, on an unambiguous statement of the accused's occupation and place of abode. Both place and county were essential to the indictment: so strict was the requirement that not even the inclusion of the county in the margin of an indictment could save it if the county was not mentioned in the body of the instrument. 'Indictments', as trial judges constantly reiterated, were 'not to be taken by intendment'.[2] Assize practice, however, scarcely mirrored legal theory. Two separate lines of inquiry indicate quite clearly that in a large number of cases the occupation attributed to the accused in an indictment, or his place of abode, or both, are entirely fallacious. By collating the details contained in recognizances for appearance to stand trial or give evidence with those given in the relevant indictments, it is possible to show that perhaps even a majority of assize indictments, while technically satisfying the legal requirements, are factually worthless.

There are at least four major grounds for assuming a high standard of accuracy in recognizances. First, actual supervision was an essential element of the recognizance system: the device would have been rendered worthless if sureties for a suspect's appearance had been drawn from a community fifty or more miles from his real place of abode. Second, where there are several recognizances, taken by different magistrates at different times, they are mutually consistent. Third, recognizances were taken locally, by local agents, and involved local characters and locally-known circumstances. This strongly suggests a climate for circumstantial accuracy. Fourth, where recognizances can be tested against evidence from sources other than indictments, they are found to be substantially accurate.

In literally dozens of cases the indictment and its associated recognizances are in direct contradiction on occupation, domicile, or both: [indictment] Richard Smith of Bishop's Stortford, labourer, *or* [recognizance] of Towcester, Northamptonshire, linen-draper; William Barnes of Royston, labourer, *or* of London, yeoman; John Wells of Bennington,

1 Marowe, *De Pace,* ed. Putnam, 390; W. West, *Symboleography* (London, 1627 ed.), ii, 94. For full references to and further discussion of this topic, see Cockburn, 'Early-modern assize records', 227.

2 *R.* v. *Elnor* (1590) Cro. Eliz. 184; *R.* v. *Child* (1598) ibid., 606; *R.* v. *Ludlow* (1600) ibid., 738; *Hamond* v. *Reg.* (1600) ibid., 751.

labourer, *or* of Long Lane, London, 'horscorser'; John Atts of Royston, labourer, *or* of Lichfield, Staffordshire, ostler; John Fowler of Bunting-ford, labourer, *or* of Ratcliffe, Middlesex, brewer; Thomas Clarke of Barkway, *or* of Halifax, Yorkshire; John and Prudence Pickott of Pirton, *or* of Wellingborough, Northamptonshire.[1] (The suggestive precision of occupations given in the recognizances needs hardly be stressed). And even where there is no direct contradiction between the two sources, all too often the sureties for the suspect's appearance are men living at great distances from his indictment 'domicile'.

The collation which reveals this massive discrepancy is of course possible only where recognizances have survived in quantity. For Essex they have not; and it is therefore unfortunate that the first published work attempting to quantify indictment data should rest on the records of that county.[2] Nevertheless, even if the contradiction implicit in the recognizances is discounted, the discrepancies revealed where one suspect is the subject of multiple indictments drawn by different clerks have still to be explained. It is surely no accident that this body of mutual inconsistency (present in the records of all the circuit's five counties) points in exactly the same direction as the recognizance evidence. As far as domicile is concerned, the clerk's general rule is to make the suspect's abode fit the crime: indicted for a burglary at Horsham, William Topsall is 'of Horsham', indicted for a similar offence at East Grinstead, he is 'of East Grinstead'; indicted in Hertfordshire for a highway robbery at Amwell, the three principals are said to be 'of Amwell', indicted in Essex for a similar offence at Hatfield, they become 'labourers of Hatfield'.[3] Which, if any, is their true place of abode is, in the absence of collateral evidence in the shape of recognizances or other documents, impossible to ascertain.

The legal requirement that every indictment should also include the date of the offence, accurately stated, was also in practice frequently disregarded. Once more the critical nature of this requirement is under-lined by a series of leading cases decided in the later years of Elizabeth's reign.[4] And once more it is possible to prove that in a significant number of assize indictments the divorce of fact from theory is com-plete. Further correlation of indictments and recognizances indicates that the date of the offence given in the former is inaccurate (in that it

1   Full references to these examples are given in Cockburn, 'Early-modern assize records', 225, note 62.

2   Samaha, *Law and Order in Elizabethan Essex.*

3   For references and illustrations, see Cockburn, 'Early-modern assize records', 225, note 64, and plate I.

4   E.g. *R. v. Buckler* (1551) Dyer 68, §28; *R. v. Wingfield* (1600) Cro. Eliz. 738; *R. v. Plowman* (1600) ibid., 752.

post-dates the recognizances associated with it) in between 30 and 50 per cent of all instances in which this comparison is possible. The margin of error ranges between one day and three months, differences of between one and two months being quite common. All the evidence examined so far indicates that this phenomenon is fairly consistent: recognizances survive in twenty-six of the forty-two Jacobean assize files for Hertfordshire, and in all twenty-six cases they reveal dating discrepancies in one or more indictments.[1]

Even allowing a fairly generous margin for genuine scribal error — there is of course a sprinkling of offences dated 31 November, and so on — discrepancy on this scale poses serious problems, particularly for the sociologist. For the benefit of legal historians, it is only fair to add that a minority of judicial opinion considered that indictments should not fail on mere technicalities. As Coke put it in an appeal of mayhem in 1586, 'an indictment shall not abate for form, if it be sufficient in substance of matter'.[2] Rolle reported a case in 1618 in which the King's Bench actually instructed the Western Circuit clerk of assize to amend the record where the error was purely formal, 'lest an infinite number of indictments should be rendered void through clerical negligence'.[3]

But the general rule excluding defence counsel from Crown cases meant that matters of form were seldom raised at assizes. Nor were indictments monitored and corrected as a bureaucratic formality: alterations *were* made during the proceedings, but such amendments followed set patterns and were made for other reasons to which we will come shortly. A moderately alert attorney could probably have made mincemeat of perhaps half of the indictments considered at assizes. In the rare cases — almost all, significantly, involving influential defendants, and most, unusual charges — where counsel are known to have been retained, their intrusion brought a rash of exceptions to the indictment and, in most cases, secured its removal into King's Bench. Thus when John Mercer, parish clerk of Hawkhurst, was indicted in 1600 for striking a woman in Hawkhurst churchyard two years earlier, his counsel, Edmund Pelham (retained, no doubt, because of his residence just across the border in Sussex), pointed out that:

1   To the grounds earlier adduced for accepting the general reliability of recognizances can now be added the improbability of recognizances for appearance and to give evidence being taken before any crime had been committed.

2   *Anon.* (1586) Godb.67, pl.80. See also *R.* v. [*Heydon*] (1586) Godb.65, pl.78, *per* Coke ('if indictments have sufficient substance, they are not to be overthrown for trifles'); differently reported in 4 Rep. 41.

3   *R.* v. *Delbridge* (1618) 2 Rolle Rep. 59 (translated). I owe this reference to Dr J.H. Baker.

(i) it appeareth not where John Mercer dwelleth; (ii) 'parish clerk' is no sufficient addition; (iii) it is not shown in what county Hawkhurst is; (iv) it is not laid certainly when the said striking was, but in this sort, *viz.* about the 30th day of June 40 Eliz., which word (about) comprehendeth no certainty; (v) the striking is laid to be in the churchyard of the said parish church of Hawkhurst, and showeth not in what county that churchyard is; (vi) it is presented that John Mercer 'did violently strike, etc', where the words of the statute be that 'none shall strike or lay violent hands', which words be not preferred. For which causes, and diverse others I do take the presentment to be insufficient. And pray that it may be so adjudged.[1]

Perhaps fortunately, such expositions of the lawyer's craft were a rare feature in Crown proceedings at assizes. Very occasionally, a suspect charged with a newly-created statutory felony might be remanded while doubts about the form of the indictment — upon which he had already been convicted — were resolved.[2] But the hard fact remains that in some 5000 indictments I have discovered only six instances of trial being delayed because of doubts about the form of a routine indictment.[3]

One's attention is drawn, rather, to the great bulk of obviously defective indictments to which no exception was taken and the consistency with which certain information is misrepresented. These features suggest that we should examine very closely the connection between offence, prosecution, evidence and indictment. In particular, it focuses attention on the sources and nature of prosecutorial energy and on the possibility that some stages of criminal process may have been deliberately simplified or even avoided altogether. We will return in due course to this line of enquiry. First, however, it is necessary to introduce a further body of indictment evidence which suggests that the uncomfortable accommodation of fact and theory in criminal indictments extended far beyond the rather vague borderline between 'form' and 'substance'.

By the late sixteenth century a number of pressures — some stemming from social changes, others generated by inadequacies or contradictions in the law itself — were perverting the form of many indictments. For example, a long-established rule stipulated that it was legally unacceptable to give a heretic, dicer, carder or vagrant his true 'addition' because, in essence, these were pejorative terms, implying the practice of occupa-

---

1   ASSI 35/42/5, mm.9, 11 [*Kent*, I, 2767-8]. Pelham was created serjeant-at-law in 1601, and appointed Chief Baron in Ireland in 1602; he died in 1606. For another illustration (1593), see Cockburn, 'Early-modern assize records', 229.

2   E.g. ASSI 35/41/1, m.15 [*Herts*, I, 910]: indictment in March 1599 of a deserter wandering contrary to 39 Eliz.1, c.17.

3   To the references given in Cockburn, 'Early-modern assize records', 229, note 88, add: ASSI 35/14/4, m.37 [*Essex*, I, 586]; 35/50/9, m.1; 35/53/8, m.8; 35/59/7, mm.14, 15 [*Sussex*, II, 108, 206, 436].

tions forbidden by law.[1] Satisfaction of this principle, particularly in the case of vagrants, clearly involved drafting clerks in a significant degree of deliberate misrepresentation. Not only had indictments on the vagrant statutes to be framed in non-prejudicial terms, but the considerable criminal activity attributed to vagrants by Harman, Hext, and others[2] had to be concealed behind additions as misleading to us as they were innocuous at law. Thus, while sociologists are undoubtedly correct in assuming that many vagrants were out-of-work labourers,[3] by a strangely insensitive irony many of those indicted as 'labourers' were in fact vagrants.[4]

Underworld aliases, a feature commonly associated with the vagrant culture and prominent in Harman's list of Home County vagrants,[5] posed another problem. Felons professing no conventional surname — Black Will, Shakebag, Dick of London, Black John, Black Nan, or William with the Wry Mouth — were technically unindictable, a realization which possibly prompted the worried note on Wry Mouth's indictment apparently suggesting that his real name was, or for the purposes of indictment could be, 'Wood'.[6]

Of more central significance to the administration of justice were fictions used to minimize limitations in the criminal law itself. For instance, the prosecution of receivers, as Professor Milsom has pointed out,[7] presented considerable difficulties. They could not be indicted for theft because their offence was not *contra pacem* — there was no taking. Attempts to prosecute tham as accessories were complicated by the fact that an accessory could not be tried before judgment had been entered against the principal,[8] and they were, even then, of only limited value in that the law in general prescribed more lenient penalties for acces-

---

1 Lambard, *Eirenarcha*, 465. Cf. Marowe, *De Pace*, ed. Putnam, 386.

2 T. Harman, *A Caveat or Warning for Common Cursitors* (London, 1566), reproduced in *The Elizabethan Underworld*, ed. A.V. Judges (London, 1930), 61-118; Edward Hext's letter of 1596 (Brit. Lib., Lansdowne MS. 81, ff.161-2) printed in F. Aydelotte, *Elizabethan Rogues and Vagabonds* (Oxford, 1913), 168-73; *William Lambarde and Local Government: his 'Ephemeris' and 29 Charges to Juries and Commissions*, ed. C. Read (Cornell, 1962), 181; Dalton, *Countrey Justice*, 96-104.

3 E.g. A.L. Beier, 'Vagrants and the Social Order in Elizabethan England', *Past and Present* 64 (1974), 12.

4 E.g. ASSI 35/16/2, mm.51-2 [*Essex*, I, 701-2]; 35/63/2, mm.21, 70 [*Herts*, II, 1143]; 35/15/1, m.24; 35/31/3, m.49; 35/32/5, m.77 [*Kent*, I, 646, 1759, 1858].

5 Appended to *A Caveat for Common Cursitors*.

6 Illustrated in Cockburn, 'Early-modern assize records', plate III(1).

7 S.F.C. Milsom, *Historical Foundations of the Common Law* (London, 1969), 372.

8 E.g. *R. v. Syer* (1590) 4 Rep. 43.

sories. For a time receivers were reached through the processes of appeal and *de re adirata,* commenced against possessors. But between the decline of these devices and the first attempt to reach them directly by statute in 1702[1] many receivers enjoyed practical immunity, often, as the statute observed, by themselves concealing the principal. It is difficult to believe that the law felt itself so trapped in legal form that it tolerated the continuing existence of this gaping hole in the prosecution of dishonesty; and in fact it seems likely that it did not. For a number of instances in which evidentiary points have been noted on the indictment itself, or in which associated recognizances include details of the offence, suggest very strongly that the principal in a larceny indictment is often not the thief himself but an accessory, most commonly a receiver.[2] That this crude but effective fiction was utilized fairly widely is suggested by the large number of indictments in which the occupation of the accused, as entered, is closely related to the nature of the goods stolen: butchers stealing sheep or cattle; blacksmiths stealing iron utensils; curriers stealing hides and leather. 93 per cent of the butchers charged as principals in larceny indictments in Elizabethan Sussex had stolen livestock; virtually all the curriers charged were said to have stolen hides or leather. While it may be slightly difficult to envisage the village butcher systematically combing the countryside for meat on the hoof, it is quite reasonable to suppose that, innocently or otherwise, he would accept the carcases of stolen beasts and that his premises might be a natural focus for the suspicions of victims and law officers. It is also not unreasonable to assume that in the interests of prosecution he might be represented as a thief. However, the maintenance of this fiction throughout the proceedings leading up to his conviction at assizes again raises some intriguing questions about the practical nature of prosecution and evidence.

The growing suspicion that in these areas of trial process, too, the division between theory and application may have been significant is reinforced by a group of assize cases in which the record also tells us something of the facts behind the indictment. At Sussex assizes in 1616 a man was convicted, and executed, on an indictment alleging simple larceny at Horsham, Sussex; the evidence, as noted by the court clerk himself, proved the offence to have been a highway robbery committed in Surrey.[3] In a similar case tried at Essex assizes in 1586 two men were convicted of simple larceny at Thaxted. On the face of the indictment the clerk wrote, 'this stuff was taken by burglary in the night time and

1 1 Anne, stat.2, c.9.

2 See Cockburn, 'Early-modern assize records', 222.

3 ASSI 35/58/7, m.27 [*Sussex*, II, 341], reproduced in Cockburn, 'Early-modern assize records', plate III(2).

68

in another shire, as did appear upon the evidence'.[1] On an infanticide indictment tried in 1580 the clerk noted, 'it was not directly proved the child was in life'. The accused was, nevertheless, convicted and sentenced to death.[2] Acute problems are raised by the conviction of two men in 1568 for raping an unknown woman.[3] Instances in which the trial jury returned a special verdict on the facts of the case are equally suggestive. Perhaps the most compelling recital is that of the facts behind the indictment upon which four men were charged at Essex assizes in 1594. The jury's special verdict revealed that the accused had broken by night into a vessel lying in a tidal reach of the Thames and had forcibly taken away money and a gun from its occupant.[4] They were indicted and convicted for robbery in the highway at Purfleet. Other assize indictments on similar facts were removed to the Admiralty Court for trial,[5] and one cannot help wondering whether the court's desire to retain jurisdiction over the case may have influenced the form of the indictment. But other cases in which there was no possibility of jurisdictional conflict show not only equally startling mutations of the facts but also something of the thinking which motivated them. Particularly interesting is a case which, although tried at Hertford assizes about 1616, is apparently missing from the assize records. The reasons for its omission are unclear, but since Dr Baker has discovered two mutually consistent manuscript accounts of the case there seems little reason to doubt the authenticity of its facts.[6] Briefly, these were as follows. A man was having an adulterous relationship with the wife of his next-door neighbour. The couple eventually resolved to do away with the husband so that they could marry. They agreed to bore a small hole in the partition wall between the two dwellings through which the adulterer would shoot the husband with a handgun as he was getting ready for bed. The plot misfired when the bullet struck the folds of their victim's shirt and only wounded him. He had the pair bound over to Hertford assizes, where the trial judge, Houghton J., caused an indictment to be drawn against the adulterer for burglary, apparently citing the adulteress as an accessory. Upon this *both* were found guilty and executed. Significantly, both reports add that King James, on being informed of the trial, commended

1 ASSI 35/28/2, m.28 [*Essex*, I, 1674].

2 ASSI 35/22/10, m.27 [*Essex*, I, 1129], reproduced in Cockburn, 'Early-modern assize records', plate II(2).

3 ASSI 35/10/3, mm.37-8 [*Surrey*, I, 346-7].

4 ASSI 35/36/2, mm.21-2 [*Essex*, I, 2571].

5 E.g. ASSI 35/33/8, m.29 [*Sussex*, I, 1297]; 35/37/5, m.3 [*Kent*, I, 2251].

6 J.H. Baker, 'Criminal Justice at Newgate 1616-27: some manuscript Reports in the Harvard Law School', *Irish Jurist* 8 (1973), 307, at 317-8 and note 30.

the judge for an excellent piece of justice, 'the most rational of any that he had heard in the common law'.

One would not presume to cavil with such a regal verdict — rational, if slightly rough, justice it may well have been. But it is also a brand of justice not readily accommodated within the framework of trial process as we have hitherto imagined it. Under what circumstances, for instance, was the indictment in such cases drawn? How were they prosecuted — if they were prosecuted at all? Did the trial judges' power to initiate and dictate the form of a criminal prosecution, so clearly evident here, extend to other areas of process, enabling them also to prejudice the outcome of criminal trials and thus to give effect to coordinated policies towards the punishment of crime?

As far as indictment and prosecution goes, several points are fairly clear. Most immediately, virtually all the indictment evidence now before us seriously weakens the case for a formal prosecution procedure at assizes. Dr Langbein has recently revived Plucknett's view that the Marian bail and committal statutes turned the justice of the peace into 'something between a detective and a juge d'instruction', and he has argued persuasively that local magistrates did indeed 'orchestrate' the prosecution case, utilizing depositions as a kind of policeman's notebook to 'buttress [their] oral performance'.[1] There can be little doubt that, in theory, the justices' duties included the general supervision of criminal administration from preliminary enquiry down to trial — investigating complaints, examining and binding over witnesses and accused, and trying petty offences. But on two separate grounds we must now question whether they retained the initiative to conduct a formal prosecution at assizes.

First, we are obliged to ask by what process they (or indeed anyone else) managed successfully to prosecute cases in which the evidence they themselves had supposedly certified into court was materially at variance with the indictment upon which the accused was being tried. What, for instance, could the prosecution make of a situation which allowed local trial and conviction on indictments alleging crimes committed locally when the evidence proved the offences to have been of a materially different character and committed in another county? Is not any attempt to mount a formal prosecution in such circumstances likely to prove simply an embarrassment?

In this, as in other features of courtroom procedure, it looks as if we may have relied too much on the account of the absentee civilian Sir Thomas Smith and on the dedicated Lambard's record of his own work,

1   J.H. Langbein, *Prosecuting Crime in the Renaissance* (Cambridge, Massachusetts, 1974), *passim*.

in the *Ephemeris*,[1] and too little on the records themselves. Attendance lists in the assize files confirm that Lambard, and some of his fellow justices, were regularly present at assizes.[2] But the same lists also show that a majority of the so-called 'working' commission failed to attend. The average rate of absenteeism in Kent and Essex during Elizabeth's reign was almost 60 per cent; regularly only between one-fifth and one-third of the justices turned up. Since they are not directly related to the committal of suspects, these figures are only suggestive. But from 1579 — possibly in a further attempt to enforce responsibility and attendance — the names of committing magistrates were entered regularly on the gaol calendar beside the names of the suspects they had committed, and it thus becomes possible to estimate accurately how many were discharging their statutory responsibilities. Over the next twenty-five years an average of 43 per cent failed to do so. Often, well over 50 per cent of the magistrates who had committed suspects to gaol were not present at their trials to certify or prosecute anything.

These statistics need not surprise us. Absenteeism in the commissions is a constant theme in governmental complaints throughout this period. Natural wastage — death, illness, and old age — was an obvious problem. In addition, the commission, particularly in the Home Counties, was full of men whose responsibilities extended to most walks of public life. Utility administrators like the Mildmays, Bacons, Waldegraves and Walsinghams were constantly engaged on government service, on business connected with the courts of law, or in Parliament. Paradoxically, local diligence ensured wider responsibilities, leaving local matters to the less dedicated. Lambard's attendance at assizes fell off markedly after he became a master in Chancery, although he continued to commit Kent suspects. Since these, like those committed by other absentee magistrates, were, nonetheless, successfully convicted, we might well wonder whether justices played any significant role in other assize trials. Could it perhaps be that the Marian legislation[3] so exhaustively glossed by Dr Langbein not only as the basis upon which crime was prosecuted in this period but also as the means for transforming criminal process through the formation of a law of criminal evidence, represents an unattainable ideal largely irrelevant to sixteenth- and early-seventeenth-century trial procedures; bearing in fact the same relationship to actual trial as

---

1   T. Smith, *De Republica Anglorum* (London, 1583); *Lambarde and Local Government*, ed. Read.

2   These remarks are based on an examination of the *nomina ministrorum* and gaol calendars for Essex and Kent included in the Home Circuit 'indictment' files (ASSI 35).

3   1 & 2 Phil. and Mar., c.13; 2 & 3 Phil. and Mar., c.10.

Marrow, Lambard's *Eirenarcha,* West's *Symboleography,* and the reported cases bear to actual indictment? The weight of evidence suggests that procedural niceties were not a feature of routine assize trial. On both negative and positive grounds, it seems much more likely that it was the clerical establishment at assizes, in consultation with the presiding judge, which coordinated prosecution materials. It was the clerks who 'orchestrated' courtroom proceedings by preparing the calendars, drawing the indictments, and keeping (as well as altering) the records. We have already touched on evidence suggesting the critical nature of these functions, and more will appear later. But however one interprets this, it seems clear that much of the evidence of actual trial provided by the court records cannot be accommodated within the theoretical procedural framework suggested by the Marian statutes.

The practical roles of the grand and trial juries are less easily discerned. Theoretically, by virtue of their powers of presentment and of preliminary inquisition, grand juries held the key to all Crown proceedings. But whether in this period they habitually exercised their powers in the responsible fashion urged in assize charges or simply to rubberstamp process initiated by other agencies is unclear. Before 1632 few *ignoramus* returns survive: indeed, only those on indictments upon which other accused went for trial. Very occasionally, these indicate that the grand jury did consider the form of indictments, returning *ignoramus* those they found defective. A Sussex jury, for example, struck out several names from a recusancy indictment in 1588 because both time and place were uncertain.[1] But all the evidence of independence discovered so far refers to indictments for recusancy, an offence with class and kinship overtones which render it obviously atypical. And against this must be set all the evidence of formal and substantial defects in assize indictments endorsed 'true', presumably by the grand jury. Whether this reflects a decline attributable to the introduction of regular pre-trial examination is at present impossible to ascertain. But the indictment evidence does suggest that the view of the grand jurors' work as 'but matter of course, a ceremony, matter of form', may have reflected practical reality well before it became common in the later seventeenth century.[2]

Like the grand jury, trial jurors could, in theory, have a decisive impact on the outcome of criminal trials. Through their powers to acquit (either on or contrary to the evidence), to return a special verdict (in effect reserving difficult cases for full judicial discussion), or a

1   ASSI 35/30/7, mm.26-8 [*Sussex,* I, 1077].
2   *A Guide to Juries* (London, 1703), 41. For a recent contrary view see J.S. Morrill, *The Cheshire Grand Jury 1625-59* (Leicester, 1976).

'partial' verdict (finding the prisoner guilty of a lesser offence) trial juries could, in theory, override both law and evidence and significantly mitigate the harshness of the penal system. In practice, however, the impact of these theoretical advantages depended on the degree of independence enjoyed by petty juries. Most of the evidence indicates that this was severely curtailed. Despite Sir Thomas Smith's pious disclaimer,[1] Elizabethan jurors were regularly bound over to appear in the Star Chamber for returning verdicts 'contrary to the evidence'.[2] Judicial bullying and less overt forms of coercion, such as sending the jury back to reconsider an unacceptable verdict, are well attested.[3] Similarly, there is little doubt that special verdicts, when found, were usually directed by the court so that the issue could be reserved for discussion by the judges assembled in Serjeants' Inn. As a method of regulating both law and procedure, this device has perhaps been underestimated — a possibility which will be illustrated in due course. For the moment, however, it can hardly be said to illustrate the independence of trial juries.

Their power to reduce the scale of the offence — most commonly by simply undervaluing stolen goods to reduce the offence to petty larceny — seems in practice to have been the most potent of the jury's discretionary powers. By this period its obvious mitigating potential had earned this device the respectability of inclusion in the textbooks,[4] and the assize files include numerous examples of the apparently straightforward exercise of this 'pious perjury'. But even this respectable fiction appears to have been affected by practical complexities. Contemporaries, reflecting the ambiguity of the legal authorities, were obviously confused about the borderline between grand and petty larceny. Eleven Cambridgeshire justices could claim in 1583 that they had condemned a woman to death for stealing 10d. 'by a general mistaking the law'.[5] It is hardly surprising therefore that trial jurors, like modern commentators,[6] were uncertain whether the theft of goods valued at exactly 12d.

1 Smith, *De Republica Anglorum*, 88-9.

2 E.g. ASSI 35/3/4, m.21; 35/10/1, mm.10, 20, 31; 35/16/8, m.19 [*Sussex*, I, 66, 240, 248, 260, 487]. A number of instances appear in T.G. Barnes, *List and Index to the Proceedings in Star Chamber 1603-25* (Chicago, 1975).

3 J.S. Cockburn, *A History of English Assizes 1558-1714* (Cambridge, 1972), 123-4.

4 Pulton, *De Pace*, 129.

5 Brit. Lib., Harleian MS. 6993, f.61. The standard authorities were unhelpful: e.g. Pulton, *De Pace*, 129 ('if the goods do not exceed the value of twelve pence, it is not felony, but petit larceny').

6 D. Veall, *The Popular Movement for Law Reform 1640-60* (Oxford, 1970), 2, note 1.

constituted petty larceny, punishable by whipping, or grand larceny, punishable by death. The files yield several instances in which a trial jury reduced burglary or grand larceny to, so they thought, petty larceny of goods valued at 12d., only to find the court sentencing the convict for grand larceny.[1] At the very least, this phenomenon suggests a lack of harmony between judge and jury. Does it also mean that the court might actually misrepresent the law where the jury favoured leniency and the judge severity?

A second, related phenomenon indicates quite clearly the practical amendment of traditional procedures. For the first thirty years of Elizabeth's reign confessions of guilt are virtually unknown at assizes: in each of the five counties there are perhaps a dozen in all. Quite suddenly, between 1587 and 1590, 'guilty' (*cognovit*) becomes a routine plea; at every assizes thereafter five or six prisoners — sometimes as many as half the calendar — confessed to their indictments and were sentenced without further process. The fact that a number of the indictments concerned have obviously been altered alerts us to the nature of this change. The alterations are, consistently, in two areas: first, the valuation of stolen goods is altered to a sum below 12d., reducing the offence to petty larceny; second, the wording of the indictment is amended, most commonly to convert a burglary indictment into one alleging simple larceny (to which of course benefit of clergy applied). It is worth noting that the latter process was often roughly effected, producing a legally unacceptable 'garbled' indictment. But for our purposes this is just as well, since it shows unmistakably what was being done. Quite clearly, the court was engaged in widespread 'plea-bargaining', reducing the scale of the offence in consideration of a 'guilty' plea. Further clerical amendments suggest that in some of these cases the law was considerably stretched to accommodate the 'bargain' so that, for example, a prisoner claiming clergy after confessing to a reduced count was allowed the benefit whether he could read or not.[2]

Lambard hints, with disapproval, at the existence of 'plea-bargaining' in respect of misdemeanours,[3] but this appears to be the earliest clear evidence of its use in felony trials. The abrupt introduction of the procedure is puzzling. One obvious possibility is a wish both to accelerate and simplify Crown proceedings, and there is some reason to think that pressure on the court's time and resources became particularly acute in the late 1580s. In practical terms it meant that from about 1590 onwards

---

1   E.g. ASSI 35/33/2, m.18; 35/42/3, mm.25, 26, 35d [*Herts*, I, 508, 943].

2   E.g. ASSI 35/31/1, m.47; 35/32/1, m.37; 35/33/1, m.21; 35/34/1, m.10 [*Essex*, I, 1949, 2067, 2167, 2301].

3   Lambard, *Eirenarcha*, 554 ('a mockery of the law').

the petty jury and formal process became redundant in between 15 and 20 per cent of the routine felonies tried at assizes. It is also a reasonable presumption that the coordinated appearance of this procedure throughout the circuit and its continuation until at least the end of this period implies central initiative or, at least, approval. Another puzzling development, the appearance of clerical signatures on indictments drawn at assizes from July 1586 onwards, has similar characteristics, and may possibly be connected. In any event, it is difficult to imagine a system of 'plea bargaining' at this period in which bench and clerical establishment were not intimately concerned, the one negotiating the 'bargain', and the other making the necessary amendments, *ad hoc*, to the record.

Formal consideration of the court's impact on criminal process cannot be further delayed. In fact the pervasive nature of judicial control — through the charge, constant interference, formal direction, bullying, and discretionary sentencing — underlies virtually all contemporary accounts of criminal trial. Modern commentators have tended to assume, therefore, that the critical variables in actual trial were judicial temperament and, much more doubtfully for routine trials, the political demands of particular régimes. The possibility of amendment in response to social and economic pressures or to changes in professional thinking, a process we nowadays take almost for granted, has been largely ignored.

The court's power to predetermine the nature of indictments has already been illustrated. Assize judges had ample opportunity to consider Crown cases in advance, since the calendar was delivered to them in chambers by the sheriff or his deputy, and to discuss them with the relevant clerk of assize — a barrister with his own chambers in which he commonly kept circuit records. It is fair to say that there is no direct evidence that indictments were drawn in advance as a result of such deliberations, but they undoubtedly helped the professional establishment to assume the initiative as soon as the trial began. Dr Baker has recently commented on the frequency with which, at early-seventeenth-century Newgate sessions, judges and clerks discussed legal and procedural points during the trial.[1] The impact of such dialogues on the development of criminal law should not be underestimated. For although most were not reported, and it might, in any event, be argued that rulings by single judges were not authoritative, contemporary writers on the criminal law incorporated such material in their accounts with an approval which rendered it, practically speaking, authoritative. More than forty assize rulings, for example, found their way into Crompton's justices' manual; Dalton included about twenty in his even more pervasive *Countrey Justice.*

1   Baker, 'Newgate Reports', 311.

Unfortunately, it is extremely difficult to distil from the records the evidence of judicial attitudes which is so obviously essential to our understanding of criminal law and process. Something can be learned from occasional accounts of the informal discussion in Serjeants' Inn of cases reserved from assizes. Analysis of the sentencing data noted on virtually all felony indictments tried at assizes allows one to approach the same problem from a different angle.[1] In combination, the two sources produce some interesting variations on the traditional theme of judicial severity.

Clemency, a feature noticeably absent from Stephen's standard account of the criminal law, is a recurrent feature, trial judges being prepared to take into consideration a variety of extenuating circumstances. At Kent assizes in 1590 Nicholas Wylton, convicted of highway robbery, was remanded and ultimately released because 'he gave back again 2s. and delivered the robbed party out of danger of other of his companions'.[2] Hawarde reports how at Southwark assizes in 1605 Serjeant Daniel saved a convict's life by lending him his spectacles so that he might read the 'neck verse'.[3] There are numerous instances of felons being remanded after conviction, and eventually released, because they were juveniles.[4] More generally, only about one-fifth of all females convicted at assizes suffered the full legal penalty for their misdeeds. Not surprisingly, the pursuit of mitigation often ran counter to legal theory. For example, clergy was occasionally allowed to convicted burglars after 1576 despite the statute of that year which expressly excluded them from it.[5] More intriguingly, a female burglar, Alice Keeler, who in 1617 stood mute and was sentenced to *peine forte et dure,* was allowed, in direct contradiction of legal authority, to obtain a postponement of execution by pleading pregnancy at the next assizes; in fact the sentence was never carried out and she was eventually released.[6]

Conversely, the trial records indicate a marked unwillingness to allow notorious criminals to escape their deserts, and an overriding desire to convict may well explain many instances in which facts and indictment are materially at variance. Whether the court had dictated the nature

1 A full analysis of the sentencing data is now in preparation.

2 ASSI 35/32/5, m.29 [*Kent,* I, 1830].

3 *Les Reportes del Cases in Camera Stellata 1593-1609, from the original MS. of John Hawarde,* ed. W.P. Baildon (London, 1894), 233.

4 E.g. ASSI 35/20/2, m.103; 35/36/1, mm.3, 20; 35/43/1, m.2; 35/44/2, mm.4, 5 [*Essex,* I, 969, 2490, 3058, 3236].

5 E.g. ASSI 35/28/2, m.8; KB 9/702(3), m.370 [*Essex,* I, 1655, 3334].

6 ASSI 35/59/6, mm.24, 37 [*Sussex,* II, 404].

of the indictment or not, it could always direct the jury to change an unacceptable verdict and, if necessary, coerce it into doing so. Alternatively, a judge might simply ignore the time-honoured verdict of the community, treating an acquittal as if it were a conviction and sentencing the unfortunate offender as 'a man of ill fame' or 'evil reputation'.[1]

The most important area of discretionary control, however, was in the administration of the ancient right to benefit of clergy. The last pretence of a religious connection was cast aside in 1576 when control of all aspects of clergy was transferred to lay authorities by an Act which also conferred the useful discretionary power to order up to a year's imprisonment for successful claimants, presumably when they were considered 'notorious'.[2] Much reported legal discussion about the distinctions between simple larceny and burglary, and between manslaughter and murder was occasioned by concern about the availability of clergy. That this concern could have significant practical effects on indictment, evidence, and prosecution is graphically illustrated by a note in Popham's reports of a Serjeants' Inn discussion in 1594.[3] Briefly, the assembled judges resolved that the nocturnal breaking of a house, with an intent to commit felony, constituted burglary, although noone was in the house at the time, Since this had always been the law, their resolution, on the face of it, seems superfluous. It had, however, been necessitated by a significant practical perversion of the law. A statute of 1532, renewed in 1552,[4] had taken away clergy from burglaries in which someone was present in the house and had been put in fear. This, Popham tells us, had encouraged Elizabethan judges to include in burglary indictments the statement that named persons had been present in the house, whether they had or not, in order to deny *all* burglars benefit of clergy. Oddly enough, they had maintained this fiction for eighteen years after 1576, apparently unaware of the change in the law which had rendered it redundant by taking away clergy from *all* burglary, whatever the circumstances.

As an illustration both of the gulf between theory and application and of the unpredictable perversities which might be produced by statutory regulation of the law, this example has certain merits. It also throws

1 E.g. ASSI 35/62/4, mm.6, 16, 22, 32, 53d [*Herts*, II, 1100, 1105]; 35/58/8, mm.23, 25, 31, 40d [*Sussex*, II, 371, 373, 377]. Conversely, at least one man who was said to have confessed was found 'not guilty': 35/47/6, mm.2-12 [*Sussex*, II, 39].

2 18 Eliz.1, c.7.

3 Poph. 42-3, 52-3. Also noted in Dalton, *Countrey Justice*, 224-5; 4 Rep. 40; Moo. K.B. 660, pl.903.

4 23 Hen.8, c.1; 5 & 6 Edw.6, c.9.

further light on another of our problems. For although Popham is emphatically silent on the point, his account clearly implies that for some thirty-five years it had been possible to obtain convictions on a capital charge without proving a material allegation in the indictment. This is a striking comment on sixteenth-century rules of evidence as they were applied to routine felony trials. And it chimes perfectly with suggestions in the records themselves that prosecution procedures were cursory and conflicts between evidence and indictment largely ignored. It also of course opens up yet another avenue through which judges could impose rough equity on the 'systematized barbarity' of the criminal law.

Even if the court did not in this way destroy the accused's right to benefit of clergy at the outset, it might prejudice it at a later stage by making the reading test as easy or difficult as the circumstances were thought to demand. We have already noticed how clergy might be allowed in offences to which it was legally inapplicable; it was also apparently allowed to felons who had been branded before and were thus statutorily debarred, and, after a hurried education, to some who had failed the test at the first attempt. Conversely, a judge might, at his discretion, vary the test to the prisoner's disadvantage by himself choosing the test verse or by asking him to read more than one passage.[1]

But the most dramatic and puzzling evidence of the exercise of judicial discretion through the application of clergy comes from the indictments. Between 1559 and 1589 the assize files do not reveal a single instance in which clergy was denied because the claimant failed the reading test. In a few cases the clerk noted that a convict had been denied clergy because he had had the book before; but never that he was unable to read. However, at the assizes for all five counties in the summer of 1589 a number of men were recorded as having failed the reading test; thereafter, until the end of the period under consideration, such failures are a regular feature. This evidence is quite unambiguous, and one can only assume that it indicates the re-emergence of benefit of clergy as a meaningful test of literacy. The beginning of this development at almost the same time as the introduction of 'plea-bargaining' at assizes is striking, as is its synchronized appearance in all five counties of the circuit. A connection is implied; and the evidence, again, strongly suggests central direction. It begins to look as if the late 1580s brought significant practical modifications to criminal process. Obviously these

---

1 J.H. Baker, 'Criminal Courts and Procedure at Common Law 1550-1800', *Crime in England 1550-1800,* ed. Cockburn, 41.

fell short of a wholesale rationalization of trial and sentencing procedures. But in so far as the changes appear to have been initiated and co-ordinated by a central intelligence, and that the revised procedures were maintained until at least as late as 1625, they may, perhaps, mark something of a watershed in criminal administration.

It is difficult to isolate the occasion for this mini-revolution. Indeed, it is less likely to have been stimulated by dramatic change than by a growing realization that existing trends in the administration of criminal justice could not be allowed to continue. We do know that by June 1586 the Privy Council was seriously perturbed by the widespread failure of justices of the peace to attend or remain at assizes until their duties had been discharged.[1] In an attempt to ensure that Crown pleas were despatched before those justices who had attended returned home again, the Council instructed the assize judges to sit together to discharge the gaol calendar before proceeding to the trial of civil causes. The response of the Western Circuit judges, one of them the Chief Justice of the Common Pleas, exposed not only the Council's flawed logic in assuming that two judges could discharge criminal business more quickly than one, but also what amounted to the wholesale breakdown of established procedures for criminal trial. Proceedings had frequently to be halted because felons could not 'be arraigned and tried *for want of indictments* and through diverse other occasions not being the slackness or will of the judges'; many could not be indicted until the last day of the assizes (by which time most justices had departed) *'for want of evidence, bringing in of the prisoners, and default sometimes in some of the justices of peace';* towards the end of the assizes, they observed, *it is hard to find a jury for the trial of any one cause';* and, finally, *'the number of prisoners be very many'.*[2]

This unique, judges'-eye view of routine criminal process raises several intriguing possibilities. It suggests a traditional system foundering on the compound problems generated by failing trial procedures and increasingly heavy gaol calendars. Since absenteeism among justices of the peace, as evidenced by the statistics adduced earlier, had long been a constant feature, it seems more likely — despite the Privy Council's diagnosis — that the critical variable was the marked increase in crime suggested by the assize records themselves and, to some extent, by contemporary commentators.[3] Faced by the need to process more than twice as many suspects in 1590 than in 1560 in a circuit of substantially

1 PC 2/14, pp.119, 134.

2 Brit. Lib., Lansdowne MS. 49, ff.59-60 (Emphasis added).

3 J.S. Cockburn, 'The Nature and Incidence of Crime in England 1559-1625: a Preliminary Survey', in *Crime in England 1550-1800.*

the same duration and also, presumably, concerned to check what they saw as an unacceptable surge in criminality, the need for judicial initiative seems plain. Is it possible that the judges' response was, quite literally, to take the law into their own hands in routine felony trials? Did they perhaps in practice dispense with notoriously weak links in the submission and consideration of evidence, relying on the cryptic forms of the indictment to conceal the wholesale jettisoning of procedural niceties? Such a 'bureaucratization' of criminal process might help to explain not only the central fact of conviction on indictments apparently unsupported by formal evidence, but also the sudden introduction of plea-bargaining, with its obvious attractions both as a method of accelerating the proceedings and of avoiding a search for jurors and the uncertainties of trial by those 'twelve silly men'. The new harshness with which benefit of clergy was controlled after 1589 also suggests an abrupt hardening of judicial attitudes.

Much more work needs to be done on this problem. Detailed analysis of the conviction and sentencing data noted on indictments should reveal the pattern of procedural modification and changing judicial attitudes, not only during the 1580s but over a much longer period. For the moment, the possibility of further practical adjustments along the lines of those detected in the 1580s suggests that criminal justice in this period was perhaps more flexible than we have supposed. The judges' perceived ability to bend established law and forms to the rough demands of moral or 'natural' justice, coupled with the practice of reserving difficult criminal matters for discussion in Serjeants' Inn, ensured that behind its archaic façade the criminal law was neither entirely cut off from the stream of discussion which shaped other branches of the common law nor wholly divorced from demographic, social, and economic pressures operating to change the nature and incidence of crime. Contemporaries preferred, no doubt, to talk about the application of 'natural' law, James I's 'rational justice', rather than about the social and administrative pressures which still find only a limited place in the lawyers' view of legal history. And in the sense that most amendments to criminal law and process were obviously made within the framework of established forms, the process of change was essentially conservative. But in so far as we can now glimpse its direction through a fog of legal theory and traditional misconception, it looks remarkably like a rough version of that 'social engineering' which is often claimed as a peculiarly modern function of criminal justice.

ENFORCING LATE-MEDIEVAL LAW:
PATTERNS IN LITIGATION DURING HENRY VII'S REIGN

DeLloyd J. Guth

Did late-medieval Englishmen see a system in their laws and law courts? Was there a system at all? It is relatively easy to find evidence from any period for individual perceptions of 'the law'. And, from time to time, we all speak of 'the law' as if it is a single and generic thing, which of course it can be. If asked to say what we mean by 'the law', our minds can easily trip over our tongues: is it anything more or less than a collection of each and all laws, whether enforced or unenforced? We may choose to feed more philosophical appetites by grappling with the universal and the particular meanings that we can impose on 'the law'. Or, like most legal historians, we can remain reluctant to speak of 'the law' without specific reference, limiting studies to particular laws, particular cases, and particular law courts. In so doing we follow the lawyer's practice, one case at a time. But the universal remains, if only in the all-embracing references to 'the law' that frequent popular language, then and now.[1]

At least one late-medieval preacher saw 'the law' as a simple class conspiracy: 'and iff [a poor man] goy to the lawe ther is non helpe, for trewly lawe goys as lordshipp biddeth hym'.[2] Such eyes saw all law and each law court in the one light. A much more laudatory light shone on 'the law' of Sir John Fortescue, making it his prince's guide for wise and just governance. Here it meant all laws, the sum of '. . . customs, statutes, and the law of nature, from which all the laws of the realm proceed'.[3] Fortescue's prince must know that law of nature as the universal source for the validation of all human law, even when made by princes.

Further examples are common in late-medieval evidence where people refer to 'the law' in different meanings but in the same off-handedly comprehensive manner. They threaten to go to law, or

---

1 The historiographical implications are explored in D. J. Guth, 'How Legal History survives Constitutional History's Demise: the Anglo-American Traditions', *Ius Commune* 7, ed. F. Ronieri (Frankfurt, 1977), 117-53.

2 *Middle English Sermons*, ed. W.O. Ross (209 Early English Text Soc., 1940), 238-9.

3 *Sir John Fortescue: De Laudibus Legum Anglie*, ed. S.B. Chrimes (Cambridge, 1942), 21.

they try to flee the law, or they wage their law. They identify 'the law' with its official agent, whether bailiff or king's attorney, or they mean specifically the law of debt, the law of adultery, the law of war, or whatever. And common to all of this is not some linguistic illusion, some rubbery verbalism, but the obvious fact that 'the law' appeared to its people as a cohesive, often mechanical, system of multifarious parts. Specific law, whether canon or common, made sense to them as part of a universality.

If we turn to the actual business of all courts of law during Henry VII's reign, we need to know what people did with law as they saw it. Then, as always, law and law courts offered a means between brute force and private treaty for controlling conflicts. In a minority of cases, courts even resolved the conflicts. But whether applied in or out of court, the law was a basic instrument for order. And in Henry VII's society, this meant that all sorts of law, including his own common law, could judicialize and legitimate individual acts that touched life, love, loyalty, and livelihood. All law courts, from the manor to Westminster, intervened in human affairs either to mediate in conflicts over property or to regulate behaviour, directly or indirectly. This system was discernible to Henry VII's subjects, all of whom lived and died with it, and it ought to be discernible to us. Local, ecclesiastical, and common laws combined to provide an entangling network of services and sanctions that could easily and repeatedly grip every single one of Henry VII's subjects.

Individuals confronted 'law as enforced in the courts', which is well documented, as well as 'law in everyday social activities', which is not. This could be the simple kind of summary law meted out at local leets and manors or the intricate sort requiring professional counsel and available at common law. Anyone easily and regularly became vulnerable to legal processes, as plaintiffs, defendants, deponents, informers, officers, judges, jurors, appraisers, mainpernors, arbitrators, or tithingmen. And beyond the dry surface of court parchment, every jurisdiction quickened and personalized its law in its officers, their deputies and their servants: bailiffs, wardens, constables, sheriffs, beadles, apparitors, stewards. Most acted only upon prior authorization, that is, after someone else had initiated judicial action, individually by information or writ or appeal, or communally by presentment. These officials, therefore, were the law's agents, although not modern policemen with inherent powers to arrest on the spot. But they all stood to remind people of what happened when they were accused of wrong, crime, or sin. And by their numbers and variety, they certainly disprove notions that pre-modern society was unpoliced and unofficered.

To complicate this panorama further, any person might sue another simultaneously in local, ecclesiastical, and royal courts on the same complaint, creating potential for a sort of triple jeopardy. Such collateral suits could be pursued also within different local courts, or in Chancery, Common Pleas and Star Chamber at the same time, even if under different legal labels and forms of action. All this at least showed that some litigants knew how to make their own systems out of laws and law courts. And from where we now sit, atop that surviving mountain of plea rolls, cause papers, court books, bills, and bundled writs, we may well wonder whom the whole system served. This is not a question to be idly dropped, with cynical reference to fee-grubbers or pious comments about the constitution. Contemporary men of letters, from Geoffrey Chaucer to Thomas More, both trained at common law, despaired at the sheer bulk of law and litigation surrounding them. Litigants complained fulsomely about judicial delays, if they jeopardized their own remedies. And yet the suits initiated, the sinners publicly punished, and the convicted felons hanged, continued in number with the dawning of a new century and the securing of a new dynasty.

Regardless of how complex and over-lapping were the jurisdictional parts of this system, we can easily identify those operating throughout Henry VII's England and Wales: courts of the manor, hundred, honour, forest, sheriff, bailiffs, ward-mote, leet, market, mayor, admiralty, archdeacon, dean's peculiar, bishop's consistory and audience, quarter sessions, assize, special commissions — and then the royal courts resident at Westminster: King's Bench, Common Pleas, Exchequer, Chancery, the conciliar courts of Star Chamber and Requests, and franchisal courts for Cornwall, Durham, Wales, Chester, and Lancaster. No doubt this list can be extended. And many good scholars during the past century have taken leads from Maitland, Cam, Milsom and others in describing and explaining what particular jurisdictions did at particular times and places, mainly medieval. What we still lack are integrated, comprehensive scrutinies of how all of these parts fit the whole of 'the law' at any time.

To this purpose a quantitative, case-counting method can be helpful. It will produce information from which it may be ascertained what each type of court actually did, for whom, to whom, and by whom. It therefore serves to define contexts, without which it is impossible to know which case is typical, what decision is unique, and what exactly is increasing, decreasing, or stagnating in the law. Ignorance of such quantitative contexts has rarely prevented historians from making judgments, or rather guesses, about change, both of the more-or-less and better-or-worse varieties. But generalizations based on an anecdote, a single prosecution, or the lawyer's favourite precedent, do not produce convincing history. Without case-counting, one must either believe in the mysterious workings of the historian's intuition or despair at his inability to distinguish between the one and the many.

It is this comprehensive purpose and quantitative method that will mark the book that I am preparing for publication. In this paper I can only survey and exemplify the range of analytical problems and questions raised by such a broad study.[1] The general result should be a descriptive analysis of what late-medieval English law, in its many varieties, achieved at all levels of society.

The twenty-three and one-half years of Henry VII's reign remain my focus, although I have gathered evidence broadly between 1460 and 1530, if only to discern contextual changes in litigation. This era witnessed three generations of Englishmen and marked the culmination of late-medieval, pre-Reformation society. Recent historiography presents this as a period of economic recovery and stability, certainly for per capita wealth, most notably in urban areas. This, of course, preceded by several decades those inflationary explosions found in later reigns. We are in the larger part of what Professor Du Boulay named 'an age of ambition,[2] and what Professor Ferguson dubbed with more nostalgia an 'indian summer'.[3]   It was certainly an age of ambition for law courts generally and especially for mercantile litigation. And both metaphors hold true in describing that royal recovery, particularly in prerogative, finance, and pageantry, which occurred before those even more ambitious, wintry blasts which crystallized the Crown's legal and ecclesiastical powers in the 1530s.

The first difficulty in this survey is to define exactly what each type of court did. Here, as in the book, I begin with some case-counts in order to set out the distribution of specific actions and offences from top to bottom in the jurisdictional network. How did the business of the

---

1   This paper was also read to a general seminar in the Max-Planck-Institut für Europäische Rechtsgeschichte, Frankfurt am Main, on 4 December 1975. In revising it for publication, I have had encouraging criticisms from Professor Dr H. Coing, Professor Jack McGovern, Dr Michael Clanchy, and Katherine Ratliff Guth. The numerous manuscript sources which support my synthetic arguments about specific jurisdictions will be documented in my forthcoming book, of which this paper is an abridged outline.

2   F.R.H. Du Boulay, *An Age of Ambition: English Society in the late Middle Ages* (London, 1970). A fully annotated bibliography for this period is now available: D.J. Guth, *Late-Medieval England 1377-1485* (Cambridge, 1976).

3   A.B. Ferguson, *The Indian Summer of English Chivalry* (Durham, N. Carolina, 1965).

King's Bench, for example, compare with that of the Chancery, or a consistory, or a mayor's court? Were litigants representative of a broad or narrow social spectrum in all jurisdictions? Can any 'litigious class' be discerned? Or was it all a conspiracy against poor men, as that preacher would have us believe? To what extent does our textbook division of pleas — felony, misdemeanour, civil — apply in this era? What kinds of laws were enforced, or at least cited for authority, in various courts: parliamentary statutes, natural law, customary law, case law, canon law, conscience, or local ordinance? This in turn raises basic questions about the nature of late-medieval legislative powers, in boroughs, manors, and parliaments. If cases enforcing such legislation cannot be found in court records, does this prove that those laws were unenforced, universally obeyed, or even unenforceable by intent? There are further problems, like the transcendental one of defining and relating crime, tort, and sin, or more pragmatic ones about social composition of juries or the mechanics of arbitration. Such questions, with or without answers, make little sense if divorced from the contexts of court business, which is why comprehensive case-counts are essential for solidly descriptive beginnings.

If we start at the centre, with the common law, the Court of Exchequer provides an unbroken collection of late-medieval plea rolls. By Henry VII's reign, its barons adjudicated upon actions alleging debt to the Crown, including fictional ones. It was here that royal proprietary interests could be protected or challenged. But for a variety of reasons, the Exchequer was never the only place for royal money-chasing, although it did retain the authority needed to enforce royal rights at common law. And one major right was the prosecution of alleged violators of penal regulations, where the potential penalty fixed by parliamentary statute constituted a potential debt to the king. Such penalties were virtually always monetary, involving fines, amercements, and forfeitures.[1]

Hundreds of statutes, ordinances, and royal proclamations created a web of penal rules that might ensnare anyone into Exchequer litigation. These included prohibitions against market abuses, such as forestalling or engrossing foodstuffs, usury, retaining, public games like bowling and shove-ha'penny, smuggling, bribery, shoddy manufactures, and so on. By Henry VII's reign there were more than fifty statutes for the cloth trade alone, and any glance through the *Statutes of the Realm* will confirm the range and repetitive nature of these penal laws.

1 There is a full analysis of cases for this court in my 'Exchequer Penal Law Enforcement, 1485-1509', unpublished Ph. D. thesis (University of Pittsburgh, 1967).

The common law's response to this broad category of statutory penalties was to treat them simply as civil pleas of debt, creating no new or distinct concept akin to modern misdemeanours and administrative law. Because such actions of debt rested on statutes, and because most offered to reward plaintiffs with part of the fine or forfeiture, such informers identified themselves 'qui tam pro domino rege quam pro seipso sequitur'. George Whelpley grabbed handsome profits out of such law suits during the middle years of Henry VIII's reign, as Professor Elton has shown.[1] And Henry Tofft worked assiduously as 'promoter' of Henry VII's causes, with direct if unofficial links with James Hobart, the king's attorney. Tofft's trail must be pieced together out of scattered plea rolls and indictments, and the story is complicated further with several competitors, especially the shadowy John Baptista de Grimaldis, a Genoese made denizen by Richard III.[2] Whether or not this all led to Empson and Dudley, it exemplifies one prevailing and legitimate aspect of late-medieval law enforcement.

But which of the hundreds of penal laws were enforced in the Exchequer? The case-count for Henry VII's reign shows that more than 75 per cent of all 1,806 prosecutions were for one offence: smuggling. Almost all were pursued by royal officers, the customers, controllers, and searchers, or their subordinates, in the ports. They appeared in court as individual plaintiffs suing *qui tam* for debt. These officials constituted the one coordinated, permanent administrative unit that the Crown directly possessed for systematic law-enforcement. Thus, all remaining regulatory statutes fell haphazardly to individual entrepreneurs, relatively few in numbers and disparate in social status. Such informers prosecuted as often out of malice as they did for a lucky profit based on the defendant's misfortune. For the entire reign there were fewer than one dozen accusations each against retaining, usury, guild infringements, and illicit gaming. Parliamentary rules about cloth, its size, quality, and markets, uniform weights and measures, dress, diet, and a variety of others remained uncited, at least at common law. The Exchequer itself was remarkably effective, resolving nearly 40 per cent of all 1,806 actions initiated. But most of these ordered forfeiture of smuggled goods that had been seized at the docks or on board ship, so owners often abandoned court appearances and pleadings. Where trial juries acquitted them and restored their goods in about 85 per cent of cases.

1 G.R. Elton, 'Informing for Profit', *Star Chamber Stories* (London, 1958), 78-113.

2 *CPR 1476-85*, 496 (dated 30 January 1485).

Obviously Henry VII enforced those laws which protected his proprietary rights to customs duties, which annually produced one-third of his ordinary income. He did not inherit or create legal and administrative instruments for control in any modern sense, and he limited 'state-planning' to very narrowly perceived royal needs. Common law still meant property law, and only that, as it would continue to do for three more centuries. It had neither legal theory nor legal institutions by which royal officials might administer human behaviour, outside those expansive remedies in civil actions for debt or trespass. The nobility might worry enough to legislate against the parvenu who wore luxurious dress above his or her rank, but the Crown had neither interest nor equipment for enforcing such sartorial statutes.

Just as the Exchequer offered the common law's protection for royal fiscal and proprietary interests, so the King's Bench and Common Pleas provided common law forums for private subjects wishing to secure, recover, or gamble for real and personal property. The King's Bench also entertained prosecutions for felonies, insofar as any central jurisdiction could, but that was not its main business. By Henry VII's reign, the King's Bench worked the trespass side and Common Pleas the debt side of the same proprietary street. The mass of litigation in the two courts shows how far the sophisticated medieval system of writs and processes had been reduced to the common denominators of trespass and debt. In the Common Pleas, 71 per cent of the 6,200 actions of record in Michaelmas term 1482 were for unjust detention of money or goods, according to Margaret Hasting's general count.[1] Twenty-five years later, in Michaelmas 1507, I have reckoned closer to 80 per cent of nearly 7,000 actions of record to have been for debt or, less frequently, detinue. Of the remaining 20 per cent, most are accusations of forcible seizures, asportations, or breaking closes to seize goods. Most of these actions probably signify what has become known, and was condoned, as 'self-help'. Such trespasses would qualify as modern felonies, and some as misdemeanours, but here they often suited fifteenth-century courtroom strategy: sue trespass *quare clausum fregit* in any of its variations and then, once in a royal court, join issue so as to try title to the land itself.

This is particularly true for the King's Bench where the civil side of the plea roll recorded at least 80 per cent of all business initiated before the justices. Virtually all of this civil litigation was for trespass, varying from the alleged breaking of a close to steal animals, or of a

1 M. Hastings, *The Court of Common Pleas in Fifteenth-Century England* (Ithaca, 1947), 27.

house to burgle its contents, to outright seizures of land based on allegations that the tenant was of neif, or serf, status. Marjorie Blatcher counted nearly 1,000 actions on the Michaelmas 1488 plea roll,[1] and I have indexed the complete roll for Michaelmas 1507. Occasionally each roll's formal, abrupt enrolments are extended enough to reveal the true nature of these trespasses. Behind the word *transgressio* were abductions, assaults, batteries, burglaries, grand and petty larcenies, rapes, riots – all committed 'vi et armis', usually with swords, clubs, bills, even poleaxes, and all 'contra pacem domini regis'. Such formal phrases were almost always fictional, but absolutely necessary to claim royal jurisdiction for the complaint. So the word 'trespass' can distract our modern eyes, just as it could offer remedy to the victim, with return of goods plus damages, and escape from the hangman for the culprit, by casting his or her felony into a civil plea. At least 25 per cent of such trespass actions alleged offences that should have been, or certainly could have been, tried as felony. This is especially the case in proprietary offences such as larceny and burglary. The private action of trespass could hardly become an administrative weapon for Henry VII to wield against the disorderly and the violent. And in this way tort confounded felony, just as the legal record confounds all historians of crime.

Late-medieval felons might also be pursued, as in about 3 per cent of cases, by widows, immediate next-of-kin, and surviving victims by process of appeal: for mayhem, murder, rape, or robbery. Remaining King's Bench activity included about 3 per cent of cases founded on parliamentary penal statutes, even though many could be sued there as well as in the Exchequer. But there was only a trickle of cases against illegal retaining, and the ever-cited prosecution of Lord Burgavenny was exceptional to the court's business. The rest of the King's Bench litigation began by bill for debt, and there are few signs of the other actions which could be brought there, such as covenant and replevin. And where over one-third of Exchequer actions were resolved within that court, these other two common law courts recorded judgment in less than 10 per cent of all suits initiated. Most claims for trespass and debt were never intended for judicial resolution. They merely armed plaintiffs with royal record and gave the means for formal, serious confrontations between parties out of court. Litigants could then sort out their differences through arbitration, pardon, compounding, bargaining, out-witting or simply out-living an adversary.

The topic of crime, or more accurately of felony, intrudes into any

1 M. Blatcher, 'The Working of the Court of King's Bench in the 15th Century', 14 *BIHR* (1937), 196-9.

discussion of King's Bench jurisdiction and it leads directly into records from assizes and quarter sessions. For the late-medieval era, records of these courts survive only in scattered bits that defy quantitative analysis. There is a large gap for records of Henry VII's assizes, except for references in other common law documents that indicate substantial traffic in property disputes heard mainly on circuit as nisi prius proceedings. Perhaps 25 per cent of the assize justices' time could be spent with such civil matters. The special commissions, usually oyer and terminer and gaol-delivery, were regularly associated with commissions to assize justices but each could be issued separately. Henry VII followed his predecessors by relying on this ad hoc, peripatetic system for royal prosecutions of alleged felons. But little of this activity survives in records that would allow measurement of accusations, prosecutions, and convictions. This is all the more true when we come to the Rex side of the King's Bench's plea roll. In actual amount, as noted earlier, the civil side completely outnumbered the Rex side, in terms of actions initiated and sheer bulk of parchment rotulets used. And the Rex side contained only those cases which filtered up, on *certiorari* or *mandamus,* in order to be pardoned or quashed. In fact the only quantifiable segments of any extant King's Bench records are its civil pleadings and its tiny original jurisdiction for Middlesex, where a dozen or more indictments each term were laid for nuisances, usually instigated at Westminster's whore-houses. Little wonder that students of late-medieval crime, facing such enormously elusive evidence, are usually reduced to generalizing from anecdotes and a selection of cases. In addition, the common law complicated the very definition of crime by clinging to trespass while felony, self-help, and equity continuously engulfed it.

The equity, or conscience, jurisdictions in Chancery and before the royal council offered process by English bill in actions ostensibly where common law provided little or no help. Nevertheless, a scrutiny of such proceedings indicates that at least 70 per cent involved issues of real property. The Lord Chancellor could and did hear actions that common-law courts still refused, such as for detention of deeds (where the quantity was unknown) and cancelled bonds, feoffments to uses, and to protect copyholders. Henry VII's Chancery also took the full range of actions that appeared at common law and furthermore found at least 10 per cent of its business in ecclesiastical disputes over tithes, benefices, and testaments. This last area of litigation grew naturally from the fact that all fifteenth-century chancellors were bishops, and most archbishops. As Dr Franz Metzger has recently shown in his meticulously analysed *doktorat,* this general pattern continued through the Wolsey era.

In Henry VII's council, surviving cases have been artificially and arbitrarily classed as 'Star Chamber' and 'Requests'. The historical problems of origins and distinctions between the two remain unresolved. But C.G. Bayne convincingly set out the overwhelmingly civil nature of this conciliar business,[1] mainly in real actions camouflaged with those dire allegations of riot and public violence invited by the parliamentary statute 3 Henry VII, c. 1, and paralleled in actions of trespass. In its more mature development under Thomas Wolsey, royal councillors sitting in the Star Chamber heard hundreds of suits charging riot, unlawful assembly, and forcible entry. But in most cases, according to Dr Guy's carefully detailed analysis,[2] the actual issue reduced itself to that of title to real property. I have computed several bundles for the 'Requests' proceedings as well and the proprietary emphasis equally applies there. So these non-common-law branches of royal justice hardly differ from their supposed competitors, at least in terms of overall business.

In sharp contrast to common law and royal equity, ecclesiastical law existed for the ostensible purpose of moulding human behaviour to a transcendental standard. Like parliamentary statute, the canon law was a huge accretion of legislated prohibitions given renewed urgency in synodal decrees and the *summa* for confessors. It presumed the omnipresence of sin, which required judicialized, public punishment in addition to the private, sacramental purgation in confession.[3] This judicial dimension was executed in itinerant courts, that of the bishop's commissary-general and of the archdeacon's visitation, as well as in diocesan consistory courts.

The consistory met in the cathedral, where sessions, officers, and procedures were all established and recorded in *acta*. At Wells between 1458 and 1498, there is record of 287 cases, averaging seven a year 25 per cent were matrimonial matters, 20 per cent alleged defamation, and 20 per cent charged perjury, as *causa fidei lesionis sive perjurii*, by which was meant breaches of simple contracts amounting to actions of debt. In the diocese of Hereford between 1491 and 1493, two-thirds of that consistory's litigation was for this sort of perjury. Similar patterns existed in the consistory courts for the dioceses of London, York, and Canterbury at the end of the fifteenth century. In these

---

1 *Select Cases in the Council of Henry VII,* ed. C.G. Bayne and W.H. Dunham (75 *SS,* 1958).

2 J.A. Guy, *The Cardinal's Court* (Hassocks, 1977).

3 For an excellent study of this as a problem in theology and intellectual history, based on Continental sources, see T.N. Tentler, *Sin and Confession on the Eve of the Reformation* (Princeton, New Jersey, 1977).

jurisdictions, the remaining one-third of their business involved claims by priests for mortuary fees, allegations of violent assaults against clergymen, disputes over tithes, and testamentary matters. Most bishops also kept courts of audience, which theoretically were personal and itinerant. But Henry VII co-opted most of his bishops into full-time royal service, and their absenteeism reduced the impact of this court on diocesan law enforcement to a minimum. In fact, courts of audience by Henry VII's reign reserved only a limited number of cases, sometimes on appeal from the archdeacon's jurisdiction, in matters concerning church patronage, benefices, or the occasional charge of heresy. This was usually recorded in episcopal registers, not in separate court books, showing its lack of a separate judicial identity. Dr Helmholz has shown recently how rich and numerous these episcopal records are, especially for marriage litigation.[1] He noted a decline in the relative amount of marital causes brought during the two centuries before the Reformation and pointed out what my research consistently confirms: that mercantile and property claims filled this gap for church business. Certainly the facade for debt offered by accusations of perjury seems to be routine by 1500, at least in all consistory courts.

The evidence for itinerant visitations is much more scattered, but there is enough to indicate how systematically the pre-Reformation church penetrated private lives. After piecing records and references together, there is a picture for Henry VII's reign of a serious and aggressive discipline imposed upon clergy and laity alike. In Bangor diocese in the autumn of 1504, *sede vacante,* the archbishop of Canterbury's visitor summoned defendants in 238 separate accusations. One cited a man for harrowing on All Saints Day. He was ordered to ride the wheel of his machine, with his head and feet uncovered, through Ruthin market-square in the visitor's presence. All the other 237 actions involved heterosexual promiscuity. Four were against non-cohabiting married couples, whose 'punishment' was to resume their cohabitation. The rest involved fornication and adultery, of which 17 per cent were priests keeping concubines, which accounted for one-quarter of all clergy called to this visitation. Of all female partners in the 237 citations 68 per cent were identified as widows. At Lichfield in 1466 the pattern was basically the same: 90 per cent of the offenders were charged with fornication or adultery, while the others were alleged dabblers in magical potions, sabbath-breakers, or negligent clergy. In all this illicit sex there was never a hint of sodomy, homosexuality, or masturbation. In the peculiar jurisdiction of Bridgnorth,

1 R.H. Helmholz, *Marriage Litigation in Medieval England* (Cambridge, 1975).

the record is marvellously complete between the 1470s and 1523. Here the dean of a royal free chapel sat regularly, punishing on average ten persons per session from about five parishes. Three-quarters were charged 'ex officio decani' for illicit sex or suspicious company, and the rest involved local property-disputes, basically for tithes, probate, or perjury. Judicial process was always summary and the penalties usually required bare-headed, bare-legged processions around the parish church before Sunday mass, after which the guilty stood before the altar throughout the services, with a one-penny candle in hand. Guilty parish-priests had to preface their next sermon with a public confession of their concubinage from the pulpit. Minor excommunication was invoked, rarely, against those who repeatedly refused the court's injunctions or those who were recidivists in serious sins. The only alternative to these punishments was composition by substantial fine, given to the church fabric. In a small way these fines may help to explain the late-medieval proliferation of church re-building and repair.

In all this ecclesiastical litigation the purpose was to punish and correct sinful behaviour. Good example was promoted by publicly shaming the bad, specific orders were given for future avoidance of the occasions of sin, and the church was constantly mapping the road towards salvation in its courts, thereby augmenting its sacramental offices. In practice, common law and church law shared all sorts of actions, mainly for mercantile and testamentary debts, and it is surprising that royal charges of praemunire and ecclesiastical excommunications were only rarely hurled around as a result of such jurisdictional competition. Henry VII's attorney, James Hobart, did lead a running battle with his Norfolk neighbour, Bishop Richard Nikkes of Norwich, over the use of church courts for actions of debt. Nikkes, or Nix, was a protegé of Bishop Fox, Keeper of the Privy Seal. He was also an infrequent member of Henry VII's council and the first patron of the young Thomas Wolsey. His feud with Hobart had personal and local dimensions, and it was never allowed to become a major confrontation between Crown and church. Allowing for this, the fact remained that there was more than enough property litigation to be spread amongst all jurisdictions by 1500, and the Crown evidently did not ordinarily feel threatened by church and local courts.

The third category of early Tudor litigation concerns the myriad of local, secular courts. They spent much of their judicial time actively and directly applying customary law and local enactments in a wide range of day-to-day affairs. By Henry VII's reign these courts were still the most effective because they were most immediate to the community. There was a regular amount of legislating at this level in the form of juries declaring old custom or, along with local councils, consciously creating new. Parliamentary statute is almost never cited here probably because local rules were normally adequate to local needs. It may also be that new forms of action and of behavioural regulations often germinated from these local courts, especially in boroughs, and grew into the common law by way of parliament. As to the courts themselves, the extant evidence is so bountiful and the enforcement-patterns for each type of court are so similar that only generalizations and examples can be presented here. The outline that follows is drawn from the records of about three dozen rural and ten urban jurisdictions.

In the countryside courts of the manor, forest, honour, and hundred, prosecuting public nuisances created as much business as did the protection of property rights for lord and tenant (heriots, fines, leases). The nuisance was proprietary insofar as it originated in the lord's possessory rights and duties to keep the peace. Hence, much of this enforcement involved good repair of buildings, maintenance of roads, and drainage. These were public matters and they signified community control, sometimes self-regulation. In the forest courts, rights to hunting and fishing were enforced, to the point where one might see principles of ecology at work. The straight-forward enforcement of the lord's rights in the manorial court appeared perfunctorily executed, and there was a noticeable absence by 1500 in most manorial and hundred court rolls of the customary seigneurial exactions and tolls. Public law was certainly being made and enforced in rural, and especially in urban, courts in ways that the common law could not match, even if its officers so desired.

Peeping-toms, gossips, noisy dogs, and lewd relationships were punished in rural courts but even more often in city ward-motes, borough leets, and mayoral courts.[1] In London, Great Yarmouth, Bridport, Chester, Hull, and dozens of other urban jurisdictions, the sort of ecclesiastical discipline found in visitational records was largely supplanted or duplicated by self-assuming officials who regularly cited and punished whores, vagrants, fornicators, gamesters, and other sinners in their secular courts. As in church courts, punishment publicly followed summary judgment: pillory, public processions, ostracism, and fines. In Langbourn and Cornhill wards, London, on 20 August 1494, ten women were convicted for nightwalking and being 'comon . . . of [their] bodyes'. Again, on 17 October 1498, Elizabeth Swyneford 'alias Frenche Phelip' was declared a 'common bawde and

1 Much of this local enforcement is exemplified in *Borough Customs,* ed. M. Bateson (18 and 21 *SS,* 1904-6).

an enticer of mennys daughters and servauntes of tender age bryngyng
theym from Westm[inster] to London to divers merchauntes straungers
. . . to be devoured'. She received an hour in the Cornhill pillory with
banishment under penalty of imprisonment for a year and a day if she
returned. Robert Hardyng admitted fornication with Katheryn Worsley
but only, he said, to disprove a rumour she had spread in order to
frustrate his wooings of other rich widows. She allegedly told them that
he 'had not as man shuld have to please theym and that she knewe yt
for a trouthe'. In addition to such prosecutions there were regular
numbers of alleged assaults, some with blood-letting. More of this was
cited in urban courts than in their rural counterparts. Such petty violence
was punished with small fines. One thing missing from all these local
courts are citations for drunkenness, despite the prevalence of beer and
wine in everyone's diet. Even more surprisingly, alcohol is never cited
as cause or mitigation for other offences, particularly felonies,
prosecuted at common law or in church courts.

One of the most profitable areas of local regulation came from
enforcement of the local 'assizes', such as the assizes of bread, wine, ale,
leather, or hay. These were part of a broad system of local rights
delegated usually in royal charters which urban governments· in turn
would delegate to individuals representing particular crafts or producers.
In London, York, Chester, Leicester, and elsewhere, guilds such as the
butchers or fishmongers retained power to search and seize meat or fish,
respectively, if they suspected poor quality, inaccurate measuring, or
excessive prices. This was a regular feature of late-medieval monopolies
and victims were often, but by no means always, non-members of the
particular guild. In the twice-yearly borough leets, presentment juries
were preoccupied with all such economic offences. There was a great
deal of recidivism from leet to leet, with jurors sometimes presenting
themselves for market violations, but fines were apparently collected
even if they constituted more of a licence than a penalty. When quarter
sessions were held in urban areas, much of their business was with the
same sort of prosecutions. Finally, mayors of cities and bailiffs in
boroughs held their courts weekly or at least fortnightly, essentially for
civil pleas. Throughout Henry VII's reign there had been a noticeable
increase, compared with earlier reigns, in localized, official prosecutions
of offenders against moral and mercantile regulations, both in church
and secular courts. It is still too early to explain why this happened or
if it happened uniformly in England and Wales, but one point is clear:
there is little evidence to show that the impetus came directly from the
centre, from Henry VII, his council, his parliaments, or his courts.

What does all this add up to? For local and church courts, Henry
VII's subjects faced a great and steady pressure from judicial restraints

on their behaviour, but only in that selective manner which emphasized sexual and mercantile relations. If we could crack the demographic problems, to determine population-units for each jurisdiction and the social status of everyone involved in litigation, then we could speak confidently about increases and decreases in the quantity and quality of applied law. Aside from such fundamental limitations, this survey does reveal certain functions for law in late-medieval, pre-Reformation communities. On the one hand, punishments were public, corporal, and purgative; but, on the other hand, apparently little social stigma within each community attached to them. Presentment jurors presented themselves, officials continued in office and on juries in spite of past or current offences, previous sinners and offenders obtained office and status, actions between a patron and his dependent in court often proceeded without any break in that relationship, and pardons and forgiveness seem regular features of secular and church courts. If nothing else is to be learned, our definitions of what constituted 'personal privacy', most notably in sexual affairs, and 'legal guilt', as distinct from the sinning soul, must adjust to accommodate these late-medieval realities.

For the common law by 1500, the full range of royal courts at Westminster merely provided alternative means for pleas between subject and subject where the issue was proprietary. King's Bench seems to have retained only residual responsibility in criminal proceedings, as felonies, while much that was indeed felonious was actually prosecuted as trespass in all courts. The fact is that three centuries after Henry II reserved felony prosecutions to the Crown, the whole legal machinery remained totally dependent on local initiatives, local juries of present-ment and of trial, as well as on appeals of felony (which came outside royal control) and liberal amounts of condoned self-help regarding rights of entry. All this may prove untidy for constitutionalists and students of crime. But it is the procedural dimension to what, in substantive law, Professor Milsom aptly dubbed 'the miserable history of crime in England'.[1]

Given this chaotic legal situation in basic matters of public order, one can better appreciate Henry VII's fresh attempt to use his council to pin down the problem. But in resorting to conciliar jurisdictions, all the king got, in the 'starred chamber' and elsewhere, was more civil disputes over property disguised as criminal trespasses and riots. So Henry VII's councillors went one step further, imposing ad hoc compositions and recognizances on anyone indicted or merely suspected

---

1 S.F.C. Milsom, *Historical Foundations of the Common Law* (1969), 353.

of offences, real or fictional, against public order. What the late K.B. McFarlane called 'govern[ment] by recognizances'[1] seems to have increased exponentially after 1485. All this can be pieced together from the King's Bench controlment rolls, the recognizances and enfeoffments recorded on the close rolls, the pardons noted on the patent rolls, and the individual receipts noted in the chamber books. The basic irony was that the Crown had begun to go outside the process of its own common law — through Chancery instruments, buttressed by conciliar process — in order to enforce the rule of royal law, thus trying to make common law more common throughout the realm.

This did not mean that monarchs lacked theory or instruments for intervention in social and economic activities. And this did not mean that, because statute generally was not enforced in courts of law, parliamentarians and private groups legislated in vain. It only meant that the common law and its courts were largely irrelevant to ways in which behaviour was directly regulated. When Henry VII did intervene in community and mercantile affairs, it was not through his courts, clutching parchment from his latest parliament. He acted daily on his own prerogatives, no doubt speaking reverently about 'the law' while making personal treaties of amity and commerce, licensing merchants or miners, bonding coastal towns against aid to pirates and royal pretenders, putting suspects under recognizance, making royal proclamations, pardoning felons and transgressors, threatening webs of litigation and weighty legal expenses for over-reluctant adherents to the Tudor will, and generally dispensing laws for all sorts of occasions and individuals. Beyond this, Henry VII delegated by charter the self-regulation of guilds and the self-government of cities and boroughs. He appears to have had little choice in keeping this traditional system, occasionally using *quo warranto,* and only revising charters without substantially changing them. We know how tenaciously he pursued prerogative rights, especially in wardship and escheat, and his law courts do reveal his steady pressure against smugglers and Crown debtors. Henry VII's law, his law courts, his prerogative, and the very philosophy that rationalized English kingship, were rooted in proprietary, possessory concepts and practices.

To anyone living in late-medieval England, laws and law courts formed a network designed to uphold a particular kind of proprietary and Christian order. Henry VII's subjects were expected to live within that system, maintaining orderly estates and avoiding ostracism. Common law promised to secure real and personal property, church

1 K.B. McFarlane, review of *CCR 1500-9* (1963), in 81 *EHR* (1966), 153-4.

law tried to correct sin and ensure salvation, and local law sought to harmonize vested interests. Common law left the regulation of social and economic behaviour to the church and the locality. When parliamentary statute exhorted and made common a vast network of penal regulations, it did not create any functional, national system for enforcement. This system of laws and law courts was therefore far too diffuse, in terms of judicial sovereignty, to be seen as exclusively royal or centralized. And it was far too narrow, in terms of the conflicts and human affairs it actually remedied, to be too often merely a debt-collection agency for mercantile, landed and royal interests. So, if we reduce all late-medieval litigation to one pattern only, it can be summarized as sex and business as usual.

KING'S BENCH FILES

C. A. F. Meekings*

As a complete group, the King's Bench files are virtually undocumented, because the twenty or so series that form the group have only now been completely arranged and have yet to be made fully available. Various things have caused this delay: accidents in the group's early archival history and, later, in the history of the Public Record Office; complexities in the series; the physical state of the files; and the belief, which perhaps died harder in the Record Office than outside it, that everything — at least everything of value — was in the plea roll.

The events of the files' early history had left them by the 1840s in three very unequal sections: down to near the mid-fourteenth century at the Tower; from then until 1422 at the Chapter House; and from 1422 onwards in the King's Bench treasuries.[1] Work on the recovery,

---

* Edited from the notebook on which Mr Meekings was working at the time of his death, with occasional references to the notebook from which the lecture was delivered. No substantial changes have been made by the editor. The subheadings and the whole of Appendix III are editorial additions. Appendix I is reproduced from the autograph diagram by Mr Meekings.

1 For the Tower group the main evidence is: William Prynne's accounts of his sorting and arrangement of documents when Keeper of the Tower Records (1661-9), and his use of material from early KB files in his writings; Thomas Duffus Hardy's reports and beginnings of an inventory of Tower records, made as Keeper of the Tower Records (1819-40), then as Assistant Keeper in charge of the Tower Office branch of the Public Record Office (1840-57); markings on file covers or elsewhere, indicating examination and arrangement by Prynne or Hardy or both; the known provenance of miscellanea from broken files as either avowedly from the 'Tower' or else as from 'Chancery'.
  For the Chapter House group there is less explicit evidence because most of this remained in sacked bulk until the 1930s, and Agarde's detailed press-lists of the Westminster record repositories do not include unsorted sacks. His dockets do occur in files of the main series that were in them; the earliest yet noticed being on the *Panella* for Mich. 36 Edw. 3 (KB 146/2/36/4), suggesting that the run began about 1361 at the latest. From other files — provincial trailbaston sessions, indictments, coroners' rolls or files, peace rolls or files — his dockets are rarely wanting. The plea rolls of the run to 1422 were stored in various of the chests B to Y of the Chapter House, along with the abbreviations, or extract abstracts, that he made of the complete run, and finished in 1607.
  For the King's Bench Treasury group, the commencing date of 1422 for both plea rolls and files is attested in print from descriptions by Thomas Powell (1622) and John Trye (1684) onwards. By the late eighteenth century the pressure on space at Westminster began the exile of the K.B. treasuries from their original home. a process which led directly to the comparative disorder into which the earlier reigns of many series fell. The last temporary accommodation for these was curiously enough in accommodation leased in the Rolls Houses, Chancery Lane, so that in 1843-44 these had to be transported from Chancery Lane to Carlton Ride: 5 *RDK*, 5.

sorting, and arrangement of one or more of these sections has been done — like much wartime active service — in energetic bursts, usually in unpleasant conditions, which punctuated long stretches of inactivity: chiefly in the early 1600s, the 1660s, the 1830s and 1840s, the 1930s, and since 1966. Before we see what was done then, and where it has brought us, it will be best to sketch the development of the group, so far as this is at present known or can be inferred, and to note the main features of each series.

The oldest series, probably coeval — at least from Henry III's time — are the *Brevia* (later renamed *Brevia Communia,* and then *Anglia*) and the *Recorda.* It is a mere accident that the earliest surviving *Recorda* file comes from 1240,[1] and the earliest *Brevia* from 1257.[2] The *Brevia* represents the court's ordinary jurisdiction; it is a file of mainly small, uniform documents; it was, until 1369, a return-day file, organised internally in that set county order which seems to have developed by the 1260s in the Common Pleas;[3] and from the early fourteenth century it was a plea-side file. The *Recorda* represents the court's appellate jurisdiction; it houses large, or unevenly sized, and very mixed documents; it soon settled as a year file, with the documents in business order; and it became dominated, eventually captured, by the Crown side. The new series were started within some years either way of 1300. The *Brevia Regis* (later renamed just *Brevia,* to torment archivists) developed, in parallel with the emergence of Rex membranes for the Crown-side business in the plea rolls,[4] to take over the growing body of ordinary Crown-side matters from the *Brevia.* It was always a term file, organised internally by return days and, within

---

1 JUST 1/1174 (Mich. 1240) [to be published in 16 *CRR*]. The error of classification by the first record in the file goes back to the Stapledon array.

2 KB 136/1/3 (quin. Joh. and tres Joh. 41 Hen. 3). The judicial writs are all tested by Bracton, whose last term *coram rege* this was. The typescript *List of Rolls and Writs of the Court coram Rege Henry III* (Public Record Office, 1957) gives illustrative examples from the file at plate 51.

3 In the King's Bench the order is only used in the *Brevia* [KB 136] and earlier *Brevia Regis* [KB 37]. The original order was: Norfolk, Suffolk, Essex, Hertfordshire, Cambridgeshire, Huntingdonshire, Middlesex, London, Kent, Surrey, Sussex, Hampshire, Wiltshire, Somerset, Dorset, Devon, Cornwall, Herefordshire, Worcestershire, Gloucestershire, Oxfordshire, Berkshire, Buckinghamshire, Bedfordshire, Northamptonshire, Rutland, Salop, Staffordshire, Warwickshire, Leicestershire, Nottinghamshire, Derbyshire, Lincolnshire, Yorkshire, Northumberland, Cumberland, Westmoreland, [Lancashire]. (As a palatinate, Lancaster disappeared 1351-61 and from 1377). The 15th-century modifications were: Norfolk, Suffolk, Cambridgeshire, Huntingdonshire, Surrey, Sussex, Essex, Hertfordshire, Middlesex . . . Nottinghamshire, Derbyshire, Northumberland, Cumberland, Westmoreland, [any order], Lincolnshire, Yorkshire, Lincoln.

4 For this, see G.O. Sayles, *Select Cases in the Court of King's Bench,* iv (74 *SS,* 1957), xlvi-li.

them, for long in the set county order. The *Panella* may have begun when the court was for some years at York and taking assize business that earlier would have gone to its chief justice or his colleagues as commissioners. With the court back mainly at Westminster, the chief section carried the case documents for actions remitted for trial, mostly at nisi prius. Always a term file, organised in business order, it was the great medieval growth file. The starting dates for both series are likely eventually to be more closely ascertained through a thorough study of the plea rolls, from the occasional cross-reference to them and from the particulars of files contained in handing-over certificates or in certificates of deposit in the Treasury of Receipt. The files in the Exchequer treasuries about 1320 seem all to have been among the many records sent to the Tower for the Stapledon array then. Nearly all were among those that did not return to Westminster, and so suffered the heavy damage common to early records left at the Tower. Survivals from Henry III and Edward I are very rare; but from Edward III, mainly his later years, just enough to provide examples of the four main series: hence his reign is taken as the starting-point for this survey. The Tower continued as a general Record Office till an uncertain date under Edward III, for the earlier part of whose reign the files are no better preserved than under Edward II.

The multiplication of series beyond these early four was caused by two developments in the court's jurisdiction: the first on the Crown side, the second on the plea side. These we must look at in some detail.

The fourteenth-century development of the court's classic criminal powers, starting with the assumption of trailbaston powers for provincial sessions, produced (probably from 1323, certainly by the 1330s) the files of indictments for irregular trailbaston sessions and their adjuncts, the files or enrolments submitted by inferior jurisdictions, including keepers' of the peace and coroners' files. It produced also spasmodic large increases in the contents of *Brevia Regis* and *Panella.* These sessions stretched irregularly to 1398, with a major gap in 1366-77, and the last revivals in 1414 and 1421. Meanwhile, as the powers crystallised into the court's classic higher criminal jurisdiction, they produced (possibly in the 1370s, certainly by 1385) the familiar term-*Indictamenta* to take over an initially small category of Crown-side documents from the *Recorda,* and the *Baga de Middlesex;* and brought in also the returned enquiry and oyer and terminer files.

The clerks could not refer concisely to the trailbaston sessions indictments and their adjuncts. For example, in the handing-over certificate of 21 April 1361, after the older series for the years

1339-61 had been listed by their succinct titles, these could only be described as 'seventy-five bags of divers presentments of felonies and trespasses, bills of trespasses, precepts and other memoranda, as well before the king in divers counties as taken before sundry justices in divers counties and afterwards sent to the king'.[1] The clerks keeping the controlment likewise referred to them by 'bag'. So *Baga*, not *Indictamenta*, was already established as the controlment reference when the term-*Indictamenta* started. It was not abandoned when this new series graduated from coverless files, docketed on a last or longest membrane, to the dignity of fully labelled covers, like other series, about 1422 when Greswold became Clerk of the Crown.[2] But authorisation cross-references on writs and precepts were always 'per indictamentum' and not 'per bagam'.

The return to the Exchequer treasury at Westminster as the place of archival deposit probably happened before this series (from 1339 to an uncertain date in or after 1361) was transferred to the archives after 1361. Certainly, with the files from the late 1340s and 1350s, the pattern of preservation improves. For Richard II, Henry IV and Henry V the four older series are as well preserved as almost any for any reign to the late seventeenth century. But survivals in these reigns from the two sorts of Indictments are much more patchy.

No more transfers were made from the court to the archives after 1422. From 1422 until almost 1500 the survival of three of the oldest series is poor to very bad; but for the term-*Indictamenta* and *Recorda* it is good to very good. From late-Henry VII the preservation of most series improves, with inevitable variations between series, and casual gaps in all. A great chasm opens in the 1630s in nearly all the then existing series, three of which plunge down this crevasse not to re-emerge. From 1660 to 1688 each of the eight regular series now extant has its casualties, but only one has major gaps. Six of these series continue to the nineteenth century, all but one still in medieval-type filings; but 1688 is the main boundary of the present survey.

Development of files on the plea side

The second development in the court's jurisdiction — that on the plea side — fell entirely within this run from 1422. The growth of the classic common-law bill procedure caused initially a swelling of the

---

1 *Select Cases in King's Bench,* ed. Sayles, vi (82 *SS,* 1965), 128-9: 87 [citing KB 27/403, m.70d].

2 Thomas Greswold was appointed King's Coroner and Attorney on 1 October 1422: *CPR 1422-9,* 3.

Panella, in which the documents of this process were at first filed; then, in little more than a century, from roughly 1503 to 1607, it caused the creation of nine series to contain the documents and the maintenance of four more as by-products. Two of the series evolved a sophisticated arrangement that greatly increased the number of potential files in a year.

Under Edward II the existing regular series probably produced thirty-two files yearly. Under Henry IV six series produced twenty-two. Under Henry VIII nine produced thirty-seven. At Elizabeth I's accession, eleven produced forty-five; but at her death, twelve were producing 180. At the brink of the chasm, fourteen series were producing 184 files a year; beyond, the picture is clouded by losses and the effects of the destruction-schedules of 1882-3 and 1907. The eight extant series about 1674 were producing twenty-nine files yearly.

A clerk in 1347 might have expected that the *Brevia* [KB 136] would soon be so big as to need filing in two parts for each return-day, like the Common Pleas *Brevia.* In fact, mortality and then bills were to cause the future of the *Brevia* to be one of steady, if at times imperceptible, decline. The great drop in business after the Black Death and the epidemic of 1361-2 caused it to change at Michaelmas 1369 from a return-day file to a file of two parts a term. The later decline in original-writ business was only very belatedly acknowledged by its becoming a term file from Easter 1642. The internal articulation remained by return days, and within them the set county order, slightly modified in the fifteenth century. Meanwhile, between 1442 and 1445 (under Fortescue C.J. and William Sonde, Chief Clerk) the title had been changed to *Brevia Communia;* then, between 1467 and 1469 (under Markham C.J. or Billyng C.J. and Reynold Sonde, Chief Clerk) to *Anglia,* which was kept, untranslated in the 1650s, down to 1703. Medieval filing ceased in 1760. From Edward II to George II there are some 2,060 files.

For most of the time from which it survives, the *Anglia* is a plea-side file for actions under the ordinary jurisdiction begun by original writ. So it contains originals, with judicials and precepts in actions begun by originals (or, in its later days, deemed to have been so begun). Its main substantive values now are: to provide examples of originals and judicials with returns and all other endorsements; and, where the series is fairly solid, to serve as an aid (through the set county order and authorisations) to cases in the plea section of the rolls, or in year books or reports, especially if the latter turn on points of process. Among its adjectival values, its original writs document activity by Chancery masters and its judicial writs activity by the chief clerk and filazers of the court. The practice of putting the issuing clerk's (not necessarily holograph) signature on writs and precepts developed in the early 1290s after the judicial scandals: at first in the centre, but eventually at the extreme right, of the bottom margin. In the King's Bench, mesne process was handled by the filazers, judgment and final process by the chief clerk or prothonotary. This body of matter supplements the information about the officers which may be obtained from plea-roll tails, but is precisely dated by date of the month.

The filazers increased in the growth period to the mid-fourteenth century. With the decline, they were organised into thirteen grouped county circuits which lasted till late in the sixteenth century;[1] then they multiplied again into individual county filazers, but with their income seemingly drawn mostly from practice as attorneys. John Trye, Gloucester filazer from about 1661 and for London and Middlesex from 1673 to 1692, was unique not only in writing the one early King's Bench book to use plea rolls and files but also, among some six hundred of his fellowship in four centuries, in signing his early writs not just 'Trye' but 'per Trye filazer in Banc le roy'. But despite his battle for the Jus Filizarii, Trye knew that, through the flourishing of the firm of Rooper, Rooper, Heywode, Rooper and Rooper, from 1498 to 1616, the chief clerks had fundamentally altered the old balance between chief clerks and filazers until their amply staffed office in the Temple 'was of so great and large an extent and the Seats so many in it, that it looked more like a Church than an Office, and incited Strangers to offer up their Devotions there, when at first they came to it'.[2]

The *Brevia Regis* [KB 37] became in 1598 simply *Brevia,* translated in the 1650s as 'A File of Writtes'. From Easter 1324 to Michaelmas 1692 there are some 968 term files. Its end, as well as its start, remains to be researched. The latest extant file is clearly not the end of the series. Nor has the order which, within return days, replaced the set county order in the fifteenth century yet been elucidated. Crown-side originals are much rarer in this series than in the *Recorda* or *Indictamenta;* they all issued over the signature of the Clerk of the Crown in Chancery. Judicials and precepts all issued over the signature of the Clerk of the Crown in the King's Bench (the King's Coroner and Attorney), so shedding no light on the staffing of the Crown side. It

---

1 See Appendix III, below, pp. 133-9, for a rough list of filazers from 1399 to 1547.

2 J. Trye, *Jus Filizarii: or, the Filacer's Office in the Court of King's Bench* (London, 1684), 104-5.

will be recalled that the distinguishing Crown formula of both was against A. 'ad respondendum nobis' or the like, whereas the plea-side formula was against A. 'ad respondendum B.'

The King's Bench trailbaston sessions brought precepts and panels for presenting and trial juries, for gaol delivery, and other Crown-side instruments, on to the *Brevia Regis*. Thereafter it settled into the form which Vernon Harcourt, knowing of it only from references in fifteenth-century controlments, aptly called the 'default list' in contrast to the *Indictamenta* as 'cause list'.[1] From the fifteenth century it is largely a file of mesne-process writs and precepts, including jury process, arising from Crown cases in *Indictamenta* and *Recorda,* either directly or through roll and controlment.

For the *Recorda* [KB 145] between 1312-3 and 1688 there are 288 files, nearly all for years. From the early sixteenth century they mostly have markers to divide terms. By the late sixteenth century each term section was usually on its own subsidiary thong as well as the main thong; so with later, broken, files one or more term sections have sometimes been recovered intact, when the rest is wanting. Earlier, the debris from broken *Recorda* has tempted the methodiser in archivists. As with much of the *Panella,* the *Recorda* was by nature a file of files, with many batches, each batch of from two to a dozen documents which made up the record and process of a case, secured together by left-hand sewings in thread or twist. This sewing usually held if the main thong broke and spilled its contents. So archivists from the seventeenth to, alas, the twentieth centuries have used dated, county or court details in records and processes to sort them into quite an array of artificial collections, concealing all reference to their origin as documents from broken King's Bench *Recorda* files.

For about a century — the forty-six extant files come from between 1327-8 and 1417-8, but the series is known to have existed from at least the early 1320s — the *Recorda* had a small calf file, tethered to its dam by a linking thong: three pairs still survive thus tethered.[2] This file, called *Precepta Recordorum,* seems to have been used initially for

1   L.W. Vernon Harcourt, 'The Baga de Secretis', 33 *EHR* (1908), 508, at 522.

2   The pairs of files still tethered are those for 30 Edw. 3, 7 Ric. 2 and 16 Ric. 2. The broken tethering thongs remain on many of the separated files. There is a cross-reference to the 'precepta' in the plea roll of Hilary 1323: *Select Cases in King's Bench,* ed. Sayles, iv (74 *SS,* 1957), 110: 44 [citing KB 27/251, m.30]. The tethering is indicated in the handing-over certificate of 1351 for the records of 1-13 Edw. 3: *Select Cases in King's Bench,* ed. Sayles, vi (82 *SS,* 1965), 79: 52 [citing KB 27/363, m.71 ('recorda cum preceptis eisdem annexis')].

smallish documents that might have been hard to trace in the large, mixed contents of the *Recorda:* great and small-seal orders to the justices, including some appointments of attorneys, respites, pardons, and so on; as well as memoranda of bails, notes of transactions between justices and the like. In its last years, writs of *non molestetis* pursuant to pardons bulk largest.

Until the fifteenth century a variety of miscellaneous documents was also in the *Recorda* itself. Dr Conway Davies has given good accounts of those in the files of 1324-5 and 1330-1.[1] In the later sixteenth and early seventeenth centuries there are the term bills 'for trymminge of the Queen's benche as yereley is used' with details of nails and tenterhooks, matting and canvas, boards and planks, benches and bars, cleaning and maintenance, and gallons of ink supplied each term. If patiently analysed, we might recapture from them something of the court's physical surroundings between the days of Catlyn and Coke. This is the seasoning to the staple food provided by the *Recorda:* records and processes, returns and documents sent in under, or without, writ or small-seal order. Much of it, especially the records, was later enrolled in full; some of it was enrolled in substance; some of it, especially documents in the process and others, was not enrolled. The whole of it was the product of all the processes underlying the appellate jurisdiction of the plea side and, except for what was eventually drawn off by the term-*Indictamenta,* of the Crown side also. For some topics, like the early history of *habeas corpus ad subjiciendum,* the *Recorda* may provide a more workable source than the rolls. Beneath the variety of content lies the steady growth to predominance of Crown-side matter, until in the mid-seventeenth century plea-side business disappears; and in belated recognition of this, when in 1677 Astry became Clerk of the Crown, the cover label was changed to one of indictment style, with Astry's name included.

The history of the *Panella* [KB 146] divides sharply into growth and decline. Between Easter 1318 and Michaelmas 1518 there are 437, mostly noble, files; from Michaelmas 1522 to Hilary 1598 there are 118 skeletons, as well as some ghosts. The title began and ended as *Panella;* but between the 1350s and 1460s it was fuller and variable, the longest and most enduring style being *Panella Assise et Bille Finite.* The nisi prius records, with endorsed posteas and jury panels, for long formed the bulk and latterly the first section of the file. Such records from broken files also tempted methodisers and may be found in various

1   J. Conway Davies, 'Common Law Writs and Returns Richard I to Richard II', 26 *BIHR* (1953), 125, at 153-6.

collections. Sample testing at different dates will show whether the endorsed postea of the nisi prius session was always enrolled.

Between 1519 and 1522, except for the few from cases begun by original, this section was removed for an entirely different make-up: that late-medieval form of fastening, still used by lawyers, the packet. Folded small, with brief particulars docketed, a county's documents for a term were tied with a broad parchment wisp, on which a succinct label was penned. For some fifty years there were, additionally, small modern-type files in two divisions: *Remanencia* and *Terminata*.[1] These, and all packet posteas, lie outside the scope of the files' arrangement; but they hampered its progress. However tightly tied, the contents of packets subject to the rough treatment which these have suffered escape all too readily from their ties. Packed into sorting boxes just as they came to hand, already they fill 1,100 boxes, to a total of over 50,000 items, not more than a sixth of which are still in their neat county-term packets: an archival tragedy, since the neat arrangement by county and date would have made this an easy class to organise in modern format and an easy class to research.

To return to the fourteenth century. Trailbaston commissioners usually kept separate files of bills, panels and precepts. The King's Bench generally used the established *Panella*, both for the great increase in possessory assize matter and for the bills and precepts in suits between parties by bill, which distinguish its provincial sessions. Hence the files' amplified titles in this century. With the court back at Westminster, in 1366-7, there are only a few bills, often in the old French forms and brought by highly-placed or connected litigants. Between the 1380s and the 1420s comes the major development in Middlesex. At the start, one has still to hunt carefully for any bill; by the finish, there will be usually a dozen or score at least, with attached precepts or writs: a definite, though not yet entirely distinct, section at the end or top of the file. In this half century, Middlesex freeholders adopted the bill (generally in the Latin form) instead of the original writ, for trespasses; and they used it for a wide range of offences. Bills from other counties at Westminster sessions remain rare.

These bills are genuine. The steps during the next decades whereby a trespass in Middlesex was alleged fictitiously, so as to get the

---

1 For Hen. 8 only: 12 *Terminata* (1522-46); 6 *Remanencia* (1520-9); 5 unspecified (1523-30); 21 whose descriptive labelled tag has been torn off (1522-45). Many seem to be associated with the Chief Justice. About 25 more, some quite large, have been found for 1549-70. By 'modern-type' files is meant all those fastened through holes pierced within ½ in. of the top left corner.

defendant into the court's jurisdiction through the marshal's custody, for process to issue against him by latitat and the real grounds of action to be declared, have yet to be established in precise chronological detail: from pioneering use until, from an action available to the privileged – the officials of the court, prominent litigants with leading lawyers advising them – it became an action used by the general run of litigants. A feature of the fictitious common bills is that the precepts on them issue over the signature of the filazer for the county in which the latitat will issue and the real bill will be declared; not, as with precepts in real Middlesex bills, by the filazer for London, Middlesex and Kent.

Though for Henry VI a poor third to the *Recorda* and *Indictamenta,* the sixty-six *Panella* are spread sufficiently to make their research rewarding. Moreover, many bills contain good stories; most reveal incidental social details at many levels: so the studies that are possible extend well beyond those of substantive law alone. Perhaps, most of all, one would like to know if it was the development of the equity side of the Chancery that stimulated the King's Bench to develop the classic bill procedure under Chief Justices Fortescue, Markham, Billyng, and Huse; or rather, whether the development of the equity (and later prerogative-court) bill and the classic King's Bench bill are not part of an early-Renaissance development of new ways of litigation.

About 1500 the *Panella* lost the common bills and precepts to a *Bille Communes* series [KB 148], whose earliest extant file comes from Hilary 1503. Between 1519 and 1521, at the same time as it lost its nisi prius section, it also lost all the rest of the bill matter to a new *Bille* series [KB 147]. Immediately the *Panella* became a poor, small thing: its cover usually thicker than the few case batches it contained, itself generally tucked between the thongs of the two *Anglia* parts for the term. Soon it became an intermittent ghost, the apparition marked by the laconic note on *Anglia* covers: 'Panella nulla hoc Termino'.[1] The last file yet found is for Hilary 1598. So, we turn from the series of medieval origin to the 'bills' group.

When common bills and precepts were taken off the *Panella,* there was still a minority of bills in real Middlesex actions. These were mostly put at the start or end of the *Bille Communes* file. Until between 1538 and 1541 the fictitious trespass was generally laid at Westminster. By Michaelmas 1541, at latest, it became the breaking of a close at Hendon; and so it invariably remained, except when plague exiled the court and the common bill was briefly a bill of Berkshire,

1   See e.g.: KB 136/15/6/2; 10/2; 13/4; 21/4; 28/4; 30/4; 31/1-2.

Hampshire, or Hertfordshire. As the sixteenth century advances, the chief clerk's office seems gradually to be ousting the filazers from their earlier share of bill business. Eventually the growth of fictions made the precept, not the common bill, the starting document of the action. How near the last extant *Bille Communes* file (for Michaelmas 1605) may stand to the death of the common bill is uncertain. No file of precepts alone has been found, so it is unlikely that such a series was ever begun.

The effective start of the *Bille* series was probably Easter 1520. There are a few earlier files, but all save one with clearly labelled covers bear a cross-reference to show that they are an overflow from the term's *Panella*. The *Bille* inherited from the *Panella* the distinctive late-fifteenth century chequer cover-device, and succeeded it also as the file on which general orders about the court's sessions were filed. The documents tended to be filed in a set order, without the sections ever becoming completely self-contained. First, *Habeas corpus cum die et causa*, with returns, which seems to have come from the *Recorda;* then jury process and panels; then latitats returned 'non sunt inventi', followed by those (or precepts) returned 'cepi corpora'; then the declared bills; lastly the final-process writs and returns. The first and last sections are not yet very large during the run of the series between Easter 1520 and Michaelmas 1548, from which only six terms are wanting.

The 'bills' business fission began in 1549 and ended in 1607. The first move, coincidental with the appointment of the former Yorkshire filazer Richard Heywode as joint Chief Clerk, was to segregate the least and the most important sections. The least important formed the *Non Sunt Inventi* series [KB 153]. Its eighty-seven mostly very dirty and tousled files between Michaelmas 1550 and Easter 1590 have a big gap between 1577 and 1588. Whether these latitats continued to be filed and kept long after this is uncertain; they were by now purely formal documents, which could well be cannibalised for other uses. The most important section, the bills, remained so styled by the clerks; but after wavering long between *Narraciones* and *Declaraciones,* it was *Declaraciones* which the clerks adopted as the cover title for the new series [KB 152]. It grew enormously, while content and arrangement were subject to successive modifications.

Until Hilary or Easter 1569 individual declarations were normally undated. This made difficult the identification by term of early files that had lost their cover or cover-label, and made impossible the certain identification to a term of most loose items from such broken files. From Easter or Trinity 1569 the declarations are dated at the bottom left: from this point, debris can therefore be sorted by terms. From about 1576, files for some terms were made up into two or more parts; from 1578, the declarations in some files are numbered; from Michaelmas 1581, numbering becomes normal. At various dates in the seventeenth century, numbering commenced in the other files series, declarations being the first. From this date one can therefore sort debris with some hope of restoring its original order in the file. By 1591 the ten parts that might make up a year's files were holding some 8,000 to 9,000 declarations, in files which are very awkward and heavy to handle. At Michaelmas 1591 it was decided to file the declarations by the first letter of the plaintiff's surname. After five terms' experiment, the series settled to seventeen files each term, with composites for IJK, for NO, for EUVYQXZ, and single-letter files for the rest. They flourish up to the chasm at Hilary 1630. A few have been found for later dates, to show that the same filing system continued for many decades. There is no hope of substantial additions to this few. Some thousands of loose declarations from broken files are being sorted, a process which will continue until after the last sack of any kind has been decanted: one finds such loose declarations everywhere. Many restorations to parent files have already been made in the lettered series; for some broken files very substantial parts have been reconstituted; for almost all the gaps, in either the wanting letters after 1591 or wanting terms before then, something from the missing file has been found to show that it is not lost but broken.

As the *Bille* file had at Hilary 1549 lost the documents whence it took its name, a new title had to be found for this reduced series [KB 151]. The clerks flirted a little in the 1550s with just *Brevia* before sensibly adding *Billarum*. Style and size were soon subject to great fluctuations. By 1571 the files were very large; at Michaelmas 1571 the jury process and panels were removed. This new series [KB 154] similarly began as just *Panella* before also having a clarificatory *Billarum* added. *Panella Billarum* was a growth series with a difference. As most cases went to nisi prius at the Lent or Long-Vacation assizes, it was the preceding (in other series small) Hilary and Trinity files which became huge. The usually big Michaelmas and Easter files remained small. At Hilary 1591, a year before the remodelling of the declarations, the Hilary and Trinity files were remodelled: thirty-eight coverless files, one for each county, labelled with just county and term, without any title, and one more for *distringas* in all counties. The broad lace-like thongs of the files of counties with the same initial were wrapped round to make a pack of the group. Since for the three northern counties there were usually only summer assizes, there were normally thirty-six files for a Hilary and thirty-nine for a Trinity term. There were ten groups: B, C, D, E (Ebor' and Essex'), L, M (Midd' and Mon'), N, S, W, and a mixture made up of Gloucester, Kent, Oxford, Rutland, and *distringas*. Cities or towns that were counties of themselves, like Exeter, Gloucester, Southampton or York, might have their writs put in a very thin separately labelled file, tied up with the parent county; their appearance is naturally irregular. The Michaelmas and Easter files continued in the old form, now restyled *Venire Facias*. The series runs up to the chasm, a year later than the declarations, to disappear at Hilary 1631. Again there are just a few survivals from later in the century. In the three years after 1571, the *Brevia Billarum* had *Et H. Cor'* added to its title. At Michaelmas 1574, the *Habeas Corpora* were removed to form a separate series [KB 155]. These are the plea-side forms of *habeas corpora*, mostly 'ad faciendum et respondendum', along with 'ad prosequendum', 'ad respondendum', 'ad satisfaciendum' and so on, originals and judicials. The main adjectival interest lies in the earlier vacation writs, which give justices' addresses in the city and suburbs and appoint precise hours for the return, thus giving a good idea of the day worked by Elizabethan judges. Term writs give no such details. Later vacation writs were mostly dealt with by the judges in their chambers at Serjeants' Inn in Chancery Lane or Fleet Street, at unspecified hours.

There is a good run of 188 term files from 1574 to the chasm at 1630. On the other side, there are twenty-two files scattered between 1638 and 1653, and twenty-four scattered between 1673 and 1686. From 1653 to 1673 there are no intact term files, only Carlton Ride stringings, some of several terms together, others of a hotch-potch nature, either mixed terms or mixtures of *habeas corpus* writs and returns with other series or documents. These are still under investigation. The removal of the *Habeas Corpora* slowed, but did not halt, the growth of the *Brevia Billarum*. Now it sometimes had *Et Ce. Cor'* added to its title, or was even called *Cepi Corpora* for an odd term; but until Trinity 1589 its contents continued unchanged. At Michaelmas 1589 the latitats or other writs and precepts returned 'Cepi corpora' then became a new series *Cepi Corpora* [KB 156]. Between then and Trinity 1688 there are 282 term files, but there is only one file in the chasm between 1632 and 1645. This left the *Brevia Billarum* shorn of all mesne process, restricted to the post-judgment writs and returns: extent, *inquiras que dampna, fieri facias, scire facias, capias ad satisfaciendum*, and so on. The series was given the new title *Brevia Judicialia:* which, if understood as 'judicial writs' rather than 'judgment writs', can be very misleading. The last loss from the now *Brevia Judicialia* came at Easter term 1607 with the start of the *Capias ad Satisfaciendum* series [KB 157] for this neat category of writ and return alone. Between then and Trinity 1688 the *Ca. Sa.* series has 223 files, with an equally grievous gap between 1631 and 1646. For the *Brevia Billarum* or *Judicialia* itself from Hilary 1549 to Michaelmas 1688 there are 448 term files, which vary very wildly in size up to 1589; more than half of those wanting are in the gap between 1631 and 1646.

So we turn from the main 'bills' group to the four auxiliary series. Presumably a note was always made when someone in the court's custody was committed to bail. These notes, or 'cedule', may have been filed; but the files were apparently not permanently preserved till the rise in importance of bill procedure: the earliest surviving *Cedule* file [KB 149] comes from Trinity 1514. In it, the bail notes are cast in what are clearly long-established set forms; a good minority are in writ actions; in trespass, they quote much of the writ and marginate the alleged damages and date of the trespass; many bail-pieces are plainly fictitious, but this can only be inferred from the names; nearly all the pieces are oblong. Within thirty years, the old set forms have been recast; anything to do with writs has almost vanished, except returns on *recordari facias loquelam;* the formula 'per recognicionem' distinguishes real from fictitious bail; and the piece is now usually in the peculiar pentagonal or hexagonal shape which became its hallmark. Between Easter 1520 and Michaelmas 1558 the run is good, with only eighteen terms wanting. It is very useful for showing the shifting proportions of parties represented by filazers, by clerks of the chief clerk's office, and by other attorneys. Thereafter, as common bail became a mere appearance record, the files grew rapidly. From the mid-1570s enormous covers were made to contain them, in which they were curled like swaddled babies. Then, about 1593, the attempt to cover them was abandoned; a seven-inch square, not labelled until about 1605, became the only ready identification for files extending from three to six feet, shaped like a caterpillar or tube train: a shape extremely vulnerable to damage. Many of the later files exist only as dismembered chunks, which were spilling pieces by the score when found. Loose bail-pieces characterise any King's Bench sack or container; they have got caught up into innumerable files and other King's Bench records, and have been gathered in thousands. The last cover clearly labelled *Cedule Communes* is from Trinity 1591; the first to be styled *Ballia Communia* is from Easter 1607.

Though despised by the Record Office, and destroyed from 1661 (if not slightly earlier) under the schedules, the bail files have two qualities. As the latitat was returnable not at a conventional return day, but on a precise date, the bail-pieces are filed in order of precise dates. So from them one can readily construct tables of working days in term for nearly a century to 1632.¹ Within dates, from the mid-sixteenth century, the pieces are filed in alphabetical order of attorneys. From 1588 to 1614 docket rolls (called *Ballia Communia*, a title adopted for the files themselves between 1591 and 1607) survive [KB 162] to enable these details to be investigated with greater ease, the attorneys being listed in the right-hand margin of the rolls. By the 1560s, justices sign some special bails; but signing was not yet universal when, apparently in Michaelmas term 1572, these pieces were segregated into the new series *Cedule per Recogniciones* [KB 158]. The number of cases in which real, substantial, bail was required ensured that these files, though becoming fat, were never unmanageably large. For example, the total of entries in all four terms of 43 Elizabeth I was some 1,140, or about a tenth only of the common bails of the same year. Filing is continuous for the term, apparently in business order. The files provide a useful summary guide to the more important cases and their attorneys, numbered from 1610; they carry a superb series of judges' autographs, from Southcote and Carus to Newdigate and Twisden; and they are of use for determining the composition of the court in the late 1650s. The series leapt the great chasm with the loss of only four years, and was continuing strongly up to its destruction point of 1661 under the schedules.² There are docket rolls for it [KB 163], but only between 1589 and 1602.

The two other subsidiary series are represented by only a few files, the earliest in each coming from Michaelmas 1610. The *Committitur* [KB 159], mostly of Carlton Ride recovery, carry the record

---

1 By Elizabeth I's reign the normal boundary-dates of terms were: Michaelmas, 9 October to 28 November; Hilary, 23 January to 13 February; Easter, Wednesday after quinzaine of Easter to Monday after the Ascension; Trinity, Friday after the morrow of Trinity to Wednesday after three weeks of Trinity. If either the first or last of the normal Michaelmas or Hilary days fell on a Sunday, then the terms began on 10 October or ended on 29 November and began on 24 January or ended on 13 February. The normal number of working days (Mondays to Saturdays) was thus: Michaelmas, 43 (excluding All Saints); Hilary, 17 (excluding Candlemas); Easter, 22 (excluding Ascension); Trinity, 17.

2 For these, see P.R.O., *Rules and Schedules 1877-1913 Reprints of Statutes Rolls and Schedules governing the disposal of the Public Records* (1914), 25-75 (KB plea side, 1715-1832, dated March 1882), 108-10 (KB Crown side 1677-1854, dated February 1907), and 172-3 (KB plea side 1660-1715, dated March 1907). The destruction, from various commencing dates in the 18th century, of common and special bails, *Satisfacciones,* and *Committiturs,* was dealt with in paragraphs 9, 14, 61 and 64 of the 1882 schedule. When, in 1907, the now extended destruction date of 1660 was being applied, there was no further examination of these classes for any merits they may have had in the mid-17th century: instead, the rulings, based mainly on documents in English of a century later, were applied indiscriminately.

of committals to the marshal's custody for the execution of judgment. The *Satisfacciones* [KB 160] contain the plaintiff's acknowledgment that the defendant has satisfied him for the adjudged debt and damages, or the like. Both were entered on bail-piece shaped parchments, and from 1661 were destroyed under the schedules.

In size and appearance there was a great similarity between the earlier *Cedule* files and those of the *Warranta Attornata Recepta* series [KB 150]. The Common Pleas filed its warrants of attorney at the start of its *Brevia* files, before the Norfolk section. But the King's Bench never filed them in the *Brevia* or other early established series. If it filed them at all, the files for long were not permanently preserved. In 1967-8 six files were gradually found from between Trinity 1511 and Hilary 1515. For some time, therefore, it was believed that the series began to be preserved about the same time as the *Cedule*. But since 1970 loose sacks of writs have yielded three files between Easter 1463 and Hilary 1472, and so its probable commencing date is at present quite uncertain. The 141 files up to Easter 1610 are very scattered. They usefully supplement the attorneys' section of the plea rolls, especially where an attorney's business is grouped on one or more sheets or where one can see at a glance the connection between a filazer's circuit and the parties or corporation for whom he acts. Distinctive latterly for its elaborate engrossment, sometimes embellished with civic or mayoral arms, is the warrant (usually filed first each Michaelmas term) whereby London appointed the chief clerk or secondary as its general attorney in the court.

Archival work in the nineteenth and twentieth centuries

If these outlines of general development and of the lives of the series had been known in 1966, recent work would have been simpler, though less stimulating. They were not even dimly guessed in the 1840s, when the Carlton Ride Record Office, under Henry Cole, was the concentration centre for legal records. As part of its general work on records from the King's Bench treasuries, much was done on the files, which came to the Ride in sacked bulk, the earlier material mostly very dirty and disorganised. Acres of vellum or scrap parchment, thousands of yards of string and many thousands of printed and manuscript labels and buffers were used. The work was done backwards: to recover, identify and arrange back to about 1630 for most series, that is, to get just a toe-nail hold on the far side of the great chasm. These arranged files had dated labels, printed in black on yellow paper, stuck on them and were packed in small bags without individual reference-numbers.[1] Also,

1 Cole was Assistant Keeper in charge at Carlton Ride from July 1840 until

skirmishing forays beyond 1630 towards the fifteenth century recovered and roughly identified a small amount only of the remaining bulk. These files had less dignified temporary white labels tied to them and were resacked to await later action: which they badly needed. When, in 1857, it was necessary to move the records from Carlton Ride to the new Pennethorne building in Fetter Lane, some 300 sackfuls of the run 1422-1630 had yet to be dealt with.[1]

So there was no comprehensive survey of King's Bench files for the Deputy Keeper's Reports. Thomas's new *Handbook* guided the searcher only to truncated portions of ten series.[2] These were in the following main categories: *Indictamenta* from 1625, plea-side series II from 1629 (a double mistake, since it held undifferentiated the plea-side *Anglia* and Crown-side *Brevia*, to be withdrawn in the 1890s), plea-side series I, also from 1629 (which held the four latest developed bill series, *Brevia Judicialia, Habeas Corpora, Cepi Corpora,* and *Capias ad Satisfaciendum,* and became KB 137). From 1649 the *Habeas Corpora*

March 1850, when seconded to the 1851 Exhibition commission; from March 1843 he was also in charge of the repair shops with their staff of some 36 workmen. The moves affecting legal records and Carlton Ride 1840-58 are conveniently summarised in 20 *RDK,* Appx 10. More interesting detailed work is reported in 1 *RDK,* Appx 9; 5 *RDK,* Appx 1(8); 6 *RDK,* Appx 1(9b, 13). On the general method of work the most revealing is in 6 *RDK,* 11. The permanent labelling system, with specimen tickets, is described in 4 *RDK,* Appx 1; the colour code was, red for Common Pleas, yellow for King's Bench, and blue for Exchequer. But it was the practice in all cases to affix a printed ticket, even if temporary, to every document; thousands of these, with a few broad categories ('Bails', 'Declarations', 'Warrants' of Attorney, 'Writs') were found on pre-1630 files, especially late Elizabeth I to early Charles I, including the lettered declarations, Hilary or Trinity county packets of *Venire Facias* and *Cedule,* special and common bail files. The 'Writs' label was used for general purposes, and so for Indictments, *Recorda* or even *Bille* (though these last sometimes have a 'Declarations' label). The fact that most of this was probably the preliminary unchecked work of men of about the standing of the modern supervisory search-room attendant explains why, in these preliminary labellings, terms are usually given correctly, regnal years often have errors, while the class (unless the title is copied verbatim from the file's original label) is rarely correct.

By 31 December 1845 Cole could report the completion of the inventories, or bag lists, covering Writs Series I and II, the Indictments from 1628, and common and special bails (files from 1616 and 1625, enrolments from 1664 and 1661 respectively): 6 *RDK,* Appx 1(28).

[1] 9 *RDK,* Appx 1(1) lists the 11 original series (8 files, 3 enrolments) starting before 1660, from Indictments to Writs Series II, with number of containers (bags, parcels, portfolios) and the strongroom (A3, A4, B2) in which they were to be placed in the new Chancery Lane building on the final removal from Carlton Ride. No such detailed particulars are given of the sacks of unsorted or rough-sorted files removed to other locations for storage only.

[2] F.S. Thomas, *Handbook to the Public Records* (London, 1853), 107 (Indictments), 116 (*Anglia*), 116 (plea-side Writs I), 107 (later *Habeas Corpora*), 113 (Record of Orders, said wrongly on p. 102 to start from 5 Wm & Mary instead of 1 Wm & Mary, 101 (bails), 103 (*Committitur*), 114 (*Satisfacciones*).

were separately bagged; but it has recently been found that most of the files in these bags were in fact *Recorda*. From 1688 the *Recorda* were bagged separately, under a shorthand version of their 1733 title 'The Records of Orders and so forth' [now KB 16]. There were three other series, now mostly destroyed under schedules. The *Handbook* could point clearly to one complete series. The *Baga de Secretis,* the offshoot started in 1500 from the term-*Indictamenta,* had always been accorded Pullman-class archival custody and had been made fully available, with a detailed printed list in the Deputy Keeper's Reports for 1842-4.[1]

The *Handbook* said nothing of a connection between the King's Bench and Tower. Prynne started work in sorting all kinds of files there in 1661. He must at least have listed for his own use as exploiter; but when Thomas Duffus Hardy began work, though the files were still neatly stacked, the listing was all to do again. In 1843 a list was printed, professedly of Chancery files only.[2] A companion for the courts was promised, along with the transfer of the relevant files to Carlton Ride when it was completed. This did not happen. The painstaking compilers of the lists unfortunately did not recognise much of what they described. Thus: 'No. 172. 12 Edward 2. Various Writs of Chancery, with some Extents of Goods, Lands and Tenements' should have read 'King's Bench *Brevia* file, octave of Hilary 12 Edward II'. So the court's earliest files, of the Tower period, in so far as they were available, were available in arrangements and under descriptions which disguised their nature. Tower debris from broken files had been partly sorted into miscellaneous collections, all reckoned as Chancery; but much was still left in packets and sacks.

The *Handbook* hinted at a connection between the King's Bench and Chapter House only by including the Assize and Quo Warranto Rolls under Queen's Bench: an inclusion maintained until 1908. Many files and some collections of debris bear marks of Agarde's work. He did not apparently touch the (presumably sacked) bulk of the four oldest series but, perhaps because their bags were lost or decaying, he concentrated mainly on indictment files of the provincial trailbaston sessions and their many adjuncts. His county arrangement of these and other rolls was expanded by Palgrave to form the Assize and Quo Warranto Rolls collection in the 1830s. Palgrave's presslists show that he never understood that this collection included King's Bench files: a small number originating in, and a much larger collection returned into, the court.

1   3 *RDK,* Appx 2, 213-68; 4 *RDK,* Appx 2, 217-97; 5 *RDK,* Appx 2, 131-244; Thomas, *Handbook,* 100.
2   'Inventory of Records in the Tower': 4 *RDK,* Appx 2(5a), 113-7.

So these lists also could not signpost King's Bench files of the middle period for the searches, while the King's Bench sacked bulk from the Chapter House continued untouched, along with much debris. No more was done until the need came to clear attics and cellars of the Rolls Yard complex of its vast quantity of unsorted bulk in sacks and containers (King's Bench among them), so as to empty the old buildings for demolition and the erection of Taylor's Chancery Lane frontage. Harley Rodney's King's Bench work was done mainly in 1886-95. Some choice pieces were removed, but generally there was only a superficial examination and the writing of a descriptive label before the sacks were moved for storage elsewhere. In resacking sacks in poor condition, matter from Common Pleas seems often to have been tipped in with King's Bench. Such sacks, when opened, presented archaeologically distinct layers, usually with bric-a-brac of the 1890s at the division or bottom. Sacks with files predominating were assigned or confirmed to reigns. Those with posteas or debris had descriptive labels, sometimes accurate; later they were all labelled as 'King's Bench Loose Writ Sacks'.

Many operations stemmed from this work. Three affected King's Bench files. A great rearrangement of Chancery and Tower material was started, and is only now approaching its end. Early in it, Hardy's arrangement of files was dismantled. The other operations were done mainly by Scargill Bird. Starting in 1886, the *Indictamenta* from before 1625 were looked for in the sacks and perhaps three-quarters of what was there was found; part, no doubt, having Carlton Ride preliminary labels.[1] This was ample for a proper understanding and arrangement of the series; but the chance was missed. Dates then assigned ignored the terms; many coverless files were cobbled together. To these recoveries were added the Carlton Ride run for 1625-75 and a few dozen bits from broken files, not all indictments. The sensible mid-Victorian 'Early Indictments' was replaced by the 'ninetyish 'Ancient Indictments'. Between July 1912 and April 1921, following (but not meeting) criticisms about the class by Vernon Harcourt and Bertha Putnam, these files were stripped and given their present format.[2] All thongs, sewings, stops — everything which would show

1   No precise details in *DKR*, but Repair Register 1 has an entry dated July-September 1886 to show that the senior repairer (A.S. Watson) working for Scargill Bird assembled the Q.B. Indictments for Edw. 3 to Hen. 8 in bundles by reigns preparatory to listing: PRO 12/1. The class title was changed from 'Early' to 'Ancient' Indictments between 1891 and 1896: Scargill Bird, *Guide to the Public Records* (1st ed., 1891), 164; (2nd ed., 1896), 170.

2   The criticisms were voiced, at first very tentatively, in 'The Justices of Labourers in the 14th Century', 21 *EHR* (1906), 517-38; and then, with great emphasis, in B.H. Putnam, 'The Ancient Indictments in the Public Record Office', 29 *EHR* (1914), 479-505; and, with great trenchancy, by L.W. Vernon

whether the file in its previous state had kept its integrity or had suffered losses from beginning, end, or in the body — were destroyed. Many covers were ruthlessly cropped, and membranes were numbered in reverse order, from end to start of the file. But the jumbled files, even those noted by Vernon Harcourt as being in 1908 but recently cobbled together, were now united with all the apparent sanctity of the single and indivisible document.

The second operation, caused partly by new items being fed from sacks, was the remodelling in 1889-91 of the Assize and Quo Warranto Rolls collection into the three sections of the Justices Itinerant group.[1] So far as concerns the King's Bench, the twenty-six transfers then made to Indictments were uncertain and incomplete. The printed list of plea rolls did not attempt to identify the remaining King's Bench files, whether they had originated in the court or belonged to the much larger number returned into it.[2]

General work on the sacks was resumed after World War I, with the active interest, though never the immediate supervision, of Hilary Jenkinson. The assault on King's Bench sacks came between 1930 and 1938, when the late Charles Drew and Bernard Wardle decided to

Harcourt, 'Baga de Secretis', 23 *EHR* (1908), 508-29. Harcourt, whose early death was an immense loss to such studies, showed that the archivists of the Record Office had only to understand and use properly a fully available series, the Controlment Rolls [KB 29], to be able to understand and arrange properly both the trailbaston and term-Indictment files. Miss Putnam scandalised the Office's senior staff by urging that no publication should be allowed of any documents from the classes 'Ancient Indictments' or 'Assize Rolls' until the K.B. indictments as a class had been thoroughly studied and properly arranged. There was no official reply. The young Cyril Flower, then editing *Public Works in Medieval Law*, i (32 *SS*, 1915) used his Introduction (xiv-xviii) for a reply to Miss Putnam which shows only too plainly the extent of official ignorance about the early history of the K.B. files. The same weakness is shown in Flower's datings of undated indictments and presentments in this and his second volume (40 *SS*, 1923). The Selden Society should prepare a list of corrigenda to the datings of documents in these volumes.

PRO 12/2 (5 July 1912) notes the repair of KB 9/1-4. Thereafter, by year's ends, the documents reached were: 159 (1912), 363 (1913), 451 (1914), 497 (1915), 591 (1916), 662 (1917), 689 (June 1918): PRO 12/2. Followed by: 708 (December 1918), 806 (1919), 910 (1920), 932 (end of class, 1 April 1921): PRO 12/3. Many repairers were well beyond active or reserve service age, and so continued progress was made during the war.

1 PRO 12/1 shows that between January and June 1891 the senior repairer (W. Winwood) worked on 254 coroners' rolls [JUST 2] and 220 gaol delivery rolls [JUST 3] for Scargill Bird. Then, between July and December 1891, many repairers combined to work on 1,657 assize rolls [JUST 1] for Bird. [The JUST class was formerly referred to as JI].

2 *List and Index IV* (1894, 2nd ed. 1910).

attack from the medieval end, other colleagues assisting at times.[1] They struck first where the medieval growth seemed best and most representative: the Chapter House bulk of Richard II to Henry V. They then moved through the far end of this bulk to the now dismantled Tower files; and then, unknowingly, imitated Carlton Ride by forays forward into the King's Bench treasury sacks, decanting a few for most reigns to the 1620s. A provisional arrangement was made, covering some 1,350 files (or the remains of them) from Edward I to Richard III: but compressing all the different series into one class.[2] As in 1857, the fruits of the forays beyond 1485 were resacked: these files were sometimes labelled, in brave attempts to relate casual items of the later abundance to the simple series of 1400. A demonstration of the work at the Office's centenary celebrations in 1938 crowned the operation, which the threat of war, and then the war itself, brought to an end.

The present work began in 1966 with the conclusion — from the discovery of the *Panella* for Trinity 11 Henry VII among the indictments[3] — that there must still be indictments in the remaining bulk sacks. These, having been mainly in the Clock Tower since the 1890s, had recently gone to Hayes: giving what had been denied workers since Carlton Ride, a prospect of ample room for recovery

[1] For an account of the work I am grateful principally to Mr D.B. Wardle himself. Messrs L.C. Hector and R.E. Latham, among others, have told me of their experiences as assistants. The work, known popularly as 'writ'-picking, was one in which all new Assistant Keepers in the 1920s and 1930s were expected to do a stint. For the larger story of work on the general file and other miscellanea and debris between the wars I am grateful also to the late J. C. Collingridge, C.S. Drew and H.C. Johnson. The accent in the 1920s had been heavily on individual items, for example single writs, from early broken files; these, especially from the 13th century, were often individually of great interest. But archivally this attack was not satisfactory, for its object was the placement of the items in various classes (or rather collections) of modern origin and not the reconstitution of the original broken files. Drew and Wardle saw this, and therefore determined to attack instead by first sorting intact files, and so establishing the gaps where broken files or their scattered contents might be expected to be found; leaving the final sorting of individual items from such broken files until later.

[2] The provisional references used in this one class arrangement may be seen in the citations of KB 136 by Conway Davies in 'Common Law Writs and Returns', 147-52. They have all been superseded. It would be ungrateful to a pioneering study to say more in criticism than that both the article's factual and statistical accounts of the five early main King's Bench files contain many inequalities, while its general theory about the development of the group seems mistaken.

[3] Found by Vernon Harcourt with the indictment file for 1 Ric.3 [KB 9/366], it was then thought to be a file of 11 Hen.8: 23 *EHR* 527. By order of Mr E. Salisbury, then in charge of the Search Room, who correctly identified its reign, it was then stitched up with the indictment file for Trinity 11 Hen.7 [KB 9/409]. Met with during the revision of the Indictments list, it was removed, first to a place in the provisional one-class arrangement and then finally to its *Panella* file [KB 146/9/1114].

and arrayal. It was therefore decided, while looking for indictments, to sort out also the contents of the 350 or so remaining sacks that were labelled, or were readily identified, as having King's Bench files, posteas, or debris; eventually likewise to clear the north-west vault under the Round Room (or Strong Room D38), where the contents of many scores of both Common Pleas and King's Bench sacks had long ago been stacked and tipped.[1]

More than half the sacks had, or had lost, reign labels.[2] Except for some undisturbed Carlton Ride sackings of roughly sorted files, in or

---

1 The hurried removal of all bulk sacks to Hayes in 1964 was caused by the (abortive) plan to build new search rooms on the roof at Chancery Lane, with public access by lifts to be driven through the Clock Tower. At Hayes the sacks were eventually stacked in rows by categories in C Building, under the general direction of the Officer in charge; but under the immediate supervision and organisation of the late Herbert Kitney (Resident Officer, Keeper at Hayes 1953-71), an incomparable adjutant for arranging sack and box moves and supplies, and familiar to the immediate post-war generation of researchers as the then police constable on gate-duty at Chancery Lane. In the winter 1966-7 he moved all labelled K.B. sacks by reign groups to D Building, and in Spring 1967 laid out for examination in batches some 322 sacks which had lost labels. The examination and identification of the latter had to be sandwiched in to the start of work on the run of labelled sacks for Hen.7 to Phil. & Mary. It produced sacks of potentially whole or part K.B. files etc., and broadened one's knowledge of the range of sacked bulk by producing sacks of files from Exchequer, prerogative courts, and even medieval assizes, in addition to the preponderant C.P. and miscellanea, mostly of Chapter House or Treasury of the Receipt provenance. The N.W. Vault under the Round Room (D38) had been filled by the 1920s, if not much earlier, by an emptying from (it proved) sacks of mainly C.P. files for Eliz. 1 to Geo. 2, and K.B. files from the 15th to 17th centuries. The workers of the 1930s believed they had removed all K.B. matter, but the level in about half the area was still some 5 feet deep and in both this and the shallower 3-foot seam elsewhere layers were found where C.P. was richly leavened with the usual K.B. mix of files. Work in great heat and dust was greatly forwarded by the assistance of C.J. Kitching. Some 1,917 files were found to include 302 KB files, besides K.B. enrolments.

2 The approximate reign totals were: Hen.6, etc., 4; Hen.7, 7; Hen.8, 17; Edw.6, and Mary, 7; Eliz.1, 92; Jas 1, 52; Chas 1, 141. There were also 32 unreigned sacks labelled as containing bails. The many misdatings are partly explained by Cole's use of expert workmen for sorting and partly by the great difference in cover-label styles between files before and after about 1460. The containers were mostly large document transit boxes, apparently supplied either in the 1930s or also during the 1964 move by junior officers to replace sacks about to burst open; they were equal roughly to another 10 sacks, and were dealt with in 1970. The K.B. files recovered in 1970-1 in clearing D38 were similarly equal to another 20, mostly reign and bail sacks. The number of sacks for Hen.6 to Ric.3 cleared in the 1930s is not known; but the total of sacks with a reign or bail label for the period 1422-1630 was probably about 250 when they were moved from Carlton Ride to Chancery Lane in 1857. The sacks for Hen.7 to Mary were emptied in 1968, the other reign sacks in 1969. Where any sack contained debris not belonging to any file found in it, a debris box was established for later action, except that loose bails, declarations, membranes of *Venire Facias* or *Warranta Attornata,* were immediately put into sorting boxes of those categories. The debris boxes were mostly sorted out later,

near the 1620s, a sack of any reign might yield files of any other, in the range Henry VI to Charles I at least. Some sacks or containers in the range Richard II to Richard III, overlooked or left in the 1930s, also turned up. A minority, disturbed in the 1890s or later, yielded also some hundreds of Common Pleas files in the range Richard II to Charles II. It was found, too, that the Carlton Ride workers had often been short of scrap parchment for wrapping files which needed, or seemed to them to need, protection. They put these, usually small, files into the middle of any large, robust, well-secured file which was at hand, often of another reign and invariably of a different series. Less than half the sacks were, or had probably been labelled 'Loose Writs'.[1] Many were genuine King's Bench sacks with posteas in, or escaped from, packets; fewer held substantial debris. Most of both sorts were leavened with files, sometimes richly. Other sacks were mixtures of files debris, mostly made in the 1890s or later. Some were older Chapter House sacks, with contents varying from integral documents, or sizeable pieces of files or rolls, to bulk sweepings of fragments; in these there were usually a few files, along with documents of many sorts from any court or department whose records were ever deposited in the Chapter House or allied treasuries from the 1220s to the early nineteenth century. Individual documents, or batches, from broken King's Bench files in the debris included little from the thirteenth century, some from Edward II, a lot from Edward III to Henry V, but the greatest bulk from Henry VI to Charles I.

as opportunity arose; much of the contents was arrayed in chronological order. Matter from C.P. etc. was separated. The bails sacks were dealt with in 1970; many large debris boxes had to be established to take badly spilling or unidentified chunks.

An editorial slip, 5 x 3 in., was made out for most individual files up to the late sixteenth century, after which some routine or prolific series were digested in multiples to a slip. The slips carried notes of such basic details as physical dimensions, condition, labelling style, content, and peculiarities. For Hen.7 to Mary, draft tabular lists were prepared on a duplicated form, in three copies (for the officer in charge of the search rooms, Library, and Hayes); but the labour involved in making the necessary yearly insertions to these lists, as a result of the later piece-meal recoveries (some 400 in 1968-73), was such that no lists were provided for earlier or later reigns except for the relatively simple *Recorda*. These lists merely indicated the existence of the files, not their condition and availability. Draft lists with such details were maintained with the editorial slips for each reign series of every class.

1 Including cartons, but excluding any allowance for matter recovered in 1970-1 from D38, there would seem to have been some 158 loose writ sacks. Of these, 128 were examined in 1969-70; at September 1974 there were still 12 unexamined. Early in 1969 all were superficially examined with mouths open, and assigned to three categories: I (mainly posteas and files, 110); II (mainly large debris, 20); III (small debris, or completely coagulated files, 28). Of the first category, 16 were wrongly labelled, being sacks of files with little or no posteas or debris and assignable to a reign or mixed reigns; 5 were entirely C.P. files of later 17th century.

The space available at Hayes, which was increased as work proceeded, made it possible to array thousands of files in order as the series were established and built up. So, eventually, at a few glances one could see the rise and fall of series from the court of Huse C.J., Reynold Sonde and Henry Harman, to the court of Hyde C.J., Henley, and Wightwick and Fanshawe. The build-up of series has been necessarily slow. Thus, of 151 potential *Brevia Regis* files for Henry VIII, only 116 had been found after the reign sacks for Henry VII to Philip and Mary had been decanted. By 1973, single recoveries had gradually raised this total to 141. Because of this very piece-meal manner of recovery, it was necessary to devise a reference system for each series which would be permanent yet would enable the reference of a particular file to be assigned immediately if it was found. The only major delay would be with new series, while the reign in which they commenced was being firmly established. The call-number is then built up of the following elements: the KB class number (the next available plea- or Crown-side number) followed by an oblique stroke; a number from 1 upwards by reigns (with 1 the first reign of the series) followed by an oblique stroke; a number corresponding to the regnal year of the reign. This completes the reference for year files: *Recorda* and *Precepta Recordorum*. Most series, being term files, need an additional number, from 1 to 4, indicating the term. The terms are reckoned as they fell in each reign; the difficulty presented by the occasional death and succession in term had usually been met and solved already by the contemporary clerks, who decided whether a broken term be reckoned first or last of a year. A few term files need a further sub-reference, where the series exists in parts, like the *Brevia* or *Anglia* up to 1642, the term *Declaraciones* of the 1570s and 1580s, the lettered declarations from 1591, the bill-panels county packs from 1591, and a few casual items. Thus: *Recorda* for 20 Elizabeth I is KB 145/13/20. *Brevia Billarum* for Hilary 20 Elizabeth I is KB 151/3/20/2. *Anglia* for the morrow and octave of Candlemas (part 2) in Hilary 20 Elizabeth I is KB 136/15/20/2/2. Two errors of reign-numbering have, however, occurred. The workers of the 1930s were certain that there was no surviving *Brevia Regis* file earlier than Edward III's reign, so when the classification started with Henry VII and Henry VIII these reigns were reckoned as 9 and 10, and so back to Edward III as 1. But when the 1930s arrangement of the Edward II files was checked much later it was found that two *Brevia Regis* had been mistaken for *Brevia*. Again, in 1967, the earliest *Warranta Attornata Recepta* found came from early Henry VIII and this remained so after all the files-sacks and most of the others had been cleared. But in 1971 the first of three such files from Edward IV was found. Lastly, a fuller knowledge of file contents has shown that the *Bille* file of Hilary

3 Edward VI is the last *Bille* file, and not the first *Brevia Billarum,* as was at first believed.

In all, by the end of 1973, for the main period 1485-1630 (that is, in the gap between the work of the 1930s and of Carlton Ride) some 8,290 files, excluding indictments and nisi prius filings, have been recovered, arranged in the series already described, and mostly boxed. Over a hundred have been found for the period from Edward III to Richard III. This, and the discovery of some inequalities in the provisional list drafted in the late 1930s, made it necessary to check the earliest files; the provisional single-class arrangement of these was dismantled and these files were also arranged in the new established series. Nearly a hundred files were formed from after 1630. This made it necessary to examine and dismantle the plea-side series II; and to follow by dismantling the Carlton Ride *Habeas Corpora* and plea-side series I to 1688, arranging them also in the established series. Excluding indictments, the whole run of classes from Edward II to James II now amounts to some 10,820 files, all but a few hundred of which have been checked and had references put on them; and most of which have been boxed. Summary descriptions of each class are given in Appendix II. In addition, 149 term-*Indictamenta,* from between 1405 and 1653, are being passed through conservation for reduction to modern format and addition to the class, along with some of the irregular trailbaston sessions and returned oyer and terminer files from between 1353 and 1494. The revision of the KB 9 list, with a conspectus of term files for each reign from 1385, has reached the 1630s.

Between arrangement and general availability there is naturally a gap, the size of which depends partly on progress in boxing and writing fair-copy lists, but mainly on the physical state of the files. Many of these are fit and robust enough for production in their original format. But many are not fit and their sheer number is far beyond the capacity of a Conservation Section whose resources have to be rationed carefully between many demands and which, for some years ahead, will have little if any available for work on King's Bench files beyond what is committed already to clearing the indictments. The more obvious is general physical damage, usually caused by some form of wetting, and resulting in all stages from heavy coagulation to a universal powdery decay, though often affecting only a part of the file. The less obvious is damage to the central filing thong, especially when the documents on it are all perfectly preserved. At one extreme this may have reduced a file to a small still on-thong batch from which all the rest has spilled away: to turn up perhaps in sundry associated loose batches, some still held together by the tension of the edges of the empty filing hole, others completely dispersed through many collections of miscellanea. At the other extreme, the file may appear to be intact and quite producible, with all its contents apparently excellently preserved; but the hidden break will be somewhere in mid-file; to handle it for consultation would be to risk reducing it in a few moments to utterly disordered debris by one incautious movement. As for the debris, much has been restored to parent files during recovery. Larger batches, especially of *Recorda* and *Indictamenta,* have been arrayed, some of the latter being also restored to parent files. Some has been rough-sorted by series, reigns, years or terms. But most could only be isolated for a later generation to work on, in conjunction with what is already in the various artificial collections, much of which (at least for the medieval period) comes from the same parent files. The same generation may complete the recovery of all the files now still in sacked bulk. Since hundreds of Common Pleas files were found in sacks labelled King's Bench, it is very probable that some of the still missing King's Bench files are hidden in the bulk of the labelled Common Pleas sacks for Henry VI and for Henry VIII onwards; and, along with files debris, in the Common Pleas loose-writ sacks and the smaller number of 'Chapter House sacks', all of which have still to be decanted.

So the first generation of scholars to whom the files may be generally available, and from whom we may expect studies far more detailed and definitive than those just summarised, based as these have been on the minimum research needed to understand series – either to organise them or identify their individual files – should not forget the last generation of archival faceworkers. They will be both practising the faith and undergoing the experience shared by all such faceworkers from Agarde to the present century, and which is epitomised in a letter from one famous member of Lincoln's Inn to another. William Prynne writes on 9 September 1661 to Sir Harbottle Grimston M.R.[1]

> Whiles you are sucking in the fresh country ayre I have been almost choked with the dust of neglected Records (interred in their own rubbish for sundry years), their rust eating out the tops of my gloves with their touch, and their dust rendring me twice a day as black as a Chymney Sweeper. I have, at last, tumbled them all over, and distributed them into sundry indigested heapes, which I intend, God willing, to reduce to order by degrees.

---

1 Grimston papers, Hertfordshire Record Office, MS. Verulam VIII.B, 157.

APPENDICES
TO
KING'S BENCH FILES

APPENDIX I

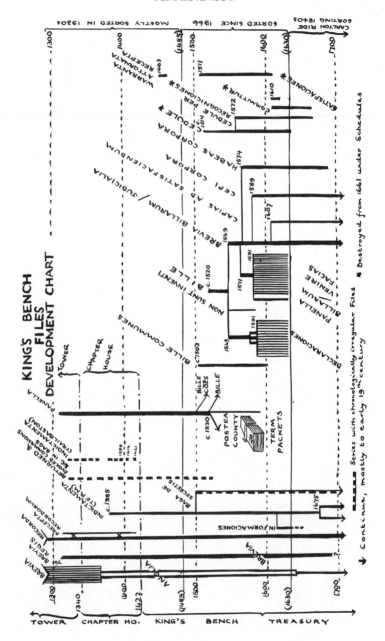

APPENDIX II

Summary Details

The classes KB 37, 38, 136/2-24 and 145 to 167 are at present stored at Hayes. They are not yet generally available; but regnal sections for some reigns are being made available, and as this is done the relevant part of the class-list is included with the Search Room King's Bench class-lists. Such files may be seen either at Hayes, or by arrangement they may be brought to Chancery Lane.

Dates without round brackets mark the definitive start or end of series or of parts here covered. Dates within round brackets are those of the earliest or latest file yet discovered for a class. Figures in square brackets are the totals for the files yet discovered for each class. All files are from the plea side unless otherwise stated, and all are term files unless otherwise stated.

KB 136   *Brevia* (to 1442 x 1445); *Brevia Communia;*
             Anglia (from 1467 x 1469 to 1708)
                               Edward II to George II [2065 files]
             Return-day file to Trin. 1369; two parts a term, Mich. 1369 to Hil. 1641; term file, Pas. 1642 to 1760. Continues as 'Writs Special and Original', arranged in 1840s, listed in 1857, and available until about 1890, when apparently withdrawn.

KB 145   *Recorda*   (1312-3) to 1699 [289 files]
             Year file, with internal term divisions. Became Crown side in seventeenth century. Continues as KB 16 (*Recorda* to 1732, then *The Record of Orders* from 1733), as bundled in 1840s in small sacks, without individual references.

             Precepta Recordorum   (1327-8) to (1417-8) [46 files]

KB 37   *Brevia Regis* (to Mich. 1598); *Brevia* (1599-1682)
                          (Pas. 1324) to (Mich. 1682) [968 files]
             Crown side.

KB 146   *Panella; Panella Assise* (early fourteenth century);
             Panella Assise et Bille Finite (late fourteenth century);
             Panella Assise Finite (1444-65); *Panella* (by 1474-1598)
                         (Pas. 1318) to (Hil. 1598) [555 files]

KB 147   *Bille*   casual (Henry VII & Henry VIII) [5 files]
                      regular (Pas. 1520) to Hil. 1549 [110 files]

KB 148   *Bille Communes*   (Hil. 1503) to (Mich. 1605) [241 files]

KB 150   *Warranta Attornata Recepta*
        (Pas. 1463) to (Pas. 1610) [141 files]

KB 149   *Cedule; Ballia communia* (c. 1593)
        (Trin. 1514) to (Hil. 1632) [276 files]
    Dismembered files, additional, Hil. 1564 to Hil. 1632 [60 files]
    Destroyed from 1661 under schedule.

KB 158   *Cedule per Recogniciones*
        Mich. 1572 to Hil. 1661 [293 files]
    Destroyed from 1661 under schedule.

KB 151   *Brevia Billarum* (to Mich. 1589); *Brevia Judicialia*
        Pas. 1549 to Mich. 1688 [448 files]
    From 1688 continued in small sacks of the 1840s.

KB 152   *Declaraciones*   Pas. 1549 to Trin. 1591 [164 files]
    Term files
    [Contd]   Mich. 1591 to (Hil. 1630) [2184 files]
    Lettered files
    There are 17 lettered files each term: A, B, C, D, F, G, H. J-K, L, M, N-O, P, R, S, T, W, E-U-V-Y-Q-X-Z.

KB 153   *Non Sunt Inventi*   Mich. 1550 to (Pas. 1590) [87 files]

KB 154   *Panella Billarum*   Mich. 1571 to Trin. 1590 [65 files]
    All terms
    Venire Facias   Mich. 1590 to (Mich. 1630) [71 files]
    Michaelmas and Easter terms only
    Distringas and untitled county files
    [Contd]   Hil. 1591 to (Hil. 1631) [2285 files]
    Hilary and Trinity terms only

KB 155   *Habeas Corpora*   Mich. 1574 to (Hil. 1686) [242 files]
    From 1660 still under arrangement.

KB 156   *Cepi Corpora*   Mich. 1589 to Trin. 1688 [284 files]
    From 1688 continued in small sacks of the 1840s.

KB 157   *Capias ad Satisfaciendum* Pas. 1607 to Trin. 1688 [223 files]
    From 1688 continued in small sacks of the 1840s.

KB 159   *Committitur*   (Mich. 1610) to (Mich. 1659) [18 files]
    Destroyed from 1661 under schedule.

KB 160   *Satisfacciones*   (Mich. 1610) to (Hil. 1612) [4 files]
    Destroyed from 1661 under schedule.

CROWN SIDE

KB 9   *Indictamenta*   (Mich. 1385) to Hil. 1675 [959 files]

The examination of files already in the class, and the revision of the list, have reached 1630 (KB 9/792); the addition of recoveries has included most of those to the end of Elizabeth I. Continues as KB 10 (London and Middlesex) and KB 11 (out counties).

KB 8   *Baga de Secretis*   1500 to 1813

Completely calendared in 3, 4 and 5 *RDK*. When created, a file from 1477 was included retrospectively in it.

[KB 9][1]   *Informaciones*

Files for James I - Charles II are being found. There was a great increase in the informations filed in the *Indictamenta* in 1616-8, which seems to have resulted in this offshoot series starting about then.

DOCKET ROLLS

Chief Clerk:

IND 1322-1384

     Remembrancia   Pas. 1390 to Hil. 1656

In the 1920s these were at first made KB 120, but were later transferred to the IND class.

KB 161	*Intitulamenta Omnium Brevium*	1552 to 1553 [2 rolls]
KB 162	*Ballia Communia*	1588 to 1614 [73 rolls]
KB 163	*Recogniciones*	1589 to 1602 [42 rolls]
KB 164	*Habeas Corpora*	1613 to 1629 [4 rolls]
	28 term and 21 vacation sessions.	
KB 165	*Scire Facias*	1610 to 1631 [5 rolls]
	43 term and 39 vacation sessions.	
KB 166	*[Latitat]*	1619 to 1632 [26 rolls]
	43 term and 27 vacation sessions.	
	[Secondary] :[1]	
KB 167	*Remembrancia*	1552 to 1603 [115 rolls]

1   It seems that Mr Meekings at one stage contemplated putting these files into a new separate class (KB 38), but eventually decided to keep them with the Ancient Indictments (KB 9). When the informations are made available in the search rooms they will be distinguished in the KB 9 class-list from the indictment files proper.

2   Editorial conjecture. Mr Meekings describes them as 'series from the clerks/ attorneys Sandbache and Kemp'. George Kemp was Secondary from before 1588 until 1606.

APPENDIX III[1]

Clerks of the King's Bench, 1399-1547

The officers of the common-law courts have received little attention from historians, even though they constituted a far from negligible branch of the legal profession and some of them were distinctly important, both in terms of the personal fortunes which they amassed and of the influence which they had on developments in the legal system. No doubt one of the obstacles to research has been the want of any list of office-holders. Since very few of the officers were appointed or paid by the Crown, the preparation of such lists requires prolonged study of the records in which they left their mark. In the King's Bench all the 'clerks' (except the Clerk of the Crown) were appointed by the Chief Justice for the time being. By the seventeenth century, at least, it was the practice for the Chief Justice to present his nominee on appointment with a parchment roll recording the gift;[2] but these instruments were not enrolled except in those few cases where, by consent, a filazer was allowed to surrender to the use of another.[3] The books of admission which once existed,[4] though probably not from an early date, have likewise been lost. In the course of arranging the King's Bench files, Mr Meekings produced a rough working list of filazers to assist in the dating of loose items; and in the course of correspondence he furnished the editor with various draft lists which, when assembled, produce fairly reliable tables of succession to the thirteen filazerships and the two chief clerkships from the reign of Henry IV to that of Henry VIII. The list is not, let it be understood, chronologically or biographically perfect. It would be possible to produce a more definitive version by collating the files and the filazers' rolls (in KB 27) term by term; but it would be an immense labour, and it seemed to the editor that it would be useful for historians to have forthwith the succession of names in the imperfect form which follows. Anyone interested in a particular name may, without excessive difficulty, discover the precise dates for himself.

---

1 Written by the editor. Mr Meekings did not intend the list for publication and is not responsible for errors which the editor has failed to remove.

2 Trye, *Jus Filizarii*, sig.B1v. There are some extant specimens of such documents for the Common Pleas in CP 4/1.

3 E.g. KB 27/796, m.73d (Styrop to Merland, 30 April 1460); KB 27/993, m.107 (Gogh to Holme, 28 November 1495). Trye cites some later precedents.

4 Trye said the Keeper of the Sign of the Latitats kept a book with the names of the filazers and the dates of their admission: *Jus Filizarii*, 274.

The 'signatures'[1] of the filazers in the files and rolls do not use Christian names, and so the lists prepared by Mr Meekings were mainly of surnames. It is sometimes possible to discover the full names from the enrolment of bills or attachments of privilege in suits brought in the King's Bench by or against a filazer; in rather more cases the full names can be ascertained from the rolls of warrants of attorney (in KB 27), since most filazers practised as attorneys, but this method fails when there is more than one attorney with the same surname. The editor has supplied Christian names for the period before 1422 from Professor Sayles' lists,[2] and for the remainder of the period from his own notes on the plea rolls.[3] Dates of death, where discovered from inquisitions, wills or monuments, have occasionally been supplied.

In the middle of the fourteenth century the King's Bench had about twenty-five clerks of the standing which entitled them to 'sign' membranes. By the end of the century, perhaps as a result of administrative reforms under Clopton C.J., perhaps of some accommodation between the clerks themselves, the number (besides the Chief Clerk and Clerk of the Crown) dwindled to thirteen and each of the thirteen clerks came to be associated with a particular group of counties.[4] The county demarcation was not rigidly observed at the beginning of the fifteenth century, and sometimes more than one name was written on a single membrane; but the principles on which business was then shared have not yet been brought to light. Nevertheless, the thirteen offices (which were legally distinct by 1469)[5]remain distinct until some time after 1547, when, somewhat inappropriately, in view of the filazers' declining business, the number was increased.[6] It is not certain when the thirteen clerks began to use the title 'filazer',[7] though

---

1 Not necessarily holograph, for the filazers probably had their own entering clerks. From the later part of Henry VII's reign, the first membrane of each KB 27 bundle is often elaborately decorated, with some canting allusion to the name of the filazer responsible: see the full descriptions in E. Auerbach, *Tudor Artists* (London, 1954).

2 *Select Cases in King's Bench,* vii (88 *SS,* 1971), xvi, lxix-lxx.

3 Valuable assistance was given by Miss Blatcher, whose important book on the King's Bench is nearing completion. The editor, however, retains sole responsibility for the shortcomings of this appendix.

4 M. Blatcher, 'The Working of the Court of King's Bench in the Fifteenth Century' (London Ph.D. Thesis, 1936), 21-4; *Select Cases in King's Bench* ed. Sayles, vi (82 *SS,* 1965), xxxv-xxxiv; vi (88 *SS,* 1971), xvi-xvii; J.B. Post, 'King's Bench Clerks in the Reign of Richard II', 47 *BIHR* (1974), 150, at 154.

5 Pas. 9 Edw. 4, 3, pl. 12, *per* Laken J. (affirmed by Billyng C.J. and Yelverton J.).

6 See p. 102, above.

7 The usual spelling before the eighteenth century was 'filaciarius' in Latin, and (after the fifteenth century) 'philizer' in English. The ph-spelling suggests an associa-

the term is used in a petition of 1410 and a statute of 1432[1] and was common to both benches. In their own rolls they described themselves as 'the king's clerks of his Bench before the king himself'. The more descriptive title became established in the fifteenth century. At Wonersh in Surrey there is a brass effigy of Thomas Elyot (d. 1467), described as 'custos filacii Surrie et Sussexie in banco regis', an idiosyncratic but apt form of the title. Three years later the defendant in a Common Pleas case pleaded that he was a servant of John Gogh 'unus filaciariorum Curie domini Regis de Banco suo coram ipso Rege, videlicet filaciarius de comitatu Devonie et Dorsetie' and was attendant on him in the parish of St Clement Dane's (presumably in Clement's or Lyon's Inn), and so demanded the privilege of the King's Bench; the outcome was a debate which reached the year books.[2] The same John Gogh surrendered his office in 1494 to the use of John Holme, and the transfer was noted by the Chief Clerk in the plea rolls.[3] A more factually interesting case concerning a King's Bench filazer occurs in the year books for 1483. Richard Whele, filazer for Yorkshire and the northern counties, sued one Richard Reynold for false imprisonment on 26 February 1481 in a house in the parish of St Clement Dane's; Reynold offered to plead that his master had a warrant to arrest Whele as an enemy alien (a Scot), and that in obedience to his orders he locked Whele in the house. The plea roll records only a plea of not guilty, and the year book tells us that the defendant was driven so to plead 'because the plaintiff was one of the clerks of the Place'. This being a King's Bench entry, Whele described himself not as a filazer but (in the traditional way) as 'unus clericorum domini Regis in Curia ipsius domini Regis coram ipso Rege'.[4]

The first literary description of the filazers occurs in a note written in 1532 by Robert Maycote, Clerk of the Papers. In his book of entries, Maycote inserted a list of names headed: 'Nomina filaciariorum in Curia domini Regis coram ipso Rege et quot comitatus assignantur

tion with *chartophylacium.* Mr Meekings preferred 'philizer', but in deference to modern usage we have here used the f-.

[1] 3 *RP* 624: 63 ('filacer' of either bench); 10 Hen.6, c.4, confirmed by 18 Hen.6, c.9 ('filicer' or 'philicer' of the King's Bench). The *Revised Medieval Latin Word-List,* ed. R.E. Latham (London, 1965), 191, gives 'filator' (1439).

[2] *Wallyng* v. *Meger* (1470) CP 40/835, m.325; Pas. 10 Edw.4, 4, pl. 9; Pas. 10 Edw.4 (47 *SS,* 1930), 42; Brit. Lib., Additional MS. 37488, f.77 (entry).

[3] KB 27/933, m.107. Gogh was also Custos Brevium: KB 27/789, m.92 (vacated entry relating to another servant); 'signatures' as Clerk of the Warrants. Holme was described on his wife's brass in 1497 as 'unus Clericorum in Banco serenissimi principis Domini nostri Henrici septimi': J. Lewis, *History of Faversham* (London, 1727), 18.

[4] *Whele* v. *Reynold* (1483) KB 27/885, m.34d; Hil. 22 Edw.4, 45, pl. 9.

cuilibet filaciario prout usitatum fuit Termino Trinitatis Anno Regni Regis Henrici octavi xxiiii et ante'. The county grouping was the same as it had been since the end of the fourteenth century, and as shown in the tables below. On the facing page, Maycote described the positions occupied by the filazers in open court: 'Sessio filaciariorum in Curia domini Regis coram ipso Rege'. The filazers did not sit in the same order as the 'Nomina', but were divided so that eight sat next to the Custos Brevium and five on the left of the Clerk of the Papers; the exact disposition of the officers around the table is not wholly clear. Maycote had also commenced a marginal note on the 'divisio sive participacio Cirothecarum in Curia domini Regis coram ipso Rege', which began, 'Memorandum quod integrum feodum cirothecarum consistat in . . .' and then broke off, leaving unsolved the mystery of the 'glove fees' in the King's Bench.[1]

The highest promotion a filazer could expect was to the office of Chief Clerk, but the filazers also at first shared among themselves the subsidiary offices in the King's Bench, such as that of Custos Brevium and Secondary. For some reason yet to be discovered the filazership for Yorkshire and the northern counties seems to have been a path to promotion more often than the other offices: no less than three holders became Chief Clerk, and at least one became Secondary. A fifth, Porter, may also have been Secondary; he acted as Chief Clerk in Michaelmas term 1491 between Sonde and Bray,[2] and held as many as five of the filazerships in turn. The office of Custos Brevium was held by filazers — Chaumbre, Dabernon, Pill, Sonde, Gogh — until the third quarter of the fifteenth century, after which it was always held by a distinct officer. No Secondary is known for certain before Lucas, the Yorkshire filazer, but as late as the reign of James I a filazer was appointed to the office. During the century after Maycote, the filazers began to lose the competition for business with the Chief Clerk's office, which was engrossing to itself all the new bill business, so that in the massive KB 27 bundles of Elizabethan times the filazers are less prominent than in the much thinner rolls of the fifteenth century. The encroachments of 'the office' were belatedly resisted in Charles II's time by John Trye, whose biography has been published by Mr Meekings.[3] Trye made as much use of history as he could. Whereas the Secondary and other clerks of the King's Bench office were really

---

1 Library of Congress, Washington D.C., MS. Ac.1093.2, ff.142v-143. This will be further discussed in an appendix to the introduction to *Spelman's Reports*, ii (94 *SS*, 1978), at *354-5*.

2 Signatures in KB 27/921.

3 C.A.F. Meekings, 'John Trye (1634 - after 1692)', *Irish Jurist* 10 (1975), 352-5.

under-clerks of the Chief Clerk, the filazers had always been 'clerks of the lord king' with the Chief Clerk as *primus inter pares*. But such had been the transformations of King's Bench business and procedure since the fifteenth century that the squabble could hardly be resolved by recourse to history. Trye took the matter as far as litigation with Sir Robert Henley, the Chief Clerk, but without success.[1] For the purpose of mastering the later procedure of the King's Bench as reflected in the files, Trye's interesting but scarce little book should be studied in conjunction with the *Instructor Clericalis*.

CLERKS OF THE CROWN[2]

1399 to 1422	Thomas Covele [d. 1422]
1422 to 1458	Thomas Greswold
1458 to 1465	Thomas Croxton [of Gray's Inn, d.1465]
1465 to 1478	John West [of Lincoln's Inn, d.1483]
1479 to 1480	John Werall [d.1480]
1480 to 1502	Henry Harman [of the Middle Temple, d.1502]
1502 to 1509	John Mervyn [of the Middle Temple]
1509 to 1542	William Fermour [of Lincoln's Inn, d.1552]
1542 to 1559	Thomas Whyte

CHIEF CLERKS[3]

1399 to 1413	John Hulton [formerly sole Chief Clerk] and Hugh Holgot
1413 to 1434	Hugh Holgot
1434 to 1458	William Sonde [resumes office 1461]

1 R. Gardiner, *Instructor Clericalis* (3rd ed., London, 1700), 254. Trye himself appears to be alluding to the case when he recalls a trial at bar between 'a' filazer and a clerk of the Chief Clerk: *Jus Filizarii*, 203-4. Neither Gardiner nor Trye mentions any verdict or judgment.

2 Full chronological and biographical details in 94 *SS* (1977). The Clerk of the Crown, or King's Coroner and Attorney, was appointed by patent; his 'signatures' occur in the controlment rolls [KB 29], at the top right-hand corner of the membrane.

3 Full chronological and biographical details 94 *SS* (1977). The Chief Clerk, or Prothonotary, was appointed by the Chief Justice; his 'signatures' occur in the plea rolls [KB 27], on the left of the roll-number at the foot (or, in the case of joint holders, on the left and right respectively). After about 1450 the Chief Clerk's rolls nearly always begin at m.20, but there was no fixed practice before then: Blatcher, *Working of the King's Bench*, 34-5.

1458 to 1461	William Brome [d.1461]
1461 to 1468	William Sonde [d.1473]
1468 to 1491	Reynold Sonde [d.1491]
1492 to 1498	John Bray
1498 to 1518	John Rooper [of Lincoln's Inn]
1518 to 1524	John Rooper [d.1524] and William Rooper
1524 to 1548	William Rooper [of Lincoln's Inn, d.1578]

FILAZERS[1]

1. Norfolk, Suffolk and Norwich

< 1399 to 1432 >	Robert Hore
< 1435 to 1458	John Lynton
1459 to 1466	Robert Cumberford
1466 to 1482	William Porter [below: 6, 10, 11, 13]
1482 to 1513	Richard Coton
1513 to 1535	John Palmer [perhaps of Lincoln's Inn]
1535 [June] to 1540	John Rant [of Thavies Inn, d.1540]
1541 to 1547 >	George Waldegrave

2. Cambridgeshire and Huntingdonshire

1377 to 1410	Alexander Dominyk
1410 to 1420	Thomas Thwaytes [below: 4; probably of Furnival's Inn]
1420 [31 Oct.] to 1425	—— Floyer [probably of Lincoln's Inn]
1425 to 1438 >	Thomas Burgeys
< 1441 to 1441 >	John or Henry Wakefield
< 1446 to 1474 >	Thomas Strete
< 1483 to 1508	Thomas Lacy [below: 4]
1508 to 1532	Richard Hawkes [d.1532]
1532 to 1547 >	John Fox [perhaps of Lincoln's Inn]

1 In these lists < and > indicate some uncertain date before (<) or after (>) the date immediately following. But all the dates should be regarded as approximate or tentative.

3. Essex and Hertfordshire

< 1399 to 1420	Thomas Crowe [clerk of the peace for Kent 1395-1420]
1420 to 1442 >	Adam Mundeford
< 1444 to 1458	John Gamell
1459 to 1482	John Beell [clerk of the peace for Herts., 1472-82]
1483 to 1501	Thomas Ingram [below: 9; clerk of the peace for Herts., 1483-1501; d.1501]
1501 to 1514	Thomas Morley
1514 [Feb.] to 1517	—— Clerke
1517 [July] to 1521	William Webbe
1521 to 1539	John Percyvall [d.1539]
1539 [Oct.] to 1543	George Aleyne
1543 to 1547 >	—— Montgomery

4. Middlesex, London, Kent and Canterbury

< 1399 to 1410	Thomas Holm
1410 [5 May] to 1414	Henry Chaumbre [Custos Brevium 1412]
1414 [24 Nov.] to 1426 >	Thomas Thwaytes [above: 2]
< 1427 to 1438 >	Alexander Kyngeston [reversioner to Clerk of Crown, but never succeeded]
< 1441 to 1458	William Coton
1459 to 1483	Thomas Lacy [above: 2]
1483 to 1500	James Starky
1500 to 1508	Edward Cheseman [below: 11; Cofferer to Henry VII; d.1510]
1508 to 1533	William Nood [of Clement's Inn; d.1533]
1533 to 1534	—— Hayes
1534 [June] to 1536	—— Cressweller
1536 [Mar.] to 1545	—— Martyn
1545 [Nov.] to 1547 >	George Symcott [of Lincoln's Inn, d.1558]

5. Surrey and Sussex

< 1399 to 1418	John Solas [M.P. Southwark; d.1418]
1419 to 1422 >	John Corve

< 1425 to 1467	Thomas Elyot [clerk of the peace for Surrey 1427-67; d.1467]
1467 to 1495	Richard Elyot [not the Richard Elyot of the Middle Temple who became a judge and d.1522]
1495 to 1515	George Godeman
1515 [Nov.] to 1533	William Fraunceis [of Lincoln's Inn]
1533 to 1547 >	Henry Warde [of Gray's Inn, d.1557]

6. Hampshire, Wiltshire, Somerset and Southampton

< 1377 to 1420	Thomas Beston
1420 to 1435 >	John Hengstecote
< 1437 to 1441 >	Richard Bye
< 1444 to 1485	Thomas Luyt [clerk of the peace for Midd. 1440-8; d.1487]
1485 to 1487	William Porter [above: 1; below: 10, 11, 13]
1487 to 1495	John Jebbe [d.1496]
< 1497 to 1525	William Draper
1526 to 1536	Richard Bucland
1536 [May] to 1547 >	John Hannam [d.1558]

7. Devon and Dorset

< 1399 to 1408	John Hordere [clerk of the peace for Dorset 1395-1411]
1408 to 1420	Henry Chorley
1420 to 1426	John Dabernon [Custos Brevium 1413]
1426 to 1444	Thomas Dourissh [M.P. Plympton 1427]
1444 to 1495	John Gogh [below: 9; Custos Brevium 1458]
1495 [28 Nov.] to 1515	John Holme [KB 27/933, m.107]
1515 to 1518	—— Sheldon
1518 to 1525	—— Davy
1526 to 1536	Thomas Bonefaunte [of Lincoln's Inn]
1536 to 1539	—— Rous or Rowse
1539 to 1541	—— Moyne
1541 to 1547 >	Richard Rusburgh [of Lincoln's Inn, d.1560]

136

8. Cornwall, Gloucestershire, Herefordshire, Gloucester and Bristol

< 1399 to 1419	John Wynchcombe
1419 to 1441	John Prudde
1441 to 1448 >	William Lovell [below: 10]
< 1457 to 1481	John Sarger [see Pas. 21 Edw. 4, 22, pl.6]
1481 to 1491	Robert Haukyns
1491 to 1495	Roger Porter [d.1523]
1495 to 1502	—— Warton
1502 to 1503	—— Askham [perhaps Richard Askham, justice of gaol delivery at Gloucester 1500]
1503 [31 Oct.] to 1515	John Lucas [of New Inn, and later of Lincoln's Inn; below: 13]
1515 to 1520	—— Smyth
1521 to 1524	Thomas Barnwell [of Middle Temple]
1524 [Nov.] to 1531	—— Case
1531 to 1534	—— Pyne
1534 [Nov.] to 1541	—— Hert
1541 to 1545	Clement Tusser
1545 to 1547 >	—— Turge

9. Oxfordshire, Berkshire and Worcestershire

< 1399 to 1414	Brian Huscarl [clerk of the peace for Berks. 1392-5]
1414 to 1427 >	Richard Corve
< 1429 to 1442	Andrew Pill [Custos Brevium 1426]
1442 to 1444	John Gogh [above: 7; Custos Brevium 1458]
1444 to 1460	William Styrop [M.P. Chippenham]
1460 [30 Apr.] to 1470 >	Henry Merland [KB 27/796, m.73d]
< 1473	Thomas Payne [not in Meekings' list]
< 1476 to 1504	Thomas Ingram and Thomas Vyncent [Meekings has them in succession, but both names occur in the rolls at first and later only Vyncent appears; Vyncent was clerk of the peace for Berks. 1472-96]

1504 to 1508	—— Wolryche
1508 to 1515	—— Swyllyngton
1515 to 1545	Christopher Payne [of Clement's Inn]
1545 [Feb.] to 1547 >	Jeronimus Songer

10. Northamptonshire, Rutland, Buckinghamshire and Bedfordshire

1381 to 1414	Thomas Bedford [M.P. Bedford; clerk of the peace for Beds. 1390-1422]
1414 to 1442	Simon Wellys
1442 to < 1446	William Lovell [above: 8] and John Prudde [above: 8]
< 1448	William Bastard and John Prudde
< 1448 to 1462	William Bastard [of New Inn]
1462 to 1466	William Porter [above: 1, 6; below: 11, 13]
1466 to 1473 >	Robert Dene [of Lincoln's Inn; clerk of the peace for Suffolk c.1456-74]
< 1476 to 1497	Thomas Holbache
	[Meekings listed Thomas Gate here 1487-97; but Miss Blatcher is of opinion he may have been acting as Secondary]
1497 to 1545	Thomas Robertz [of Clement's Inn, and later of the Inner Temple; possibly two men in succession, since one of this name d.1535]
1545 to 1547 >	Andrew Tusser

11. Shropshire and Staffordshire

< 1399 to 1413	Hugh Holgot [joint Chief Clerk; sole from 1413]
1413 to 1427 >	Thomas Whatton
< 1429 to 1432	—— Laweley
1432 to 1453	William Betley
1453 to 1481	John Rowelond
1482 to 1485	William Porter [above: 1, 6, 10; below, 13]
1485 to 1500	Edward Cheseman [above: 4]

1501 to 1503	Oliver Southworth [formerly a servant of Cheseman; below: 12]
1503 to 1520	Hugh Hykman
1520 [Mich.] to 1541	Thomas Skrymsher [clerk of the peace for Salop 1511-12, d.1551]
1541 [June] to 1547 >	James Wolriche [clerk of the peace for Staffs. 1548-51, d.1552]

12. Warwickshire, Leicestershire, Nottinghamshire, Derbyshire, Coventry and Nottingham

< 1399 to 1418	Thomas (or, possibly, John) Whatton [for Thomas, above: 11]
1418 to 1422 >	Thomas Greswold [Clerk of the Crown 1422, d.1458]
< 1424 to 1433	William Holder
1433 to 1459 >	John Greswold
c.1460 to c.1480	John Hawe [probably not the John Hawe who became a serjeant in 1486, a judge in 1487, and d.1489]
c.1480 to 1488	Robert Andreux [perhaps of Lincoln's Inn]
1488 to 1499	Richard Palmer [probably of Furnival's Inn]
1499 to 1500	——— Turnar [not in Meekings' list]
1501 to 1505	Richard Moton [d.1506]
1505 to c.1510	Richard Wyllys
c.1510 to 1537	Oliver Southworth [above: 11; of Clement's Inn; attorney of Common Pleas; fishmonger of London; d.1537]
1537 to 1538	——— Charneley
1538 to 1544	——— Fytzherbert
1544 to 1547 >	——— Bray

13. Yorkshire, Lincolnshire, Westmoreland, Cumberland, Northumberland, York, Lincoln, Kingston-upon-Hull and Newcastle-upon-Tyne

1371 to 1406	Thomas Ellerbek
1407 to 1427 >	William Waldeby
< 1429 to 1434	William Sonde [Chief Clerk 1434, d.1473]

1434 to 1458	William Brome [Chief Clerk 1458, d.1461]
1458 to 1487	Richard Whele [above: p. 130]
1487 to 1493	William Porter [above: 1, 6, 10, 11; d.1493]
1493 to 1511	William Fyssher [formerly clerk to Reynold Sonde, Chief Clerk]
1512 to 1515	Thomas Yemmez
1515 to 1525	John Lucas [of Lincoln's Inn; above: 8; clerk of the peace for Kent 1506-25; Secondary to Rooper; d.1525]
1525 to 1535	William See [d.1543]
1535 to 1547 >	Richard Heywode [of Lincoln's Inn; joint Chief Clerk 1549]

AN EPISCOPAL AUDIENCE COURT

Dorothy M. Owen

The late Brian Woodcock remarked, in the introduction to his important study of the medieval diocesan courts of Canterbury, that little had as yet been done to remedy the complaints made by Maitland in 1898 that there was no material in print for the reconstruction of the history and organization of ecclesiastical courts.[1] Had Mr Woodcock lived he would perhaps have published some of the Canterbury material; and, since he wrote, a number of other students have collected scattered evidence to illuminate the workings of various provincial and diocesan courts of the later middle ages.[2] But specimens of medieval church court records have not attracted many record-publishing societies: it is true that Mrs Bowker's edition of an early sixteenth-century Lincoln audience court book has recently appeared, and that the London Record Society is contemplating the publication of a London act book of the late fifteenth century;[3] but for any earlier period there is nothing at all, at least for the Southern Province, for the very good reason that very few records survive. The Canterbury and York Society, in publishing the entire register of Bishop Martival of Salisbury, was doing better than it knew, since the last section contains what appears to be the act book, and a reasonably complete one at that, of the episcopal court of audience in the years 1315 to 1329.[4]

Professor Cheney has demonstrated the way in which the family or chancery of the bishop took shape during the twelfth and thirteenth centuries, and gradually assumed the place, as judicial adviser to the bishop, once taken by the synod of the clergy.[5] Bishop Simon of Ghent, Martival's immediate predecessor at Salisbury, was on one occasion

---

1 B.L. Woodcock, *Medieval Ecclesiastical Courts in the Diocese of Canterbury* (Oxford, 1952).

2 C. Morris, 'The Commissary of the Bishop in the Diocese of Lincoln', *Journal of Ecclesiastical History* 10 (1959), 50-65; R.M. Haines, *The Administration of the Diocese of Worcester in the first Half of the Fourteenth Century* (Church Historical Soc., 1965).

3 *An Episcopal Court Book for the Diocese of Lincoln 1514-20*, ed. M. Bowker, Lincoln Record Society 61 (1967); *Act Book of the Vicars General: 'Foxford' 1520-39*, ed. C. McLaren, London Record Society (forthcoming).

4 Canterbury and York Soc., vols 55, 57-9, 68, ed. K. Edwards, C.R. Elrington, S. Reynolds and D.M. Owen (1959-75). Citations below refer to the last volume.

5 C.R. Cheney, *English Bishops' Chanceries* (Manchester, 1950).

at least to call the members of his chancery 'the clerks of my council', and from among them he and his fellow bishops were choosing auditors or commissaries to whom they committed some of the hearing of correction cases arising during a visitation, the examination of witnesses, and even the hearing of entire cases when these were outside the competence of their officials. A leading clerk, or chancellor, had usually appeared in the English episcopal's household before the end of the thirteenth century, and he seems to have become (in some cases at least) the presiding judge who, if the bishop were not himself present, heard all such cases. Dr Haines quotes an example of 1342 from Worcester in which Bishop Bransford appointed his Chancellor John de Severley 'ad audiendum cognoscendum etc. omnes causas et lites ad audienciam nostram extra consistorium nostrum'. In other places these functions were already being performed by an official who was called either 'auditor of causes' or 'commissary-general'.[2]

The jurisdiction which was exercised by the bishops and their commissaries in the audience court was what remained, after the commission to the official of all minor cases between parties and the evolution of special arrangements for corrections during visitations, of the ordinary jurisdiction of bishops as set out in the Sext in these words:[3]

> Since the bishop is known to have ordinary jurisdiction in his whole diocese, there is no doubt that he may freely sit in judgment either in person or through another, to hear causes belonging to the ecclesiastical court in every place that is not exempt from that jurisdiction.

Thirty years ago Professor Hamilton Thompson printed a surviving fragment of a Lincoln court book of the early fifteenth century, and used it as the basis for an account of medieval audience courts. He came to the conclusion that they were primarily courts of correction ('officium merum') for serious offences and he quotes, in support of this, a list of cases reserved for his own audience by Archbishop Courteney: perjury in matrimonial causes, wilful murder, usury, breaches of sanctuary, attacks on the property of the Church, and

---

1 *Registrum Simonis de Gandavo,* ed. C.T. Flower and M.C.B. Dawes (Canterbury and York Soc., 1934), no. 862.

2 Haines, *Diocese of Worcester;* see also n. 3 on p. 142, below. *Registrum Gandavo,* no. 342, has an appeal to the Arches from Peter de Periton 'se auditorem causarum audiencie vestre seu commissarium generalem pretendente'.

3 Sext 1.17, c.7. I have discussed this jurisdiction at some length in 'Ecclesiastical Jurisdiction in England, 1300-1550', *Studies in Church History* 11 (1975), 199-221.

similar serious matters.[1] Certainly his list accounts for most of the cases published by Mrs Bowker, and for the material to be found in the later audience court books at Lincoln. But there seems no doubt that at an earlier period, despite the existence of the official and his consistory court, a number of instance causes came directly to the bishop's audience — whether because of the social importance of the parties or of the gravity of the matter, it is as yet impossible to say. Similar causes could also be heard in the episcopal audience court on appeal from lower courts, or from the bishop's own commissaries, or even, on occasion, when they had been remitted there from the Court of Arches.

The diocesan administration by which Martival's register was compiled is still somewhat hazily known. As early as 1251, and probably long before, an Official of Salisbury was in existence, although his functions are not known. The earliest surviving register, that of Simon of Ghent, shows a well established consistory court which sat in the cathedral in Salisbury, which had its own seal, and a clerk who was also sequestrator of vacant benefices in the diocese.[2] The presiding judge there was the official, who was sometimes called on by the bishop to act as commissary in audience business. Appeal from the official in the consistory lay not to the bishop, whose *alter ego* he was, but to the Court of Arches; his judgments as commissary, however, might well be the subject of an appeal to the bishop. On one occasion Bishop Simon instructed his official to remit to him for personal hearing a cause so appealed. There were in addition the courts of the archdeacons, of the Dean of Salisbury, and of several prebendaries who had jurisdiction within the manors which formed part of their endowments. In the early fourteenth century, appeals from all these courts lay to the bishop in his audience, from which in turn appeals lay to the Court of Arches and to the papal Curia. No surviving commission shows that Ghent had ever nominated any single clerk to hear all audience matters with which he could not deal himself, but his clerk Peter de Periton was once described by the Official of Arches as 'auditor causarum audiencie vestre seu commissarius generalis'; and this title for the presiding judge of the audience court was undoubtedly in regular use in Salisbury by the middle of the fourteenth century.[3]

1 A. Hamilton Thompson, *The English Clergy and their Organization* (Oxford, 1947), 206-46.

2 *Victoria County History of Wiltshire*, 3 (1956), 17-19.

3 *Calendar of Entries in the Papal Registers relating to Great Britain and Ireland; Papal Letters*, ed. W.H. Bliss and others (London, 1893), iii, 201: an expectancy granted to Richard de Netheravon 'commissary-general of the bishop of Salisbury, 1345'.

Ghent's surviving register contains four sections: presentations and collations, licences, divers letters emanating from the Chancery, and a small *sede vacante* register. There are no ordinations, nor do the visitation rolls (which contained corrections) survive, except in brief quotations in the registers of his successors. The chief evidence of judicial activity is in occasional commissions which empower clerks to try cases or to cite parties and in the certificates of inhibitions returned to the Court of Arches, which are all found among the divers letters. With Martival's register we move on to something much more specialized, reflecting either a more developed diocesan organization or, more likely, a bishop of more precise habits. No ordinations or correction rolls have survived, although quotations from them appear among materials sent up to the Arches; but the register has two new sections (royal writs, and inhibitions and acts) in addition to the sections of institutions, licences, and divers letters. This last section is no longer the only record of the bishop's judicial activities; as in Ghent's register, it contains commissions and mandates for citations, and it also has full recitals of several cases delegated to the bishop from the Curia, and requiring a certificated return. This is like many other contemporary English registers, but the section of inhibitions and acts seems to be something quite new in record-keeping. It is a record of judicial acts in the bishop's audience court, including the reception and certification of inhibitions from the Official of Arches, and it suggests the beginning of crystallization, or specialization, in that section of the bishop's household which was concerned with legal matters. It is, in fact, a chronologically kept journal or court book. It certainly does not include a record of all the cases for which commissions or citations survive, and so cannot be called complete; it may well be that occasional cases heard by the official as commissary were included in his consistory court records, as was sometimes done at a later and much more formal period, and so have been lost. But the register covers the whole period of the episcopate, and provides more evidence than has previously been available about the functioning of a court of this type.

At the very beginning of Martival's episcopate two members of Bishop Simon's household, William de Selton and John Tarent, had been given a temporary commission to hear and determine all instance causes in the consistory court; soon after, Simon's official, Mr Peter de Periton, was commissioned as official by Martival, with powers of correction of faults discovered during visitation. Four years later, in 1319, Selton had taken his place as official, with the same powers, and in addition was permitted to hear promoted office causes arising during visitation. From this time on, Selton regularly served as a commissary in audience business.

The title of the register ('De inhibicionibus, actis et aliis infrascriptis') covers its contents exactly: it contains acts or narratives in instance and office causes heard in the audience court, memoranda of documents exhibited there, submissions made, or oaths sworn before the court, announcements of definitions or arbitrations in difficult administrative problems, and the receipt and certification of large numbers of inhibitions, remissions and mandates for the production of evidence, emanating from the Court of Arches.

Much of the business dealt with in the court was undoubtedly correction, arising from visitation presentments. Many of the causes heard in this way were prosecutions of clerks for lapse into moral offences which they had previously sworn to abjure. The charge brought in such cases was *fidei lesio.* A characteristic defendant in such a clerical prosecution was the litigious rector of Oaksey, who was also Prior of the Hospital of St John of Cricklade. There were four articles against him: (1) non-residence at Oaksey and waste of the hospital's goods at Cricklade; (2) breach of the oath he had taken before Bishop Simon to see no more of certain sisters of the hospital; (3) conduct of a case in a secular court on behalf of the community of Cricklade, in spite of his oath to Bishop Simon to meddle no further with hundred courts and their like; (4) failure to observe the excommunication laid on him for violence to one of the lay brothers of the hospital. There were also prosecutions for thefts of tithe sheaves, which began with a general excommunication of all such thieves in a single deanery, and the discovery by means of inquisitions of the names of the guilty men. As in the Oaksey case, these prosecutions usually ended with a confession on oath and a petition for absolution. Two of the matrimonial causes also began as office prosecutions. One arose from the presentment at visitation of a couple who had been married without the proper proclamation of banns. They were served with articles alleging this, submitted to the truth of it, but added in extenuation that there was no impediment to the marriage. They produced witnesses to prove this, the witnesses were admitted by the court, and the marriage was pronounced valid. The other case is a much longer and more complicated matter, which eventually disappeared to the Arches. It begins with the presentment of a husband and another man for cruelty to a wife and waste of the goods of the matrimonial home, presumably at the promotion of the wife. It continues with the husband's counter-claim for restitution of conjugal rights, and ends, so far as this court is concerned, with the wife's successful claim of 2s. maintenance per week while the case is *sub judice.* An important tithe cause involving a lay proprietor arose from his presentment at the visitation, for non-payment of tithes, by the parochial chaplain to whom they were due;

and *ex officio* articles were used by the bishop to implead the officers of St Nicholas's Hospital, Salisbury, who had refused to admit Thomas de la More to an almsman's place in the hospital.

Instance cases directly recorded in the register are of two types. On the one hand, there is the straightforward case between parties of some importance, about alimony or divorce, or a presentation to a benefice, though these last are chiefly known from the inhibitions. The case against Alan Pluknet, Lord of Kilpeck, for alimony, which was begun in April 1321 by his wife Sybil, who resided in the diocese of Salisbury, was to go through eleven sessions before it was finally removed to the Arches; the narrative or *materia* of the case was sent up 'in tribus rotulis hiis annexis' in December 1321, and was still under discussion there in July 1323. In the course of the case Alan's proctor said that his lord's estate was worth £1,000 *per annum* and the bishop, weighing this, assigned to Sybil alimony of 50s. a week. Another instance cause arose between the executors of the late Prior of the Hospital of St John of Devizes and the parishioners and burgesses of that town, who had opposed the executors' intention to exhume the body of the prior from the parish church, and to re-bury it at Potterne, in accordance with the prior's *ultima disposicio*. In extenuation, the men of Devizes, who now submitted to the bishop, said that they had been misled by John Frene, a royal clerk then keeper of the castle, who had pretended that the case ought to be heard in the royal courts. They said, moreover, that the brothers of the house had always previously been regarded as parishioners of Devizes; yet, after consultation with his council, the bishop declared in favour of exhumation.

This last case approximates in type to the disputes submitted to the bishop for a ruling or *diffinitio*. In this way Martival pronounced in favour of the archdeacon's right to visit the church of Uphaven, for which the proprietors (the Priory of St Wandrille) had claimed exemption. He also settled, by a judicious compromise, a long-lasting and very difficult dispute between the parishes of Cookham and Bray about the status of the chantry chapel on Maidenhead Bridge. These *diffinitiones*, which are solemnly attested by witnesses from the bishop's household, although cast in the form of acts of court, seem to be entered in the register for record. The same appears to be true of the witnessed entries which begin with the words 'memorandum quod' and which include exhibitions of proofs in causes, relinquishments of prosecution, oaths, submissions and abjurations, and even the formal refusal of a papal provisor to accept an offered living 'because it was insufficiently rich'.

Much the most numerous class of entries in the register is concerned with the Court of Arches. There are eighty-one inhibitions, twelve relaxations, and twenty-three mandates for the production of evidence in cases to be heard in the Arches, besides those inhibitions used only as delaying tactics and buried in the narratives of cases heard in the audience court. Of the eighty-one, sixty-three relate directly to presentation disputes and had, in almost all cases, begun with a *querela* of injustice suffered at the hands either of the bishop or of another claimant to the benefice. If a second claimant is introduced into the suit, the bishop is ordered in the inhibition to cite him into the Court of Arches, and no more is heard of the case. In seven of the benefice cases, however, the appeal had been against the bishop himself, who was therefore cited to the Arches. The remaining inhibitions arise partly from the bishop's alleged failure to act in appeals made to him from his own commissaries, or from the peculiar jurisdictions, and partly from appeals against his judgments in correction cases. There are only six explicit appeals for the tuition of the Arches during the prosecution of a suit at the papal court, but some at least of the cases remitted to the bishop because of failure to prosecute may have been of this type, since (according to Miss Churchill)[1] such cases were to be remitted if the appeal were not prosecuted within the year. The sort of complicated case which might be produced by this apparatus of appeals is admirably illustrated in the dispute about the tithes of Bisham. It opened in July 1320 with Andrew of Northampton initiating a case in the Arches against the bishop for failure to institute him to Bisham, while the bishop in his audience court began an *ex officio* prosecution against Andrew for removing tithe corn while the benefice was sequestrated by the episcopal officials. The original Arches cause was remitted to the audience after two years and decided against Andrew, who thereupon appealed for tuition in the office case but failed to prosecute his appeal, which eventually lapsed; the last entry relating to the case shows Andrew excommunicated by the bishop for contumacy in non-appearance. All told, one has an impression of the very considerable business done by the Court of Arches for even a moderately sized diocese such as Salisbury.

Several groups of diocesan statutes of the thirteenth century had enjoined on lesser ordinaries the transmission to the bishop's audience, with all due respect, of appeals from their jurisdiction, and certainly such appeals occupied a fair proportion of this court's time. There are three appeals from the bishop's own commissaries, one of which was

[1] I.J. Churchill, *Canterbury Administration*, 1 (Church Historical Soc., 1933), 463.

taken to the Arches, and one appeal each from an archdeacon, from the commissary of the Dean of Salisbury, and from a judge-delegate in a papal provision case. Where these cases are fully recorded they begin with a statement of the subject of the appeal in a *suggestio* addressed to the bishop, who then inhibits the inferior judge, cites the parties, and hears the case. The reason usually given for the appeal is the failure of the inferior judge to do justice, but it is clear that such appeals were often used merely as delaying tactics and were never proceeded with.

It is difficult to distinguish any formal organization in Martival's audience court, yet the survival of a separate register and the indication that files of libels, depositions, and judicial acts were kept by the court suggest some degree of professionalism among its servants. This may have been forced upon Martival by increasing business. It may even have begun in Bishop Simon's time, for one should not forget that both Simon and his successor had legal experience in Bishop Sutton's household and as successive Chancellors of Oxford. It may equally have arisen from the increasing employment of professional lawyers ('iuris periti') among the household clerks. These were the men to whom both bishops referred as their council and from whom 'tunc assistentibus' Martival sought guidance in the difficult matter of St Wandrille's claim to exemption. They witnessed, and presumably had advised on, all the formal *diffinitiones* and, alone or in pairs, they acted as commissaries when the bishop did not preside in court. Some thirteen of them, almost all Oxford masters, were active at different times during the episcopate. It is probably not accidental that one of them, Thomas de Astley, was a lecturer in civil law at Oxford and had acted as a royal proctor at the Roman Curia, where he was closely associated with Adam Orleton. Orleton's legal expertise had helped to give a professional air to Walter Reynolds' Worcester register, and among the Worcester lawyers were Robert Worth and Peter de Periton, who were officials for Simon and his successor.[1] Martival thus inherited a legal tradition which had probably already formalized and professionalized the Salisbury courts.

It is not possible to say that any one commissary is used more than any other, or can be distinguished as chief commissary or commissary-general, until almost the end of the episcopate, when William de Lubbenham and Robert Worth are described in a witness list as 'my auditors of causes' and a similar description is applied to Worth alone in an inhibition. Three years later, in 1329, Mr Walter Stratton is also called 'auditor of causes' and it may well be that a regular organization

---

[1]   This emerges from various entries in A.B. Emden, *Biographical Dictionary of the University of Oxford* (Oxford, 1957-9).

of the audience court and its servants had evolved during the episcopate. There is, nevertheless, no reason to suppose that all causes had been handed over to a single auditor; and, indeed, of the twenty-nine cases fully reported in the register the bishop acted as sole judge in ten, and presided in some stages of all the others. There was even an occasion, in 1320, when a decision was postponed in a suspension case 'until the Lord shall have returned from Parliament'.

The sessions of the court were held wherever and whenever it suited the bishop and his entourage or the commissary concerned. Once, during the Lincoln Parliament of 1316, there was a hearing at Lincoln, and during 1319 and 1320 when parliaments were twice held at York there were sessions of the court in Beverley and Blythe, and at York itself. Moreover, there were clearly times when a commissary, for his own or the suitors' convenience, held a session at some place other than the resting place of the bishop and his household. Much of the court business was undoubtedly transacted, or at least initiated, during visitations; it was thus that the bishop's attention was drawn to such scandals as the Devizes dispute and the long interdict on the Maidenhead chapel. The sessions were irregularly spaced according to need; a plaintiff only once objected because he was summoned on a *dies non sessionis*. Some attempt must have been made to allow for the suitors' difficulties in following the bishop's court. Martival's register has many fewer examples than his predecessor's of citations to 'wheresoever in his diocese the bishop may be found', and precise locations are regularly given. The citations are addressed to the rural deans and other suitable local agents, and certificates of their service are duly admitted in court. For the rest, the procedure is that described in the legal manuals and admirably discussed by Fournier: it would serve no purpose to discuss it here or to rehearse the details of any of the voluminous cases.[1]

It was suggested earlier that some of the men who actively influenced practice in the Salisbury court, and those of neighbouring bishops, might well have been trained in the papal courts. Miss Edwards has pointed out that during the pontificate of John XXII, who was himself a lawyer, many appointments to the English and other sees were undoubtedly made from the ranks of professional lawyers,[2] but the professionalizing of the bishop's legal staff probably began before this time. It is a subject which deserves a more thorough investigation,

1 P. Fournier, *Les Officialités au Moyen Age* (Paris, 1880).
2 K. Edwards, 'Political Importance of the English Bishops during the Reign of Edward II', *EHR* 59 (1944), 311.

over a much wider field, than is possible here; but a few points may be
pertinent. The registers of Sutton of Lincoln, Cantelupe and Swinfield of
Hereford, and Greenfield of York, all of them a little earlier than the
Salisbury registers discussed here, contain many commissions and acts
in audience cases which, while obviously competent reports of business
competently conducted, are unsystematically recorded and scarcely
distinguishable from the rest of the diocesan administration. Reynolds'
Worcester register contains much fuller legal reporting, with articles and
libels formally set out. Orleton's own Hereford register has similar
entries, and also regularly registers inhibitions, without separating them
from other business. For a separate audience register like that
of Martival we have to go to Rochester, where, in Hamo de Hethe's
register, there is a long section covering the years 1321 to 1330, which
Mr Charles Johnson called 'consistory records' but which is undoubtedly
the register of proceedings in the bishop's court of audience. The
Worcester register edited by Dr Haines also contains a brief section of a
similar register.[1]

These records apart, Martival's own register is an unusual specimen,
produced perhaps by a remarkable concentration of legal ability in
Martival and his predecessor, but perhaps also due to the increasing
professionalism of all ecclesiastical lawyers, who were already beginning
to assume some of the characteristics displayed by those figures
of European reputation, with whom Father Boyle and Dr Highfield
have familiarized us.[2]

1 *Rolls and Registers of Bishop Oliver Sutton*, ed. R.M.T. Hill (Lincoln Record
Soc., in progress); *Registrum Thome de Cantilupe*, *Registrum Ricardi de
Swinfield*, ed. W.W. Capes, *Registrum Ade de Orleton*, ed. A.T. Bannister, and
Registrum Hamonis Hethe, ed. C. Johnson (all Canterbury and York Soc.); *The
Register of Walter Reynolds*, ed. R.A. Wilson (Dugdale Soc. and Worcester
Historical Soc.); *The Register of William Greenfield*, ed. A. Hamilton Thompson
(Surtees Soc.); *The Register of Wolstan de Bransford*, ed. R.M. Haines
(Worcester Historical Soc. and Historical Manuscripts Commission).

2 For the evolution of the Canonist in the later Middle Ages, see my
introduction to *John Lydford's Book* (Devon and Cornwall Record Soc. and
Historical Manuscripts Commission, 1975); a paper I read to an international
colloquium on ecclesiastical history at Oxford, September 1974 (forthcoming);
and 'The practising Canonist: John Lydford's Notebook' in *Proceedings of the
4th International Congress of Medieval Canon Law: Monumenta Iuris Canonici*,
Series C. subsidia, Vol. 5 (Vatican City, 1976).

RAVISHMENT OF WOMEN AND THE STATUTES OF WESTMINSTER

J.B. Post

The early history of rape and abduction in English law remains to be described, partly because of the vagueness and ambiguity which beset so much of the medieval criminal law, and partly because a diversity of purposes was served by a relatively small group of ill-defined actions and statutes. This paper[1] is intended simply to highlight the Statutes of Westminster and their function, both as symptoms and as causes, in the strange process whereby the ordinary and straightforward remedies framed for a crude and shameful crime were effectively taken away from the victim, and put at the disposal of secondary, and sometimes opposing, interests.

The statutes themselves present slight textual problems in the relevant clauses,[2] but there is no doubt about the general terms of each.[3] In 1275 the first Statute of Westminster provided that no one should ravish nor take a maiden under age, regardless of consent,[4] nor matron nor maiden over age without her consent. Offenders convicted at private suit should have the 'common right'; if no one sued within forty days, the king would do so, the penalty on conviction in such cases being two years imprisonment and ransom. These provisions were short-lived. In 1285 Westminster II made ravishment of any matron or maiden, without her consent before or afterwards, a capital offence, and added that, in cases where the woman assented afterwards, the king should nevertheless have suit for the same penalties. Furthermore, the king allowed himself suit for the goods taken with an abducted wife; the abduction of a willing nun was to be punished by three years imprisonment, ransom, and compulsory compensation to the parent

---

1 Only partly revised from the paper as read; but I hope to incorporate subsequent research, and the helpful suggestions of several friends and colleagues, in a future study. See also 'Sir Thomas West and the Statute of Rapes, 1382', *BIHR* (forthcoming). The law of rape in many ancient codes, including Roman law, is usefully collected in J. Disney, *A View of Ancient Laws against Immorality and Profaneness* (Cambridge, 1729), 158-80. The survey of the medieval common law in B. Toner, *The Facts of Rape* (London, 1977), 89-94, is heavily but not unerringly derived from my notes and unpublished papers.

2 See Appendix, below, pp. 161-4.

3 Here and elsewhere I use 'rape' to mean 'forcible coition' (real or alleged), and 'ravishment' in its ambiguous (i.e. sexual or non-sexual) sense.

4 Westminster I, c.13 [1 *SR* 29]. This may be the first secular prohibition of coition with a minor.

house; and a wife living with her adulterer, and unreconciled to her husband at the time of the husband's death, forfeited all right to dower.[1]

It is far from clear what Westminster I meant by the 'common right' following conviction on appeal. As usual, the commentators are not entirely vindicated by the plea rolls. The author of Glanvill apparently regarded rape as a capital offence,[2] for which judgment could be respited only if the justices, and the families involved, allowed the girl to claim her assailant in marriage.[3] Since the pipe rolls provide ample evidence of amercement for rape at this date,[4] the account in Glanvill must be regarded as somewhat simplified. Seventy years later Bracton poses similar problems, though at much greater length. Parts of his discussion are Glanvill exegesis,[5] parts ostensibly go even earlier;[6] from his own day he describes the appeal procedure in careful detail, using perhaps two or three notable cases.[7] For conviction on appeal of rape, or at the king's suit,[8] he specifies the penalty of blinding and castration, to be mitigated only if the girl herself chooses to claim her assailant in marriage.[9] He supposes, however, that this notion of rape applies only where virginity or sworn chastity was lost, and he mentions a lesser scale of punishments for cases involving wives, widows, mistresses, or whores.[10] Unfortunately he does not detail these punishments, and he leaves the impression that the full penalty was the most important. So, too, does the author of *Placita Corone*, describing later in the century the same procedures and the same major penalty, relieved only by the opinion, attributed to Justice Thurkleby, that a convict's wife, as an interested party, could claim remission of the castration.[11]

1 Westminster II, c.34 [1 *SR* 87].

2 Glanvill, 176, associates the penalty for rape with that for other felonies (as we should term them), but the reference to 'death or mutilation' may have been made with rape in mind: ibid., 3.

3 Ibid., 175-6.

4 *Pipe Roll 34 Henry II* (38 *PRS*, 1925), 98. Cf. *Pipe Roll 31 Henry II* (34 *PRS*, 1913), 111; *Pipe Roll 28 Henry II* (31 *PRS*, 1910), 19.

5 Bracton, ii, 394-5 (f.140), 414 (f.147) and notes, 417 (f.148).

6 Bracton, ii, 418 (f.147): dooms of Athelstan – which might be genuine, or at least a tenth-century garbling of Alfred's dooms.

7 He cites an example of full sentence at the king's suit on failed appeal, from a (lost) plea roll of Michaelmas 1222: ii, 403 (f.143). There is one rather odd appeal of wife-stealing in 3 *BNB* 469:1597 [11 *CRR* 90:476; and Bracton, ii, 398 (f.141)]. The punishment for castration of a seducer (ii, 408, f.144v) may reflect *Millers* v. *Breton* (1248): Matthew Paris, *Chronica Majora*, ed. H.R. Luard, v (*RS*, 1880), 34-5; *CPR 1247-58*, 387.

8 Bracton, ii, 403 (f.143).

9 Bracton, ii, 414-5 (f.147), 417 (f.148).

10 Bracton, ii, 414-5 (f.147).

11 *Placita Corone*, ed. J.M. Kaye (4 *SS* Supp. Ser., 1966), 9.

It seems unlikely that Westminster I was intended to invoke such a penalty. Apart from the solitary instance from 1222 cited by Bracton, no conviction with sentence of mutilation has yet been found,[1] although a clerk, safe in his clergy, might be convicted.[2] Instead, the plea rolls show a wide range of resolutions. Very often the appellatrix was nonsuited, or failed to prosecute; very often, again, the parties reached a concord. The terms of such concords are not usually specified in the record,[3] but the exceptions to this rule fall into two categories. Some appeals were concorded by material settlements, perhaps in cash,[4] perhaps in land.[5] Rather more were concorded in the fashion allowed by the jurists, with the appellatrix marrying the defendant.[6] The regularity with which this form of concord can be traced or inferred suggests that the intention of forcing a marriage was the purpose of many appeals in the first place; this would also help to account for the high proportion of appeals which were not prosecuted. Who was forcing whom is a more difficult matter. The disparity of status which is apparent in many cases of failed and unconcorded appeals indicates, perhaps, the classic and hopeless plight, in which a ruined peasant attempted to salvage honour if not revenge from a social superior.[7] Revenge may underlie some appeals by discarded mistresses.[8] On the

---

1 Cf. *Placita Corone,* ed. Kaye, xvi, n.6.

2 *The Roll and Writ File of the Berkshire Eyre of 1248,* ed. M.T. Clanchy (90 *SS,* 1972-3), 350-1: 888.

3 E.g. 'Two Thirteenth-Century Assize Rolls for the County of Durham', ed. K.E. Bayley, in *Miscellanea* (127 Surtees Soc., 1916), no.214; *Somerset Pleas,* i, ed. C.E.H. Chadwyck Healey (11 Somerset Record Soc., 1897), 248: 848; 271: 963; 290: 1055; 291: 1065; 292: 1067; 300: 1118, 1121. (All from 1243.)

4 E.g. *The Earliest Lincolnshire Assize Rolls 1202-9,* ed. D.M. Stenton (22 Lincolnshire Record Soc., 1924), 151: 916; *Pleas before the King or his Justices 1198-1212,* iv, ed. D.M. Stenton (84 *SS,* 1967), 114: 3491.

5 E.g. JUST 1/359, m.35d (1241).

6 E.g. 'Durham Assize Rolls', nos 94-6, 116, 209 (1243); *Crown Pleas of the Wiltshire Eyre 1249,* ed. C.A.F. Meekings (16 Wiltshire Archaeological Soc., Records Branch, 1960), 240: 461; 249: 517.

7 For clear cases of poor girls appealing prosperous men, see *Three Yorkshire Assize Rolls for the Reigns of King John and Henry III,* ed. C.T. Clay (44 Yorkshire Archaeological Soc., 1910), 37 (? 1208); *Somerset Pleas,* i, ed. Healey, 248: 848; 265: 934 (and cf. 242: 811-2); 323: 1256 (and cf. 171: 542) (all 1243); *Calendar of Lancashire Assize Rolls,* i, ed. J. Parker (47 Lancashire and Cheshire Record Soc., 1904), 106 (and cf. 26, 149, 153)(1246). For the shepherdess and the lord of the manor, rather later, see *CPR 1281-92,* 406 (and cf. 215). Many cases show merely poor appellatrices: e.g. *Somerset Pleas,* i, ed. Healey, 255: 881, 885; 276: 989; 290: 1056 (1243); *Wiltshire Eyre 1249,* ed. Meekings, 182: 155; 222: 366.

8 E.g. *Wiltshire Eyre 1249,* ed. Meekings, 210: 310; JUST 1/174, m.32d (1238); *Rolls of the Justices in Eyre for Yorkshire 1218-9,* ed. D.M. Stenton (56 *SS,* 1937), 250-1: 669; *Lincolnshire Assize Rolls 1202-9,* ed. Stenton, 150: 909.

other hand, family feelings sometimes asserted themselves, again in cases where the seduction was not necessarily forcible;[1] trial jurors might detect pressure from an indignant mother,[2] or other members of the family.[3] One father, after his initial wrath, accepted the seducer as son-in-law, on condition that he provide the father with land, to be returned to the young man as the daughter's maritagium;[4] while in another instance a group of brothers gave their sister's seducer the choice of death, marriage to her, or giving her the profane kiss.[5] The emphasis here seems to have been on regularising the situation rather than on revenge; it is suggestive that the father of a Berkshire girl was one of the presenting jurors amerced at the 1248 eyre for concealing her appeal.[6] These and many comparable cases, in conjunction with the cases concorded by marriage without further explanation, indicate that accusation of rape was often used as a procedure for invoking family shame at illicit defloration, and it is arguable that some couples used the procedure to offset family objections to socially disparaging matches − a trick which has a striking modern parallel.[7]

With such various factors inhibiting the full prosecution of appeals of rape, the significance of Westminster I, c.13, was clearly in other sectors. Firstly, the appeal of rape was apparently extended to matrons as well as maidens, which Bracton had claimed to be the case in his day, but which the courts did not support: the issue of the appellatrix's virginity is a commonplace of the eyre rolls,[8] and was put firmly in context when, in 1244, Thurkleby J. allowed abatement of a widow's appeal 'because a woman can only appeal concerning rape of her virginity'.[9] It is possible

---

1 Cf. a presentment in 1279, that 'he . . . forcibly lay with her and ravished her virginity', resulting in acquittal on the girl's evidence that 'he was betrothed to [her] before he lay with her': JUST 1/876, m.50.

2 *Somerset Pleas,* i, ed. Healey, 290: 1057 (1243).

3 *Berkshire Eyre 1248,* ed. Clanchy, 392-3: 1032; 'The Veredictum of Chippen-ham-Hundred, 1281', ed. C.A.F. Meekings and R.E. Latham, in *Collectanea* (12 Wiltshire Archaeological Soc., Records Branch, 1956), no.58 and n.(1272).

4 KB 27/51, m.26d (before c.1270).

5 He chose marriage: KB 27/25, m.7d [*Placitorum Abbreviatio* (Record Commission, 1811), 267 (1276)]. For an alternative private resort, see *Millers* v. *Breton:* above, 151 n. 7.

6 *Berkshire Eyre 1248,* ed. Clanchy, 377: 983 (and cf. 296: 712).

7 The use of a declared defloration to procure family consent to a marriage, and legislative attempts to suppress this − both entirely concordant with the bulk of thirteenth-century English cases − are described by V. Martinez-Alier, 'Elopement and Seduction in 19th-century Cuba', *Past and Present* 55 (1972).

8 E.g. *Yorkshire Eyre 1218-9,* ed. Stenton, 216-7: 545; 250-1: 669; *Somerset Pleas,* i, ed. Healey, 300: 1120 (1240); *Wiltshire Eyre 1249,* ed. Meekings, 210: 310; *Lincolnshire Assize Rolls 1202-9,* ed. Stenton, 150: 909.

9 JUST 1/175, m.44d.

that such cases were previously regarded as moral rather than legal offences; in a plaint for rape of a married woman, the defendant claimed that he should answer such cause before the ordinary.[1] The statutory extension of the appeal of rape to matrons therefore brought within the purview of an existent private action the problem of ravished wives,[2] and may have been prompted by a Sussex abduction feud which had recently attracted the Crown's attention.[3] Probably more important, however, was the definition of the king's suit. It has been said that rape was a matter of presentment as early as 1180,[4] but it seems more likely that these were presentments of hue raised and of appeals brought in the county, rather than of the offences themselves.[5] The Crown interest was normally evinced in the residual prosecution of lapsed appeals, 'for conserving the king's peace'; Bracton notwithstanding, the relatively few convictions in such cases resulted only in amercement,[6] occasionally requiring compensation for the appellatrix as well.[7] The new provision enabled the Crown to take spontaneous and relatively severe action against offenders, as a matter of keeping the peace, and a clause for enquiry of ravishments was inserted accordingly among the Articles of the Eyre.[8] This does not mean that it was solely or even predominantly a peace-keeping measure, either in intent or in effect. There were now, indeed, presentments of rape, and convictions at Crown suit sometimes carried prison sentences. The procedure was even adapted to cover nonsuited

---

1 *Select Cases of Procedure without Writ under Henry III*, ed. H.G. Richardson and G.O. Sayles (60 *SS*, 1941), 131-2: 132 (1260).

2 For earlier attempts at such actions, see 11 *CRR* 90: 476 (1223); *Procedure without Writ*, ed. Richardson and Sayles, 109: 103 (abduction of daughter, 1259). A Yorkshire case of ravishment of wife was sufficiently awkward to be referred *coram rege* by the justices when the prosecution lapsed: *Yorkshire Assize Rolls*, ed. Clay, 42 [3 *CRR* 297 (1205)].

3 JUST 1/923, m.27; *CPR 1272-81*, 69 (1274-5).

4 N.D. Hurnard, 'The Jury of Presentment and the Assize of Clarendon', 56 *EHR* (1941), 402, citing *Pipe Roll 26 Henry II* (29 *PRS*, 1908), 79.

5 Apparent presentments for rape in 'Durham Assize Rolls', ed. Bayley, nos 8, 122 and 371 (1243) evidently arose from the imprisonment of the defendant after the hue; one of these (no. 8) was explicitly referred to the county, as was a similar case (no. 93). For a hundred court acting on a presentment of hue raised, despite protestations that the substantive charge was rape and beyond the hundred's competence, see 'Three Courts of the Hundred of Penwith', ed. G.D.G. Hall, in *Medieval Legal Records edited in memory of C.A.F. Meekings*, ed. R.F. Hunnisett and J.B. Post (London, 1978), no.27. Presentment of a lapsed appeal was also permitted: e.g. JUST 1/371, m.17d (1273).

6 E.g. *Yorkshire Assize Rolls*, ed. Clay, 28 (? 1208); *Berkshire Eyre 1248*, ed. Clanchy, 317-8: 787. Imprisonment might obtain pending or in default of payment, but not in its own right: e.g. JUST 1/954, m.56d (1259).

7 JUST 1/954, m.56d (1259).

8 *Capitula Itineris*, c.13 [1 *SR* 237]; H.M. Cam, *Studies in the Hundred Rolls* (Oxford, 1921), 89, 98-9.

appeals: jurors found an appellee guilty of the fact, 'but they say she was not a virgin; therefore he is to be imprisoned for two years according to the new statute, and is to make satisfaction to [her]'.[1] But from the Crown point of view the new statute served to increase the opportunities for amercement, and to promote the developing fashion for buying pardons of Crown suit.[2] In consequence, the courts were still cheerfully levying the monetary penalties which had characterised conviction at Crown suit previously,[3] and the improvement in public order must have been negligible.

More to the point, in terms of law: the king's courts were further than ever from exacting the full penalty on appeals of rape. In the decades before 1275 it is possible to find appeals abated on grounds as elaborate as those outlined by Bracton and the author of *Placita Corone*, but the points were generally substantial ones − lack of fresh suit implying lack of objection to the act, vagueness of dating, and the like.[4] A fugal pattern was developing, of increasingly meticulous exceptions to increasingly circumstantial appeals, but it had not yet exceeded mere punctilio. After Westminster I, however, it becomes increasingly clear how strenuously the justices were refusing − either from judicial conservatism or to encourage fines and amercements − to allow appeals to proceed to the proper sentence. Exceptions became trivial, and strictly irrelevant to proof of the charge: the appellatrix might fail to specify whereabouts in a grange was the door by which her assailant entered,[5] or which member the rape of her virginity had ruptured.[6] This casuistry was probably a common trend in appeals of felony; a clause in the Statute of Gloucester attempted to restrict the scope of exceptions severely,[7] but it made no odds to the justices: an appellatrix who claimed that she had been raped on the road between two named vills had the strict words of the statute cited against her, for failing to specify a single vill,[8] while another, who cited the statute against some exceptions which seem to have exceeded its provisions,

---

1 JUST 1/371, m.15d. Cf. JUST 1/784, m.17d (1279-80).

2 *PR 1216-25*, 255; *PR 1225-32*, 125; thereafter increasingly frequent (e.g. *CPR 1247-58*, 59, 389, 453, 548).

3 E.g. JUST 1/371, m.15d (1279); *Select Cases in the Court of King's Bench*, i, ed. G.O. Sayles (55 SS, 1936), 101-2: 75 (1280).

4 E.g. JUST 1/954, mm.52d (1258), 56d (1259).

5 JUST 1/924, m.60d (1281).

6 KB 27/146, m.19 (1295).

7 See the Appendix, below, 163-4.

8 *Placitorum Abbreviatio*, 221 (1290).

was simply ordered to answer the exceptions regardless.[1] These might be taken to indicate the justices' appreciation that such appeals were often if not always malicious, as in the supposedly classic case of *Seler* v. *Limoges* in 1320,[2] but some at least were genuine sexual assaults: when an exceptional jury of twelve men and twelve matrons returned a verdict of guilty on appeal, with the rider that the defendant 'deflowered her with dreadful physical violence', the justices overruled his steadfast refusal to try pleading clergy, and sent for the ordinary.[3]

It is evident from the terms of Westminster II, c.34, that Westminster I, c.13, was considered wholly inadequate. It is also evident from the structure and content of the later chapter that peacekeeping was not its main consideration; the clause making ravishment of women a capital felony was almost certainly an afterthought. Unlike the rest of the statute, it is in French;[4] it is sloppily drafted; there are numerous variants in this clause between several texts which manage to agree verbatim on the subsequent Latin clauses; and it obtrudes as the only felony treated in a long and varied statute. Moreover a Chancery clerk, jotting down some of the business of the parliament, did not identify the chapter by what eventually became its first clause.[5] Plucknett suggested that the clause was inserted at a stage too late for redrafting,[6] and the uncertainty of the text would be consistent with an addendum made verbally in the course of open discussion. This is all the more probable since the question of punishment and emendation in a particular case of rape came before the king in council on the first day of the parliament which enacted the statute.[7] The felony clause, then, was not part of Edward I's effort to simplify and enforce the criminal

---

1   JUST 3/35B, m.39 (1281). Cf. *The Mirror of Justices*, ed. W.J. Whittaker (7 *SS*, 1893), 198 ('The statute against the abatement of appeals for slight cause is not obeyed').

2   *The Eyre of London, 14 Edward II*, i, ed. H.M. Cam (85 *SS*, 1968), cxxiii-cxxiv, 87-93; *Novae Narrationes*, ed. E. Shanks and S.F.C. Milsom (80 *SS*, 1963), 341.

3   JUST 3/35B, m.38 (1282). Since it was technically the ordinary who did the claiming (Westminster I, c.2), the justices were within their rights; but the procedure was quite unorthodox.

4   See Appendix, below, 164.

5   *CCR 1279-88*, 333.

6   T.F.T. Plucknett, *Legislation of Edward I* (Oxford, 1949), 121-2. His earlier suggestion, that French was used to make certain chapters 'perfectly clear to the general public', remains improbable: *Statutes and their Interpretation in the first half of the 14th Century* (Cambridge, 1922), 11.

7   The case (*Savage* v. *Clifford*) is in *King's Bench Cases*, i, ed. Sayles, 101-2: 75. The *postea* noting the Council hearing, brought to my attention by Dr P.A. Brand, is at KB 27/75, m.22d, dated the morrow of the Ascension 13 Edw.1: which is given as the first day of the parliament by B. Cotton, *Historia Anglicana*, ed. M. Luard (*RS*, 1859), 166.

law, but an ad hoc addition to a statute already prepared. It was a short-sighted promotion. Litigants subsequently went to some trouble to circumvent its implications,[1] and the history of rape tried as a felony was even less distinguished than before — a solitary convict, in 1305, was allowed to make fine for life and limb.[2] The hasty felony clause was, at all events, subsidiary to the main chapter.

This main chapter, as contemporaries were quick to notice, was aimed at consenting sexual relationships. Both *Britton* and *Fleta* took a conventional neo-Bractonian line,[3] but *Britton* did point out, without comment, the innovations of the previous decade;[4] the author of *The Mirror of Justices*, however, pilloried with some anger and fair accuracy the oversimplification and excessively broad scope of the offending statutes, while incidentally contributing to the juristic muddle.[5] The problems arose because the chapter was aimed at the material and familial aspects of a consenting illicit relationship. Two of its clauses — the provision of penalties for the abduction of nuns, and forfeiture of dower by unreconciled adulteresses — were reasonably straightforward. The clause on nuns emphasised, by implication, the material motivation of the whole chapter: nuns, by their profession, had no property value, and sentence for eloping with them was one of imprisonment only.[6] The dower clause, which provided an excuse for heirs to retain estates intact, was invoked sufficiently frequently to show that it met a real want,[7] and it even prompted a modifying doctrine, that a husband's boorish behaviour was a reasonable ground for leaving him.[8] It also gave rise to the abortive but spectacular attempt at evasion, in which John Camoys formally released and quit-claimed his wife Margaret to William Paynel.[9]

1   It is interesting that the 1382 statute of rapes, although ostensibly sought by common petition, was the subject of another common petition three years later, complaining that it was 'too rough and ready law': 6 Ric.2, stat.1, c.6 [2 *SR* 27]; 3 *RP* 139-40, 174.

2   *Placitorum Abbreviatio,* 253.

3   *Britton,* ed. F.M. Nichols (London, 1865), i, 17, 55, 114; *Fleta,* ed. H.G. Richardson and G.O. Sayles, ii (72 *SS,* 1953), 88-9.

4   *Britton,* ed. Nichols, i, 55.

5   *Mirror of Justices,* ed. Whittaker, 28-9, 59, 103, 141, 172, 195-6.

6   The clergy objected that such matters were sin and not crime: *Councils and Synods, with other Documents relating to the English Church,* ii (1205-1313), ed. F.M. Powicke and C.R. Cheney (Oxford, 1964), ii, 965: 7; 967: 10; and see the editorial comments on the texts, 955.

7   Mich. 3 Edw.2 (19 *SS,* 1904), 145, pl.43; Trin. 5 Edw.2 (33 *SS,* 1916),228-9, pl.29. See Plucknett, *Legislation of Edward I,* 121 and n.

8   Trin. 35 Edw.1 (*RS,* 1879), 533-5; *Calendar of Inquisitions post Mortem,* iii, 391 (1290).

9   Described fully by F. Pollock and F.W. Maitland, *History of English Law*

158

But the more serious, or more immediate, problem was that of the female eloping with or abducted by an unacceptable suitor.

The statute here focussed attention on two points of considerable significance. One was the question of consent. The latter part of the felony clause made the ravishment of a woman capital, 'although she consent afterwards'. The 'afterwards' served three purposes. Firstly, it limited proof of intention to accomplished fact, which was the essence of the wrong — after all, from the family point of view the situation was only inconvenient or embarrassing if a girl stayed away, whatever her attitude in the first instance.[1] Secondly, it replaced the tacit consent of an appeal unprosecuted within forty days. Thirdly, it precluded any effective complaint of common-law encroachment upon the strictly ecclesiastical matters of simple fornication and adultery. By thus discounting a woman's consent, the wishes of others – technically the Crown, but, by extension,[2] family – were allowed to override her own, despite her nominal status as victim, and the time-honoured concord by marriage was removed. The second question concerns the ambiguity of 'ravishment'. Hitherto, whatever the true circumstances behind actions for rape, the substance of appeals invariably and explicitly related to forcible coition; where a more flexible meaning of *rapio* or *raptus* was used, to indicate or subsume an abduction, this was generally made clear from the context of circumstantial detail, and sometimes from the unorthodox form of action.[3] It is possible that Westminster I was intended to blur distinctions, or that it reflected a significant development in usage; but Westminster II, with its felony clause attached to the defence of family interests, definitively lumped all the variations together, and made them capital. The author of *The Mirror of Justices* singled out the verbal crudity of equating rape with elopement, but his own terminology is too hybrid to serve as an accurate common-law commentary.[4] More damning criticism is implicit in the pattern of lawsuits in the wake of the statute.

Westminster II, c.35, elaborating the Statute of Merton's chapter on ravishment of ward,[5] provided appropriate forms of writ; the chapter

before the Time of Edward I (2nd ed., reissued with addenda by S.F.C. Milsom, Cambridge, 1968), ii, 395-6: from 1 *RP* 146-7.

1 Some girls who were actually raped may have 'consented afterwards' rather than undergo the indignity of legal procedures: cf. S. Purdie, 'Rape – the Victim on Trial', *The Times*, 58954 (3 Dec. 1973), 16.

2 E.g. appeal of robbery and ravishment of wife: JUST 1/374, m.43 (1293).

3 11 *CRR* 90: 476 (1223); *Procedure without Writ,* ed. Richardson and Sayles, 109: 103 (1259) and 131-2: 132 (1260); JUST 1/923, m.27 (1275).

4 *Mirror of Justices,* ed. Whittaker, 28-9.

5 Statute of Merton, c.6 [1 *SR* 3]. For numerous references to actions for

on ravishment of women, not apparently offering new private actions, provided no writs. Nevertheless, it was not long before trespass writs of ravishment appeared on the scene, clearly unrelated to wardship or even to forcible coition. In 1294, in what began as a plea of conspiracy, a man whose daughter had been abducted was told that there was a common-law writ available.[1] Twenty years later, it was claimed that a writ for ravishment of an abducted daughter fell between rape, for which private action was still reserved to the woman, and ravishment of ward, for which action was reserved to a guardian; the writ was held good, although counsel for the plaintiff admitted that it was unusual.[2] The more common trespass action, indeed, was for ravishment of wife, usually in conjunction with chattels asported; such actions were certainly occurring by the end of the thirteenth century,[3] and the form of the writ leaves no doubt that it was based upon Westminster II, c.34.[4]

The rise of this action exposed very forcibly the major weakness of the statute which it speciously claimed as its parent; the collection of all types of ravishment of women under one simplistic chapter set a unique paradox which was never satisfactorily resolved. Justice Shareshill epitomised it in 1339:[5]

> That which you allege at the suit of the party is only a trespass, for a party will recover his damages in such a case. . . . But at the suit of the king it is different; for, if the defendant be found guilty at the suit of the party, the king may take such verdict for an indictment, and arraign him, and then, if he be found guilty, the judgment will be of life and limb.

Personal considerations apart, no plaintiff wanted to see his damages evaporate as forfeitures for felony, and the paradox was, predictably, eased by playing down the felony aspect. By about 1290 it could be claimed that a nonsuited appellatrix should not be gaoled as was

---

ravishment of ward, both before and after Westminster II, see S.S. Walker, 'The Marrying of Feudal Wards in Medieval England', *Studies in Medieval Culture and Society* 4 (1974), esp. 218-20.

1 *King's Bench Cases*, ed. Sayles, iii, 22-3: 10.

2 Mich. 9 Edw.2 (45 *SS*, 1928), 28-33, pl.12.

3 *King's Bench Cases*, ed. Sayles, iii, 100: 58 (1300). Some early, unstandardised forms of action may have anticipated this later development: S.F.C. Milsom, 'Trespass from Henry III to Edward III', 74 *LQR* (1958), 210-11. In 1278 the Newgate gaol delivery justices rejected a case of abduction sued without words of felony, but referred it to the sheriff as a private trespass suit: JUST 3/35B, m.53.

4 *King's Bench Cases*, ed. Sayles, iv, 59-62: 20 (1314); vi, 159-60: 108 (1364); *Early Registers of Writs*, ed. E. de Haas and G.D.G. Hall (87 *SS*, 1970), 181: R324 (c.1318-20).

5 Mich. 13 Edw.3 (*RS*, 1886), 62, pl.34, at 64.

possible with other felonies;[1] and although a year's imprisonment for nonsuit was prescribed in 1315, the same order allowed mainprise for defendants impleaded by trespass writ, whom the courts had apparently tended to regard as suspect felons and remand accordingly.[2] In 1320 the King's Bench rather unexpectedly offered the worst of both worlds, awarding the plaintiff damages and committing the defendant to the ordinary, on the basis of a recent precedent, but the reporter evidently thought the decision remarkable,[3] and even the King's Bench came to favour the lenient view.[4]

By interpretation and extension, therefore, the Statutes of Westminster turned the law of rape into a law of elopement and abduction, which inhibited the purposes of the woman herself — whether outrage at a sexual assault or the desire to further or avenge a consenting relationship — and fostered the interests of those who wanted material recompense for the material disparagement wrought by self-willed womenfolk and suitors. The appeal of rape lapsed into insignificance, the more readily since the opportunities for indictment, in cases where breach of the peace was the essence of the offence, were increasing; now conviction was even rarer, while full sentence apparently remained unknown. The law, moreoever, failed to affect behaviour, and, nearly a century after Westminster II, a further statute of rapes completed the transfer of the wrong, by giving the appeal of rape to fathers, husbands, or next of kin, and by counting eloping couples as dead, in order to maintain the integrity of family estates.[5] The history of the 1382 statute and its aftermath illustrates vividly the same priority of family fortunes over personal feelings that had characterised earlier development; but that is another story.[6]

---

1 *Casus Placitorum,* ed. W.H. Dunham (69 *SS,* 1950), lxxxvii: 33.

2 1 *RP* 290; cited in court from letters close in 1318: *Placitorum Abbreviatio,* 330. A corollary of this, that as a matter of trespass the inquest could be taken in the absence of a defaulting mainprised appellee, was not allowed: Trin. 16 Edw.3 (*RS,* 1900), 216-9, pl.64

3 Pas. 13 Edw.2 (London, 1678), 405-6, pl.[5].

4 Pardon of outlawry at trespass suit, with evidence of gree made, was accepted as justification for acquittal at the king's suit: 42 Lib. Ass. 16 (cf. 41 Lib. Ass. 9).

5 6 Ric.2, stat.1, c.6 [2 *SR* 27].

6 Post, 'Sir Thomas West'.

APPENDIX
TO
RAVISHMENT OF WOMEN AND THE
STATUTE OF WESTMINSTER

The texts which follow are the working texts used in the preparation of this paper, and are emphatically not definitive;[1] they are derived from a small number of early or interesting manuscripts, lettered here for reference: Corporation of London Records Office, *Liber Horn;*[2] Public Record Office, E 164/9, known as *Liber X* [X]; P.R.O., C 74/1, 'the Great Roll of the Statutes' [R]; Bodleian Library, Douce MS.139 [D]; National Library of Wales, Peniarth MS.329A [E];[3] and N.L.W., Peniarth MS.330A [F]. Orthographic variants are not noted; capitals, punctuation, *i* and *j*, and *u* and *v*, are editorial.

Statute of Westminster I, c.13.

There is no thoroughly satisfactory text of Westminster I, although the terms of c.13 are not in doubt. This text, from *Liber Horn,* ff.37v-38, has some alterations (additions italicised, emendations footnoted) made apparently by the glossator who collated it with a sealed Guildhall copy (see marginalium to f.35v). X, rubric f.26v; D, f.165v; E, p.18.

De rape de damysele ou de dame[4]

E le roy defend qe nul[5] ravyse ne[6] prengne[7] damysele[8] *de*[9] deinze age, par[10] soun gre ne sanz soun gre,[11] ne dame ne damisele[12] de[13] age, ne autre femme[14] maugre soun.[15] Et si nul le face,[16] a[17] la sute celuy ke

---

1 In general see H.G. Richardson and G.O. Sayles, 'The Early Statutes', 50 *LQR* (1934), 201-23, 540-71.

2 Described in detail by N.R. Ker, *Medieval Manuscripts in British Libraries, I: London* (Oxford, 1969), 27-34.

3 This MS. once belonged (prelims, f.D) to one 'Thomas . . . servant of Henry Harman'. Harman was King's Coroner and Attorney in the King's Bench 1480-1502: above, 132.

4 Other MSS. lack heading.

5 DF *nul ne.*

6 DFX *ne ne* (second *ne* interlined F).

7 X *purchase;* DEFX add *a force.*

8 D has this word and its dependents in the plural.

9 X omits.

10 EFX *ne par.*

11 D *sans lur gre ne par lur gre.*

12 D adds *ne autre femme; dedenz age . . . damesoele* interlined F.

13 D *de plein.*

14 F transposes *dage* and *nautre femme.*

15 DE *le son.*

16 Emended to *fet;* DFX *fet;* F *face.*

17 D *&,* in error.

suera *de* denz[1] les .xl. jours le roy luy[2] fra commune dreyture; et si nul *ne*[3] comence la[4] sute *de* deinz .xl.[5] jours le roy suyra,[6] e ceus qe il *en*[7] trovera copables si[8] averount la prisoun de .ij. aunz, e puis soynt[9] reinz a la volunte le roy;[10] e si il ne ad[11] dount[12]rendre ou de estra reinz[13] a la volunte le roy[14] si[15] soynt[16] puniz par plus grevous e[17] plus long prisoun,[18] solom ceo qe le trespas demaunde.

Statute of Gloucester, c.9

As indicated in *Statutes of the Realm*, i, 49 and n.2, the chapter on homicide is sometimes but by no means always followed by a clause circumscribing dilatory exceptions to appeals of felony – not, as is sometimes assumed, appeals of homicide only. It is, for example, missing from the good and early texts in Douce 139, and from the Great Roll of the Statutes. *Liber Horn* has two versions of the Statute of Gloucester. The first in sequence (f.31v), though slightly fuller in c.9, was discarded by the glossator, who refers the reader to the 'fuller and better' version at f.47. This second version did not, when first engrossed, carry the clause on exceptions, which was added, perhaps by the glossator, at the foot of the page, immediately and fortuitously following the main clause of c.9. The exceptions clause appears in both the Peniarth manuscripts, but in F it is marginated *vacat*. This text is from *Liber Horn*, f.33, italicising omissions from f.47v. E, p.31; F, f.38v.

Purveu est ensement qe nul appel *desoremes*[19] seyt si legerement[20] abatu

1 Erasure, presumably *i*, between *de*- and *nz*.

2 DE *en*.

3 Interlined later, X; omitted EF.

4 E *sa*.

5 DEF *les .xl.*

6 E *eit la sute*.

7 DEFX omit.

8 X omits.

9 Emended to *seront;* DEFX *serrunt.*

10 D continues *seint puniz . . . ,* presumably omitting the intervening matter through homoeoteleuton.

11 Followed by *iut,* presumably in error, deleted; E *ount;* F *neient.*

12 E *rien.*

13 *rendre . . . reinz* deleted, with *destre reint* interlined; X *destre reint,* concluding simply *seit puni par plus long prison;* EF *destre reint.*

14 *a la volunte le roi* after *puniz* E; F omits.

15 EF omit.

16 Deleted, with *soit* interlined; *reint* marginated at this point.

17 *plus grevous e* deleted; DEF omit.

18 F *enprisonement.*

19 E omits.

20 E *grevement.*

come avaunt[1] a este; mes si lapelour counte le fet,[2] et lan,[3] et le jour, *et le luy*,[4] et le temps le roy, et la ville ou le fet fust fet, si estoyse le appel,[5] et nies ne soyt lapel[6] abatu *par defaute de*[7] fresche sute, par quei qe il[8] sue deinz[9] lan *et le jour* apres le fet fete.[10]

Statute of Westminster II, c.34

For the problems of this first clause, see above, 156-7. The contrast of French here is not absolute: the text of Westminster II at Peniarth 329A, pp. 29-71 is entirely in French, as is a version in rhyming couplets at Douce 139, ff.119-24v and 130-9, which unhappily wants the gathering which bore the chapters on ravishment. A list of chapter headings associated in the latter manuscript gives c.36 'de femme ravye', c.37 'de femmes aspuses alopes', c.38 'de noneyne ravye', and c.39 'de enfanz heyrs reviz'. This text is from *Liber Horn*, f.62. X, rubric f.60; D, f.165v; R, m.45; E,p.58; F, f.66v.

Purveu est ensement[11] qe si homme ravise femme espose, damousele,[12] ou autre femme deshormes par la ou ele ne se est[13] assentue[14] ne avaunt ne apres[15] eit jugement de vie e de membre; ensement[16] par la ou homme ravise femme, damoysele, dame espose,[17] ou autre femme a force, tut seyt ele[18] assentue apres,[19] eit tel[20] jugement come avaunt est dist,[21] sil[22] seit atteint a la swte le roy, e la eit le roy sa sywte.

1 f.47v adds *avaunt ses houres; E sicome.*

2 *le fet et* omitted F.

3 *et lan* omitted E.

4 ? for *lieu;* here some late versions have *le heure: Statutes of the Realm,* loc. cit. E *e le heure.*

5 EF *le plee del appel.*

6 EF omit.

7 f.47v has simply *pur;* EF omit *par defaute.*

8 EF *home.*

9 E *soit dedenz age.*

10 F *soit fait;* E omits but continues *sicome il soit en la curt le roi si estoise lappel.*

11 DER omit.

12 F *dame ou damoisele.*

13 F omits; E *est pas.*

14 X *ne serrad assentaunt.*

15 F *ne avant ne apres* emended to *avant.*

16 R *e ensement.*

17 DR *femme, dame espuse, damaysele;* X *femme espuse, damoisele;* E *dame espouse, damoisele;* F *femme espouse, dame ou damoisele.*

18 F *il qele s'.*

19 D *ke ele sey apres asente;* RX *ke ele se assente apres.*

20 E omits.

21 D *cumment devauint est dit.*

22 E *e sil.*

COUNSELLORS' FEES AND EARNINGS IN THE AGE OF SIR EDWARD COKE

W.R. Prest

> For the problems of this first clause, see above, 156-7. The contrast of the Law, that have been before thee, and never shalt thou finde any that hath excelled in the knowledge of these Lawes, but . . . by the goodnesse of God hath obteyned a greater blessing and ornament then anie other profession, to their family and posteritie. . . . For it is an undoubted trueth, 'that the just shall flourish as the Palme tree, and spread abroad as the Cedars of Libanus'.

Sir Edward Coke's providential interpretation[1] stands in sharp contrast to the general contemporary view, that the worldly success of the common lawyers could best be understood as an example of the devil giving his own their due and the wicked spreading abroad like the green bay tree.[2] But among Coke's contemporaries few would have questioned the fact that lawyers − or, more particularly, members of the upper branch − did frequently amass large fortunes and substantial landed estates, even if these were widely held to be the fruit of exorbitant fees exacted from their hapless clients. The rise of the common lawyers in numbers and wealth during the sixteenth and early seventeenth centuries was indeed a truism of contemporary social comment. It is also one of the few aspects of early-modern social history on which both main parties to the recent controversy over the fortunes of the gentry seem to have found themselves in substantial agreement.[3]

This remarkable consensus may help to explain why the economic ingredients of legal practice in Elizabethan and early Stuart England have been so little discussed, although the main reason is no doubt simply the under-developed state of legal-historical studies in general for this period. Yet, whether in terms of the interests, motivation and careers of individual lawyers, the social history of the profession, or the functioning of the legal system as a whole, such matters as the size and distribution of legal earnings and the level of fees charged to clients are clearly of considerable interest. In this short paper I propose to examine how far contemporary estimates of the earning-power of common

1 *Le Second Part des Reportes del Edward Coke* (1602), f.v.

2 See E.W. Ives, 'The Reputation of the Common Lawyer in English Society, 1450-1550', *University of Birmingham Historical Journal* 7 (1959-60), 130-45; E.F.J. Tucker, 'Ignoramus and Seventeenth-Century Satire of the Law', *Harvard Library Bulletin* 19 (1971), 313-30.

3 See R.H. Tawney, 'The Rise of the Gentry, 1558-1640', *Economic History Review* 11 (1941), 20-1; H.R. Trevor-Roper, 'The Gentry, 1540-1640', *Economic History Review,* Supplement 1 (1953), 26-7.

lawyers practising at the bar are supported by other forms of contemporary evidence, especially bills of costs and counsellors' own records of their income.

Fees

Fees were received by members of the upper branch for a wide variety of professional services (including the keeping of manorial courts, arbitration, advice prior to or apart from litigation, and the drawing of legal instruments), but particularly for the representation of parties to civil suits in the central courts, assizes, and provincial conciliar jurisdictions. Fees charged for appearances at the bar were probably the main source of most counsellors' professional incomes, and certainly the main target for critics and would-be reformers of the legal system.

Unlike the fees payable to the clerks and other officers of the legal bureaucracy at various stages in the progress of a suit, which were supposedly assessed according to known prescribed scales, counsellors' fees were regulated only by convention and custom. Bills designed to extend the principle of fixed and certain fees to counsellors as well as attorneys and clerks of the courts were read in the parliaments of 1571, 1614 and 1621, and proposed by the Rump's committee on law reform (the 'Hale committee') in 1653.[1] But, as with similar schemes outlined among the Burghley papers for the mid-1580s, none of these measures was enacted. As Burghley's correspondent Francis Alford pointed out, 'to allot the councellors fee certen, either in respect of their paines or attendance, wilbe very difficile and litle hope to be observed'.[2] Apart from the fact that English barristers, like French *avocats,* held their fees to be *honoraria* freely granted by the grateful client and hence not properly regulated by any third party,[3] there were obvious objections to laying down standard charges for services of widely differing complexity performed by men of similarly various capacities. Moreover, since members of the upper branch were not officers of the law courts, who was to enforce a scale of fixed charges? In the absence of a body like the modern Bar Council, which lays down rules governing the financial

1 J.B. Davidson, 'Hooker's Journal of the House of Commons in 1571', *Transactions of the Devonshire Association* 11 (1879), 462-3, 471, 490; *Commons Debates: 1621,* ed. W. Notestein, F.H. Relf and A. Simpson (New Haven, 1935), ii, 435; vi, 157; *Commons Journals,* i, 93, 489; *Tracts of the late Lord Somers,* ed. W. Scott (2nd ed., London, 1811), vi, 184, 233.

2 Brit. Lib., Lansdowne MS. 44, ff.2v, 25-26v, 30-3; Harleian MS. 6847, ff.113v-120.

3 J.H. Baker, 'Counsellors and Barristers: an Historical Study', *Cambridge Law Journal* 27 (1969), 224-9; L.R. Berlanstein, *The Barristers of Toulouse in the 18th Century (1740-93)* (Baltimore, 1975), 25-6.

relations between barrister, solicitor, and client, responsibility for such matters could only have devolved by default upon the judges of the central courts, who as former counsellors themselves showed little enthusiasm for the tasks of defining and policing the exaction of 'excessive' fees. Like James I's proclaimed intention of 1603 to visit 'severe punishment' upon 'all Lawyers, Attorneys, officers and Clarkes' who 'extort or take any undue or excessive fees', their few recorded pronouncements on this subject are so vague that we may disregard them as evidence of any policy. By the end of the sixteenth century, at least, barristers were at liberty to charge for their services whatever their clients might be prepared, however reluctantly, to pay.[1]

It would be interesting to know whether this free-market situation had always prevailed. Dr Ives has suggested that payments to counsel in the late fifteenth and early sixteenth centuries were normally at a standard rate of 3s. 4d. or 6s. 8d. (the half or whole angel).[2] It may be that the combined impact of price-inflation and the currency manipulations of the mid-sixteenth century, the rapid expansion of business coming before the central courts in the second half of the century, the concurrent decline in the practice of retaining counsellors on an annual basis, and the proliferation of new forms of action and procedural devices, introduced a far greater degree of instability and confusion than had previously existed. This supposition receives some support from the literary evidence set out in Table I, which suggests that between the mid-fifteenth century and the mid-seventeenth century fees not only increased sharply in amount but also became noticeably more elastic. In 1452 the apprentice Robert Moyle asserted that where no set sum was promised to a serjeant for his services, he should receive 3s. 4d. 'by common right'. Eighty years or so later this amount was claimed by an anonymous group of parliamentary petitioners to be the mandatory charge levied by both serjeants and apprentices; but a hundred years after that the officers of the King's Bench testified that the usual fee charged there by barristers was 10s., and by serjeants 10s. or £1 or

---

1 *Stuart Royal Proclamations,* ed. P.L. Hughes and J.F. Larkin (Oxford, 1973), 13; Huntington Library, Ellesmere MS. 2982 ('Orders considered of by the Judges concerning the Exaccion and the excesse in takinge of fees' [1597 ?]); WARDS 14/3/20 ('Orders Set down by the Master and Council of the Court of Wards and Liveries, 11 May, 1 Jac.'); *Rules, Orders and Notices in the Court of Common Pleas,* ed. G. Cooke (London, 1742), rule 6 of Hil. 14 Jac.1 (that counsellors or serjeants taking excessive fees would be liable to reimburse their clients). Cf. Sir Thomas Egerton's undated 'Memorialls for Judicature', Ellesmere MS. 2623: 'The Fees of serjeantes and Lawyers to be moderated according to former orders heretofore taken [and sett downe in a table - *erased*] in that behalf which were sett downe in tables in every court and the same tables doe yet remayne'. No other reference to these schedules of fees has been found.

2 Ives, 'Reputation of the Common Lawyer', 152-3.

more, 'as their clients will give'. Less expert and undoubtedly more hostile testimony from the later sixteenth and early to mid-seventeenth centuries (extracts c, e, f, in Appendix I, p. 178) suggests an even steeper range of inflation.

When checked against surviving accounts, bills of costs, and lawyers' fee-books, these latter claims appear somewhat alarmist. The highest single fees I have come across in this period are two of £6 each, said to have been paid to William Hudson and Edward Herbert when they were briefed for a Star Chamber case in 1634; but as the whole bill of costs was the subject of a complaint for fraud, we cannot be certain that such large sums were ever actually handed over.[1] A sampling of the records of corporate bodies and private individuals gives the impression that before the Civil War only a very few leading serjeants and Crown law officers could ask for and expect to receive single fees above £3 or £4. The more typical level of payment was between 10s. and 20s., or just over, although slightly larger sums were often charged for giving an opinion and reading or drawing documents. In general, as we might expect, the main factors influencing the level of fees charged were the nature of the task performed, the professional standing of the lawyer concerned, the jurisdiction involved, and the social and financial standing of the client. The extracts set out in Appendix II (p. 179) may help to illustrate these points.

The first example (A) comes from a bill of charges presented to the borough of Totnes for a suit tried in the King's Bench in 1601. The £5 paid to Attorney-General Coke was presumably a single fee; the additional £2 to Serjeant John Hele 'after the verdict' need not have any sinister connotations, being probably a further fee payable for an argument after judgment, on a demurrer or special verdict. Mr Stephens is probably the senior barrister Thomas Stephens of the Middle Temple, who was called to the bench three years after this trial, but Mr Clarke cannot be positively identified. Corporate bodies were perhaps liable to be charged at a somewhat higher rate than private individuals, or so the borough of Sandwich claimed in 1642, asserting that 'counsel . . . will expect that the solicitor for such a corporation as the [Cinque] Ports should be more liberall than a private person'.[2]

The published accounts of the Founders' Company of London contain numerous entries for legal charges (B). Mr Stone, who received four 10s. fees in 1613, is probably the Inner Templar John Stone, a resident

---

1   E 215/857.
2   Quoted by D. Gardiner, *Historic Haven* (Derby, 1954), 253.

of Coleman Street, London, who was called to the bench of his house in 1613. 'Mr Garard' and 'Mr Jarrett' are very likely the same person; that is, Philip Gerrard of Gray's Inn, a great-nephew of Sir Gilbert Gerrard, and a bencher of Gray's Inn from 1611. The fee of £3. 6s. 0d. which he received in 1617 'when we met the Brashers at the Recorder's, being Councel on both sides' was presumably a reward for his services as arbitrator. Counsel did not normally appear at quarter sessions, which is hardly surprising if the 5s. 6d. paid to Mr Ellice 'for speaking at the Sessions of the Peace against Burkett' was the usual rate of remuneration for such work. The level of fees payable for counsel's services in borough and town courts seems generally to have been lower than at Westminster Hall. A handbook to the law courts of the City of London published in 1682, which lists fees in the Sheriffs' Court, states that 'the Councel well [? will] deserve 5s.'; and a return to the Caroline commission on fees, from the borough of Andover, specifies the same sum 'to the counsell for theire fee at every tryall and argueinge of every demurrer', although in the Town Court at Plymouth the fee 'to a Councell at lawe att the time of the triall' was 10s. (an anomaly for which there seems no obvious explanation).[1]

The last set of extracts (C) in Appendix II comes from the household account books of an inveterate aristocratic litigant, Lord William Howard of Naworth Castle, Cumberland. 'Belted Will' did not restrict himself to the services of north-country lawyers; apart from Sir John Jackson, member of the Council of the North and Recorder of Newcastle-on-Tyne, and John Bankes, later Attorney-General (who hailed originally from Keswick), he also retained the London barrister John Davies, Serjeant John Moore the Recorder of Winchester, and Rice (or Richard) Gwynne, a Welshman who had settled in Norfolk. The sequence of payments to the latter is slightly puzzling: on 16 November, Gwynne received 22s. for a motion in the King's Bench on behalf of Lord Howard in his suit with Mr Salkeild; two days later he made another motion in the same court, but in a different cause, for which he received only 11s.; and four days after that he again moved in the King's Bench against Salkeild, for a fee of 11s. Presumably the first motion was of a more complex and demanding nature than the other two and was charged accordingly. The draft bill for regulating counsel's fees discussed by the House of Commons in 1621 proposed a graduated scale, whereby serjeants or king's counsel might claim £3 for arguing a hearing or demurrer, but only £2 for a motion, with benchers or readers charging £2 and £1 respectively and barristers £1 and 10s.[2]

---

1 [W. Wright], *Lex Londiniensis* (London, 1680), 245; E 215/1069, 1454.
2 *Commons Debates 1621*, vi, 157.

Unfortunately, as in the present case, one usually cannot determine from bills of costs the precise nature of the services for which payments were made or claimed.

Appendix III (p. 182) analyses the receipts of individual barristers, rather than the payments made by their clients. First, Thomas Thornton, of Lincoln's Inn and Newnham, near Daventry, Northamptonshire, who kept a record of his personal incomings and expenditure from his marriage in 1582 until his death half a century later. Up until 1601 Thornton listed each suit or client and the fee received, but thereafter merely summarised his annual earnings, until in 1625 he began listing vacation earnings in full with summaries of his termly receipts. The two extracts which appear in paragraph A of Appendix III illustrate the pattern of his earnings, first as a barrister of twelve years' standing and then as an associate bencher of six years' standing. In both cases it is evident that 10s. or 20s. was his normal single fee. All three £5 fees, and four of the five £4 fees, which he received in the year 1596-7, were paid by his cousin Thomas Denton and seem to have been retainers or lump-sum payments in connection with a suit Denton was pursuing against one John Fetiplace, possibly the Oxfordshire landowner, rather than payments for a single motion or hearing. (The same may well have been the case with most of the other large sums recorded, since Thornton's accounts generally seem to have been written up as fair copies at intervals, rather than recording each payment as and when it was received.)

The second series of fees listed (B) in Appendix III comes from the financial 'memoranda books' of another Lincoln's Inn lawyer, Henry Sherfield, the puritan Recorder of Salisbury. The first of these books runs from 1608 to 1613, and after a gap until 1620 the series continues without interruption until just before his death in 1634. It may be noted that Sherfield received three times more 10s. than 20s. fees in the year 1608-9, when he had only recently begun his career at the bar; but by Easter term 1620, when he was on the eve of call to the bench, the proportion of 20s. and 22s. fees was almost equal to that of 10s. and 11s. fees, and there are significantly more still larger sums recorded.

Finally we have two extracts (C) from the fee-book kept by Arthur Turnour, a serjeant-at-law originally of the Middle Temple. As we might perhaps expect, these show a somewhat higher average level of fees than those received by either Sherfield or Thornton. Nevertheless, the normal range appears to have been from 10s. to 40s., which is still well below the sums claimed as typical by William Harrison and the two anonymous seventeenth-century critics cited in Appendix I (e, f). This fee-book is especially valuable because it normally indicates the court concerned as well as the parties to the suit in which Turnour was retained. Turnour seems to have done best out of Chancery cases; although his practice there was about as large as in the Common Pleas, he collected more than twice as many fees of 20s. and upwards from his Chancery clients as from those he represented in the Common Pleas in the term shown.

In the light of this admittedly fragmentary evidence, it seems reasonable to assert that the level of fees charged by learned counsel in the late sixteenth and early seventeenth centuries was by no means so high as hostile contemporary critics alleged. The fee most frequently paid to both barristers and serjeants was between 10s. and 20s., not £3 or more; and a rise from 3s. 4d. to even 20s. between the mid-fifteenth and mid-seventeenth centuries is hardly out of line with the general increase in the level of consumer prices over that period, which (according to the Phelps Brown index) rose more than seven-fold between the 1450s and the 1640s.[1] Nevertheless, contemporary lay complaints about the exorbitance of fees charged by counsellors were not merely malicious or mistaken. The client's chief concern was presumably less with the amount of each individual fee charged than with the size of the total bill for all fees paid to counsel during the progress of his suit. Many clients paid more than one fee to the same lawyer in connection with the same suit, while some paid five or six or even more fees in the course of a single term. Bills of costs often fail to distinguish the separate individual fees paid to a barrister; but even where only one fee appears, it is often the largest single item on the entire account, although it may still be only a relatively small fraction of the total laid out in fees to officers and clerks, witnesses, jury, and other expenses.

Earnings

While the level of a counsellor's fees was obviously of considerable importance to his clients, the crucial figure for the individual lawyer was that of his total earnings. In the middle of Elizabeth I's reign, William Harrison retailed an anecdote which suggests that serjeants-at-law could expect to earn between £300 and £400 each term, or at least £1,200 a year. Thomas Wilson asserted that the twelve judges and most of the serjeants-at-law were worth £20,000 to £30,000 a year. At the beginning of James I's reign, Anthony Atkinson contrasted the palmy days of Henry VIII when many lawyers, as he claimed, earned less than £100 a year from their practices and could buy less than £100 worth of land (in annual value) in ten years, with the evils of the present, when 'there

1 E.H. Phelps Brown and S. Hopkins, 'Seven Centuries of the Prices of Consumables, Compared with Builders' Wage Rates', *Essays in Economic History*, ed. E.M. Carus-Wilson (London, 1954), 194-5.

are now that in the space of one year can gain three, four or five hundred pounds per annum, and purchase lands in less than ten years worth one, two or three thousand pounds per annum'.[1]

Atkinson's figures are undoubtedly inflated, if they are taken to imply that the average yearly earnings of barristers at the beginning of the seventeenth century were in the region of £300 to £500. But they are certainly much nearer the mark than the guesses by Harrison and Wilson. John Hoskyns, the future serjeant and Welsh judge, who was called to the bar in 1600, wrote to his wife eleven years later that he hoped 'my practice will be in London better than 200 li. a yeare'. This letter was written in the middle of Michaelmas term, when he had already gained the princely sum of £23 in fees and had hopes of making it up to £30 by the end of term.[2] Now it is true that Hoskyns tended to paint a uniformly dismal view of his financial circumstances in correspondence with his wife, and may have been unwilling to divulge the full amount of his earnings for fear of encouraging her to domestic extravagance. Nor does he refer explicitly to assize-circuit earnings, which were an additional source of income for some lawyers, although not (as they have been recently characterised) the 'principal means of support' for 'most barristers'.[3] Apart from these reservations about this particular piece of evidence, we would naturally expect a lawyer's professional income to show quite marked yearly fluctuations, owing to the vagaries of clients, patrons, and attorneys, adjourned or sparsely attended sittings of the courts resulting from outbreaks of the plague and, after 1641, political upheaval, and the personal circumstances of the individual counsellor – his state of health, domestic distractions, and so forth. Thus it is advisable to avoid attaching any great significance to isolated figures for a single year's earnings, but rather to seek longer continuous sequences which provide some indication of a man's earning power at least a sizeable portion of his career at the bar.

Four such series are summarised in Appendix IV (p. 183) together with the much shorter but very revealing diary record of John Archer's earnings in 1658. None of the lawyers represented can be regarded as professional failures. Thornton and Sherfield both held recorderships –

---

1 *The Description of England by William Harrison*, ed. G. Edelen (Ithaca, 1968), 173-4; T. Wilson, *The State of England A.D. 1600*, ed. F.J. Fisher (Camden Soc., 1936), 25; H. Ellis, *Original Letters, Illustrative of English History* (1824-46), 3rd ser., iv, 53-4.

2 *The Life, Letters and Writings of John Hoskyns, 1566-1638*, ed. L.B. Osborn (New York, 1937), 68.

3 J.S. Cockburn, *A History of English Assizes 1558-1714* (Cambridge, 1972), 143.

Sherfield, indeed, held two – and were called to the bench of Lincoln's Inn, while Turnour was a serjeant and both Archer and Whitelocke became judges. Yet it will be observed that Thornton's earnings from his practice did not reach three figures until he had been fourteen years at the bar, and even during his most profitable decade (from 1610 to 1619) his highest single year's gain was only just over £250. Sherfield (who, incidentally, died about £6,000 in debt) did considerably better, especially in the early years of his career; when the record resumes in 1620 his gross earnings were not much below the figure Sir James Whitelocke was averaging during his second highly profitable decade at the bar. But thereafter Sherfield's receipts fell, and indeed averaged only £385 a year for the remaining thirteen full years of his life.

Given his professional rank, the record of Serjeant Turnour's takings seems even less impressive, although the disruptive effects of the Civil War may reduce the value of this particular set of data. His fee-book commences in Hilary term 1642, and lists fees received until the end of Michaelmas term that year; there is then a gap of five years until Easter term 1646, after which every term's earnings are listed up to and including Michaelmas 1651. The first figure, of only £191, does not represent a full year's profits and is further depressed by the coming of the Civil War and the consequent adjournment of Michaelmas term 1642. By Easter 1646, large-scale hostilities were over and there must have been a considerable back-log of legal business. Yet Turnour's highest yearly earnings from this date until his death were £526, collected between Easter 1647 and Hilary 1648, while his earnings dropped to as low as £362 in 1648-9 and were only £346 in 1646-7. These surprisingly low sums doubtless reflect the general unrest and uncertainty during the period covered by his fee-book, and especially the slow revival of business on the assize circuits. Turnour also seems to have been a rather lukewarm supporter of the parliamentary cause, which may have reduced his appeal to some potential clients from his native Essex. It could be, perhaps, that his state of health in his latter years adversely affected his earning capacity. But it is also possible that he belonged to that class of serjeants described by Whitelocke in 1614 as having given £600 for the preferment 'and sum of them . . . not worthe the money, and sum not likely to see it halfe againe by thear practise'.[1]

This characterisation is obviously not applicable to John Archer, whose spectacular financial record in 1658 is the last item in Appendix IV and may be left to speak for itself. Nor could it refer to James

---

[1] *Liber Famelicus of Sir James Whitelocke,* ed. J. Bruce (Camden Soc., 1858), 44.

Whitelocke himself, who (unlike Archer) was very much a self-made man, the younger son of a London merchant who could provide him with little more patrimony than a first-rate education at Merchant Taylors' School and St John's College, Oxford. By 1616 Whitelocke had nevertheless prospered sufficiently to buy the manor of Fawley, on the border of Buckinghamshire and Oxfordshire, for £9,000. Yet the 'abstract of all that ever I got by my practice', which appears in the manuscript version of his autobiography, shows that his total earnings from the law between 1600 and 1620 amounted to only £8,341 and that this sum was offset by expenses of at least £8,742, no figures being available for his first three years at the bar. Whitelocke's average annual earnings over twenty years were only just £400; although he never earned less than £400 a year after 1606, his expenses likewise never fell below £300 a year from that date, and rose very sharply indeed during his last four years at the bar. Whitelocke's fee-income between 1616 and 1620 amounted to £2,466, but his outgoings were nearly twice as much at £4,313, a sum inflated by the cost of his reading at the Middle Temple in 1619 and his payments on becoming a serjeant in 1620. Where, then, did the money come from to buy Fawley Court? There are hints in his autobiography of gains from the sale of wood, from loans at interest, and from compensation received for the surrender of a reversion to a share in Sir John Roper's King's Bench office; but the precise significance of these and other sources of income and capital cannot now be established from the surviving sources.[1]

Conclusion

Professor Aylmer has suggested that in the 1630s the average annual income of knights was about £800, and of esquires around £500.[2] If so, the figures set out in Table IV suggest that even such a highly successful barrister as James Whitelocke could have only hoped to reach a financial position concomitant with his honorific social rank after ten years' practice at the bar, while many would never achieve even that relatively modest degree of prosperity. Of course, these figures do not tell the whole story, since many, perhaps most, practising members of the upper branch were landlords, farmers, and money-lenders as well as lawyers. Thomas Thornton, for example, drew an income from rents and usury which frequently exceeded his earnings in fees. In 1658 John Archer augmented his professional income by another £500 drawn from his estates, and had no less than £8,000 loaned out at interest. For many

---

1 Cf. R. Spalding, *The Improbable Puritan* (London, 1975), 45.
2 G. Aylmer, *The King's Servants* (London, 1961), 331.

barristers the main economic significance of legal practice was as a supplement to landed earnings. Given the instability and uncertainty of legal incomes (quite apart from any social considerations), it is not surprising that barristers sought to purchase land, although their frequent prolonged absences from home must often have adversely affected the efficient management of their estates.

This necessarily hurried and superficial survey of some rather tedious statistics threatens to turn into a discussion of the role of legal practice as an avenue of upward economic and social mobility in Tudor and early Stuart England. That — an important and interesting topic — must be reserved for another occasion. But it would be unfortunate to leave the mistaken impression that this paper has only been concerned to score easy points off simple-minded Elizabethan social commentators, or to question Sir Edward Coke's insistence on the close connection between legal erudition and an abundance of worldly blessings. Of course, for many counsellors the law was a high-road to fame and fortune. But it was also a lottery, in the words of Adam Smith — whose analysis of the economics of legal practice still bears quoting at length, despite the somewhat dubious nature of its statistical content:[1]

> The wages of labour in different employments vary according to the probability or improbability of success in them . . . Put your son apprentice to a shoemaker, there is little doubt of his learning to make a pair of shoes; But send him to study the law, it is at least twenty to one if ever he makes such a proficiency as will enable him to live by the business. In a perfectly fair lottery, those who draw the prizes ought to gain all that is lost by those who draw the blanks. In a profession where twenty fail for one that succeeds, that one ought to gain all that should have been gained by the unsuccessful twenty. The counsellor at law who, perhaps, at near forty years of age, begins to make something by his profession, ought to receive the retribution, not only of his own so tedious and expensive education, but that of more than twenty others who are never likely to make anything by it. How extravagant so ever the fees of counsellors may sometimes appear, their real retribution is never equal to this. Compute what is likely to be annually gained, and spent . . . with regard to all the counsellors and students of law, in all the different inns of court, and you will find that their annual gains bear a very small proportion to their annual expense, even though you rate the former as high, and the latter as low, as can well be done. The lottery of the law, therefore, is very far from being a perfectly fair lottery; and . . . is, in point of pecuniary gain, evidently under-recompensed. These professions keep their level, however, with other occupations, and, notwithstanding these discouragements, all the most generous and liberal spirits are eager to crowd into them. Two different causes contribute to recommend them. First, the desire of the reputation which attends upon superior excellence in any of them; and, secondly, the natural confidence which every man has, more or less, not only in his own abilities, but in his own good fortune.

1 A. Smith, *The Wealth of Nations,* ed. E. Canaan (London, 1904), i, 118-9.

The records of calls to the bar at the four inns of court suggest there was no lack of 'generous and liberal spirits' in late Tudor and early Stuart England. But even Coke would doubtless have agreed that, of the many called, few were chosen to become 'Sages of the Law'.

APPENDICES
TO
COUNSELLORS FEES AND EARNINGS
IN THE AGE OF SIR EDWARD COKE

APPENDIX I

Contemporary literary estimates of fees
charged by counsel

(a) 1452   Et si nul denier en certein soit a luy promis, donques il
aura tant en comon droit luy done; come a serjeant xl d., et
al attorney xx d. de cesty que luy retenut.

Year Book, Mich. 31 Hen.6, 9, pl.1

(b) 1539? nother sergeauntes nor apprenticis woll for the preferment
of theyr cleauntes cause goe barre at any time . . .without
fee of iii s. iiii d. to them to be gevyn for eny tyme soe
goying.

SP 2/Q, f.31

(c) 1587   some of them will not come from their chambers to the
Guildhall in London under £10, or twenty nobles [£6. 13s.
4d.] at the least.

W. Harrison, Description of England,
ed. G. Edelen (Ithaca, 1968), 174

(d) 1630   Counsellors' Fees are not certaine to our knowledge butt
they usuallie take for their Fee for every cause ordinarilie x
s. Sergiantes of the lawe doe likewise practise in this Courte
and they take some x s. for a fee some xx s. or more as their
Clients will give them and accordinge to the paines they
take, but the certaintie of their Fees wee knowe not.

Evidence of the King's Bench officers
to the commission on fees, E 215/849

(e) 1631   So as the Noble or Ryall [6s. 8d.] (which within memory
was an usuall reward for a Counsellor) is now risen to 4
pound, five pound, 20 nobles or 10 pound with some.

Anon., The Just Lawyer, 18-19

(f) 1645   Nor are their fees of mean value, 3 pounds, 5 pounds, six
pounds being usual, even for making a motion of five or six
lines.

Anon., Some Advertisements for the new
Election of Burgesses for the House of
Commons, sig. A.

APPENDIX II

Fees paid to counsel (selected examples)

(A) *The borough of Totnes* (1601)

	£.	s.	d.
Item paid Mr Stephens for his fee	1	10	0
Item paid Serjeant Williams for his fee	2	0	0
Item paid Serjeant Heale for his fee	3	0	0
Item paid Mr Attorney for his fee	5	0	0
Item paid Mr Solicitor for his fee	2	0	0
Item paid Mr Clarke for his fee	1	0	0
Item paid Mr Serjeant Heale after the verdict	2	0	0

Devon County Record Office, MS. 1579A/10/17

(B) *The Founders' Company, London* (1613-19)

1613	Paid to Mr Stone, Counsell, at 4 severall times	2	0	0
	...			
	geven unto Sir Henry Montagew, Recorder, for his advise	2	4	0
1615	to Mr Garard for Counsell about the Corporacion	2	4	0
1616	to Mr Jarrett for counsel about the ordenance	1	2	0
1617	unto Mr Jarrett for councell concerninge our sherche	2	4	0
	to Mr Jarrett for his counsell against Gantlett	0	11	0
	Mr Recorder for his councel against Gantlett	1	2	0
	given to Mr Ellice, Councellor, for speaking at the Seshions of Peace against Burkett	0	5	6
	given to a Councellor for making a motion for the stainge of Gauntlette's suit and bote hiere to Westmynster that time	0	11	6

given unto Mr Jarrett when we met the Brashers at the Recorder's, being Councell on both sides	3	6	0
1619 given to Mr Jarrett at two severall times for his councell concerning the Brashers	2	4	0
given to Mr Croocke by consent for councel	1	2	0
given to Mr Dampford at the same time For his councel	1	2	0
given to Mr Townshend for a moshone to have our sewte staed till the next terme	0	11	0
given to the new Recorder	2	4	0
given to the Recorder for overlooking of our deedes for the hall	2	4	0
...			
delievered unto Mr Townsshend to retaine counsell [to] prosecut our shewtt	1	2	0

Wardens' Accounts of the Worshipful Company of Founders, ed. G. Pascoe (London, 1964), 256-99

(C) *Lord William Howard, of Naworth Castle* (Michaelmas term 1619)

Sir [John] Jackson, for a mosion in Chequer	0	11	0
...			
Mr Hudson, for pereusing the bouks in Star chamber for my Lord against Sir William Huttin and others	1	2	0
To Mr Davies for attending Sir Ewboluse Thelwall in the reference between my Lord and Mr Salkeild two tyms	1	2	0
...			
To Mr Daviese for perusing the bouks in Star chamber betwixt my Lord and Sir William Huttin and for drawing a breffe in that cause	1	2	0
To Mr Sargent John Moore for a mossion in the King's Bench	1	2	0

To Mr Greme for assisting him therein, and
for moving Mr Justeis Houghton for a Rule
thereupon   1   2   0
...

Mor to Mr Davies for perewsing the bouks in
the Star chamber, and for attending [Sir]
John Walter for his oppinyon therin   1   2   0

Sir John Walter for his opinyon therin   3   6   0
...

To Mr Gwin for a mossion in King's Bench
betwixt my Lord and Mr Salkeild   1   2   0
...

To Mr Gwin for a mossion in King's Bench
between my Lord and Slatter   0   11   0
...

Mr Gwin for a mossion in King's Bench tuching
the Tryell betwixt my Lord and Mr Thomas
Salkeild   0   11   0

Mr Banks for opinyon in that cause and
attending Mr Damport for his opynyon   0   11   0

'Selections from the Household Books of
the Lord William Howard of Naworth Castle',
ed. G. Ormsby, *Surtees Society* 68 (1877),
110-15.

APPENDIX III

Fees received by counsel

(A) *Thomas Thornton* (1553-1632; called to bar 1584; associate of the bench 1620)

    (i)   March 1596 to March 1597
            1 x 4s.; 1 x 5s.; 62 x 10s.; 1 x 12s.; 1 x 16s.; 15 x 20s.; 6 x 40s.; 5 x 80s.; 3 x 100s.

    (ii)   April 1626 to May 1627 (vacation fees only)
            31 x 10s.; 1 x 15s.; 7 x 20s.; 1 x 80s.

Northamptonshire Record Office,
MS. Thornton 2251

(B) *Henry Sherfield* (d.1634; called to bar 1606; to bench 1620)

    (i)   1608-09
            5 x under 10s.; 75 x 10s.; 1 x 12s.; 1 x 13s. 4d.; 1 x 15s.; 24 x 20s.; 3 x over 20s.

    (ii)   Easter term 1620
            58 x 10s.; 37 x 11s.; 34 x 20s.; 50 x 22s.; 1 x 33s.; 1 x 40s.; 8 x 44s.; 1 x 50s.

Hampshire Record Office, MS. 44 M 69/xxv/1,2

(C) *Arthur Turnour* (c.1589-1651; called to bar 1613; to bench 1634; serjeant-at-law 1637)

    (i)   Hilary term 1642
            31 x 10s.; 1 x 15s.; 37 x 20s.; 12 x 30s.; 22 x 40s.; 1 x 60s.

    (ii)   Hilary term 1642 (jurisdiction and fees)

            Chancery: 6 x 10s.; 1 x 15s.; 20 x 20s.; 1 x 30s.; 2 x 40s.; 1 x 60s.

            Common Pleas: 22 x 10s.; 10 x 20s.

            Exchequer: 1 x 20s.

            King's Bench: 1 x 10s.; 1 x 20s.

            Parliament: 1 x 30s.

            Star Chamber: 1 x 20s.

            Wards: 1 x 10s.; 2 x 20s.

            Advice: 2 x 20s.

            Unspecified: 1 x 10s.

Harvard Law School, MS. 137

APPENDIX IV

Annual earnings by counsel (to nearest £)

(A) *Thomas Thornton*

Year	£	Year	£	Year	£
1582-3	0	1599-1600	71	1616-7	190
1583-4	18	1600-1	91	1617-8	219
1584-5	10	1601-2	112	1618-9	252
1585-6	30	1602-3	103	1619-20	222
1586-7	9	1603-4	78	1620-1	130
1587-8	25	1604-5	102	1621-2	109
1588-9	35	1605-6	104	1622-3	131
1589-90	39	1606-7	161	1623-4	146
1590-1	46	1607-8	127	1624-5	168
1591-2	87	1608-9	57	1625-6	111
1592-3	61	1609-10	191	1626-7	124
1593-4	79	1610-1	154	1627-8	54
1594-5	70	1611-2	147	1628-9	114
1595-6	90	1612-3	[?]	1629-30	90
1596-7	85	1613-4	248	1630-1	51
1597-8	133	1614-5	162	1631-2	102
1598-9	129	1615-6	194		

Northamptonshire Record Office, MS. Thornton 2251

(B) *James Whitelocke* (1570-1632; called to bar 1600; to bench 1619; serjeant-at-law and C.J. Chester 1620; J.K.B. 1624)

Year	£	Year	£	Year	£
1600-1	34	1607-8	419	1614-5	556
1601-2	68	1608-9	402	1615-6	499
1602-3	80	1609-10	433	1616-7	616
1603-4	188	1610-1	533	1617-8	628
1604-5	254	1611-2	517	1618-9	622
1605-6	327	1612-3	531	1619-20	600
1606-7	453	1613-4	620		

Brit. Lib., Additional MS. 53725, ff.31-130

184

(C) *Henry Sherfield*

Year	£	Year	£	Year	£
1608-9	77	1621-2	403	1628-9	360
1609-10	236	1622-3	386	1629-30	505
1610-1	312	1623-4	418	1630-1	257
1611-2	355	1624-5	332	1631-2	426
1612-3	304	1625-6	192	1632-3	383
1613*	191	1626-7	311	1633**	379
1620-1	547	1627-8	495		

*   Easter and Trinity terms only
** Easter, Trinity and Michaelmas terms only

Hampshire Record Office, MS. 44 M 69 xxv/1,2

(D) *Arthur Turnour*

Year	£
1642	191
1646	347
1647	526
1648	363
1649	435
1650	303

Harvard Law School, MS. 137

(E) *John Archer* (1598-1682; called to bar 1626; to bench 1648; serjeant-at-law 1659; J.C.P. 1663)

1658:	Hilary term	289
	Lent circuit	184
	Easter term	117
	Trinity term	209
	Summer circuit	215
	Vacation post	52
	Michaelmas term	191
	Total	1,257

W.G. Benham, 'A Great Essex Lawyer's Diary', *Essex Review* 31 (1922), 188-9

THE ACTION OF WASTE IN THE EARLY COMMON LAW

Sue Sheridan Walker

The action of waste had, by the late thirteenth century, become a popular common-law remedy to halt the destruction of property and to secure both the recovery of tenements and damages for capital depredations committed by feudal guardians, dowagers or tenants for life or years. The formula in most of the writs was stereotyped: the plaintiff alleged 'waste, exile and sale made in houses, woods, gardens and men'. But the materials in the Bench writ files, when correlated with those of the plea rolls, enable us to see how pleas of waste were settled and to see the connection between legislation and the intricacies of litigation in the courts. The history of the action of waste also tells us about the working of the jury: the questions put to it, the answers made, especially in regard to points raised in pleading, and the treatment of jury-findings at Westminster.

To help in understanding the nature of the remedy in waste, I shall trace the stages by which successful litigants came to be able to recover the property wasted and obtain damages (in triple after 1278, for waste in tenements other than those in wardship). The correlation of jury inquests in the Bench writ files with the judgment-clauses in the plea rolls provides information about the relationship between judges and juries, about law-finding and fact-finding. I shall discuss as well the function of prohibition and the effect of legislation, especially the Statute of Gloucester (1278). Not every question can be answered with precision, but it may be helpful to suggest what these documentary sources cannot tell us as well as what they can. The materials are generally sufficient, however, to show the whole procedure in waste from initial process to final judgment.[1]

The earliest references to punishment for waste are in the pipe rolls of Henry II (c.1177), where guardians were amerced by the Crown.[2]

---

1 I should like to thank Morris Arnold, John Beckerman, Charles Gray, Richard Helmholz, Janet Loengard, William McGovern, Donald Sutherland, and the late C.A.F. Meekings, for their assistance.

2 E.g. *Pipe Roll 23 Henry II* (26 *PRS*, 1905), 169 ('Matheus de Wallop redd. compotum de xx m. pro wasto bosci de Wallop'); *Pipe Roll 31 Henry II* (34 *PRS*, 1910), 139 (guardian amerced for waste in woods of a minor heiress in his ward).

Magna Carta provided that wasteful guardians should lose the custody of the land and make amends for the damages;[1] the reissue of the Charter in 1225 declared that the custody would be entrusted to two discreet knights of the fee,[2] a rule which Bracton later re-echoed.[3] The earliest references show that guardians who committed capital depredations suffered amercement by the Crown, but it is not clear to what degree the injured heir was compensated. Did a like rule apply to dowagers and tenants for life or for years or by the curtesy? The plea rolls certainly contain examples of actions of waste brought against such persons; but it is difficult to determine whether or not they had been brought before the king's courts on the basis of a violation of a royal prohibition against making waste.[4] The published and unpublished thirteenth-century plea rolls contain a considerable number of cases of waste against doweresses, about half of which are brought in respect of waste 'contrary to prohibition'.[5] The proportion is the same in the fewer actions against termors.[6] But in the many more cases for waste in wardship, few mention prohibition.[7]

Waste in the sense of capital depredations must be distinguished from fines for permission to make wastes or assarts – that is, permission to bring waste or vacant land under personal cultivation. See also *Feet of Fines 10 Richard I* (24 *PRS*, 1900), 220; *Rolls of the King's Court Richard I* (14 *PRS*, 1891), 44, 59 (waste in a wood). The articles of the eyre sought out such wasters: *Rotuli Hundredorum tempore Henrici II et Edwardi I*, ed. W. Illingworth (London, 1812-8), i, 13-14 (article xxx concerns waste by escheators and sub-escheators). See also Glanvill, viii, 9.

1 See J.C. Holt, *Magna Carta* (Cambridge, 1965), 318-9, cc.4-5.

2 For cases mentioning waste 'contra regni consuetudinem', see 7 *CRR* 75-6 (1214); 8 *CRR* 68 (1219).

3 Bracton, ii, 252 (f. 87).

4 See S.F.C. Milsom,. *Novae Narrationes* (80 *SS*, 1963), cxc. And see, generally, his excellent 'commentary on the action', at cxc-cxcviii.

5 E.g. (mentioning prohibition): 2 *BNB* 492: 640 (1231), 681: 880 (1232); 15 *CRR* 72: 333, 88: 420 (1233); JUST 1/699, m.22 (1246-7); KB 26/145, mm.45, 54 (1251); KB 26/171, mm.21d. 40, 43 (1261). E.g. (without mention of prohibition): 13 *CRR* 563: 2664 (1230); *Staffordshire Record Society*, iv, 78, 83 (1230); 2 *BNB* 364: 461 (1230); 14 *CRR* 347: 1630 (1231); 15 *CRR* 22: 100 (1233), 209: 981F (1234).

6 E.g. (mentioning prohibition): 3 *BNB* 340: 1371 [9 *CRR* 20 (1220)], where the denial is of waste after prohibition. E.g. (without mention of prohibition): 2 *BNB* 531: 691 (1232); *Bedfordshire Historical Record Society*, xxi, 66: 161 (1247); JUST 1/1046, m.35 (1250-2).

7 E.g. (mentioning prohibition): 15 *CRR* 18: 77 (1233); 2 *BNB* 563: 739 (1233); 3 *BNB* 100: 1075 (1225); JUST 1/699, m.25d (1246-7); KB 26/149, m.14 (1253); KB 26/171, m.69d (1261). E.g. (without mention of prohibition): 11 *CRR* 319: 1596, 450: 2251, 477: 2404 (1224); 12 *CRR* 391: 1930 (1226); 14 *CRR* 217: 1059 (1231); 15 *CRR* 325: 1303 (1234), 342: 1358 (1235), 409: 1928 (1236); KB 26/115B, m.25d, 26d (1234); KB 26/148, m.9d (1253); KB 26/185, m.139 (1268); KB 26/205, m.20 (1272).

For many reasons we shall never be certain about the function of prohibition in waste. Initially the writs were not returnable and therefore form no part of surviving Common Bench files; those returned into Chancery by their recipients when suing a writ of waste in violation of a prohibition were probably scrapped by the issuing masters. The crisp accounts of the procedure in waste which are outlined by the editors of the *Brevia Placitata* (*c.*1260)[1] are not verifiable, because no county-court rolls or sheriffs' files survive from the period. Initial process in prohibition was supposed to have been by attachment, but in many cases it actually began with summons. The casualness of clerks in expressing the term 'contra prohibicionem', often reducing it to an 'etc.' or 'contra etc.', might argue for extreme familiarity with this procedure.[2] Some are abbreviated in such a way that reference to prohibition might be overlooked; this is shown in Dr Clanchy's important volume, where a waste case in the Berkshire eyre says only 'contra' in the plea roll but 'prohibition' is mentioned in the writ.[3] But if these abbreviations of allusions to prohibition suggest habitual usage, any sure conclusions are foiled by the enrolment of pleas that are settled. There are a few cases in which the defendant specifically denied making waste after the prohibition. In one case the jury did not support this defence, and gave damages for waste.[4] In another case the defendant went free because he had made no waste.[5] These instances may give credence to Bracton's statement that waste was actionable, prohibition or not.[6] Yet we do not know whether the inquest reflected Bracton's principle or simply the facts of the case. The paucity of writ-files or remains of broken files surviving for the reign of Henry III means that there is little chance of the record of an original waste inquest being found. It is at least comforting to recognise that, even in the thirteenth century, prohibitions in waste were misunderstood and were for this reason abolished by chapter fourteen of the Statute of Westminster II (1285). The statute said that persons

---

1 *Brevia Placitata*, ed. G.J. Turner and T.F.T. Plucknett (66 *SS*, 1951), cxli (regarding the writ of prohibition in waste).

2 E.g. in KB 26/133, m.15d, the defendant is attached to answer concerning waste and damages of so much 'etc.' His answer, however, is to deny making waste 'contra prohibicionem'; and he goes *sine die*. Various forms of abbreviation are used in the following: KB 26/136, mm.2d, 26d (1249); KB 26/137, m.3 (1250); KB 26/141, m.2d (1250); KB 26/145, mm.45, 54d (1251); KB 26/148, m.9 (1253); CP 40/8, m.9 (1278) (but written out on mm.47d, 54d, 58d); CP 40/33, m.65d (1280) ('etc.').

3 *Roll and Writ File of the Berkshire Eyre of 1248*, ed. M.T. Clanchy (90 *SS*, 1972-3), 216: 509, and 447: a115.

4 CP 40/33, m.21 (1279); CP 40/32, m.52d (1280).

5 JUST 1/483, m.22d (1271-2).

6 Bracton, iii, 411 (f.317).

188

had been deceived into thinking waste was punishable only after the prohibition.[1]

Statutory regulation of waste is naturally said to begin with the provisions of Magna Carta described above. The Crown, of course, needed neither legislation nor litigation to remove persons who were mishandling lands held by royal grant, but there are some early thirteenth-century suits between private parties whose pleas are based upon waste made in violation of 'royal constitutions'.[2] The next legislation which mentioned waste was chapter twenty-three of the Provisions of 43 Henry III (1259), which stated that farmers convicted of waste were bound to restore damages in full. Chapter seventeen provided the action of account for waste committed by guardians in socage.[3] The Dictum of Kenilworth (1275) declared (in chapter sixteen) that waste must not be done by persons holding lands of the 'king's wardship'; should they do so, 'justice' would be done against them as it was contained in Magna Carta. Chapter nineteen of the Dictum declared that woods could not be sold or wasted; and that offenders would be grievously punished.[4] Chapter twenty three of the Statute of Marlborough (1267) similarly referred to farmers within their terms, who 'shall not make waste, sale, or exile, of houses, woods, men, or of anything that they have to farm, without special licence ... making mention that they may do it'. Should farmers be convicted of making waste, Marlborough added that they should yield full damages and be punished grievously by amercement.[5] Early statutory mentions of the award of damages – in the 1259 Provisions, and repeated in the 1267 Statute of Marlborough – are anticipated by cases from the 1230s onwards where successful litigants were awarded damages.[6] But these cases seem to have been brought on the basis of violation of prohibition or of a fine made between the parties. The above statutes, however, gave a remedy against 'farmers' (meaning termors) irrespective of prohibition. The function of the two statutes, whether intentional or not, was to establish the principle that damages

1 1 SR 81-2.

2 7 CRR 75-6 (1214); 8 CRR 68 (1219).

3 1 SR 11: c.23 gave a remedy against waste by farmers, and c.17 gave the action of account against guardians in socage.

4 1 SR 15.

5 1 SR 24: c.23 provides that termors 'shall yield full damages and be amerced grievously'.

6 2 BNB 420: 540 (1231) [14 CRR 113: 576[(satisfaction and amercement for waste contrary to the fine). In KB 26/201, m.20 (1271), a case of waste in wardship. judgment is to 'indemnify and emend'; but in some parts of the estate no waste was made. In 14 CRR 347: 1630 (1231) the jury itemizes the amounts

were recoverable and pleas suable against termors without any mention of prohibition.

Thirteenth-century legal history is made less easy to understand by the fact that so few cases ended with judgment. Many of those which were resolved ended by 'concord'; but at least the details of the compromise were usually noted in the plea rolls. Most of these private agreements provide for damages to be paid to the plaintiff:[1] this must have been more advantageous to both parties than royal amercement. Some provide for the return of property, perhaps reflecting the custom described in Bracton's statement that wasters lose the land[2] and have to make good the damages.[3] Many of these concords, however, have more the nature of a true compromise: while the defendant gives damages, he may retain the wardship and the marriage of the heir, or enjoy some other concession.[4]

While the Statute of Gloucester (1278), like Magna Carta, speaks only of wasters losing the thing wasted, all cases decided after it reveal both aspects of the developed remedy — recovery of property and damages. The 1278 statute merely adopted the old terminology of Magna Carta in saying that wasters should lose the thing wasted: not that plaintiffs would receive it.[5] Yet, in case after case, the recovery of the lands in which waste has occurred becomes a principal constituent of the remedy.[6] Two cases which were pending in the courts in 1278 and 1279, and ended in concords, adopted the formula 'that the plaintiff recover the lands and damages'.[7] Recovery of the lands does

---

of damage done in waste of dower, but does not say who gets them. 3 *BNB* 215-6: 1201 (1236) suggests the loss of the custody and the obligation to repair.

1   7 *CRR* 64 (1214); 8 *CRR* 71 (1219); 12 *CRR* 145: 713 (1225); 13 *CRR* 134: 588 (1228) (orders repair and emendations); *Somerset Pleas*, i, ed. C.E.H. Chadwyck Healey (11 Somerset Record Soc., 1897), 213: 686 (1242-3); JUST 1/909A, m.14 (1248-9); KB 26/136, m.11d (1249); JUST 1/487, m.53 (1280-1); JUST 1/924, m.25d (1287-8). For concords after the view, with particulars of the agreement, see e.g.: KB 26/165, m.26 (1260); JUST 1/1055, m.18 (1278-9); CP 40/42, m.39 (1281). On the calling of the view before a compromise, see: C.A.F. Meekings, 'A Roll of Judicial Writs', 32 *BIHR* (1959), 217-8.

2   See note 3 on p. 186, above.

3   Bracton, ii, 252 (f. 87).

4   E.g. JUST 1/1055, m.18 (1278-9).

5   1 *SR* 48.

6   E.g. CP 40/68, m.64 (1287); CP 40/70, m.65d (1288); CP 40/95, m.95 (1292); CP 40/125, m.148d (1298); CP 40/138, m.35d (1301); CP 40/148, m.73d (1303); CP 40/181, m.266 (1310). There is an anticipation of recovery of land in waste in KB 27/9, m.12d (1274).

7   JUST 1/1055, m.18 (1278-9). Another like example: JUST 1/323, m.14d (1277-9).

become habitual in settlements after 1278, but this is not because of the wording of the Statute of Gloucester. The novel feature of that statute is the introduction of triple damages for waste other than waste in wardship. The plea rolls recognise this innovation by stating again and again 'damages in triple according to the statute'.[1] By its omission of any reference to prohibition, Gloucester may have helped to separate waste from the older prohibitory process. The statute helped to advertise the remedy and perhaps made it more worthwhile to pursue such actions by reason of the enhanced damages awarded. It is doubtful whether Plucknett is correct in saying that plaintiffs had to await the statute to recover cash damages,[2] but Gloucester with its triple damages did create an attractive remedy.

The part of the Statute of Gloucester which referred to wardship seemed difficult to apply. The remedy for waste in wardship was to continue as in Magna Carta: the wasteful guardian would lose the wardship.[3] According to Gloucester, damages were to be recoverable only if they exceeded the value of the unexpired portion of the wardship.[4] The practice shown in the plea rolls after 1278, however, is the recovery of the wardship and the award of single damages.[5] If the wardship had but little time to run, juries could award more than single damages to compensate for the diminished value of the recovery.[6] Besides this rather bold stretching of the statute, juries sometimes — either by misunderstanding or by an express desire to award punitive damages for waste in wardship — awarded triple damages, saying 'triple according to the statute'.[7] The fact that such findings on the

---

1 E.g. JUST 1/367, m.11 (1278-9) (damages 10s.), m.15d (damages 12 marks). These cases mention the 'new statute'. JUST 1/922, m.26 (1278-9) is a long case with itemized damages. CP 40/42, m.39 (1281) is particularly interesting in that it awards damages in triple for that waste done 'post statutum'; the last annotation is that the defendant gave half a mark for licence to agree.

2 T.F.T. Plucknett, *Statutes and their Interpretation in the 14th Century* (Cambridge, 1922), 102. Similarly, Milsom, *Novae Narrationes*, cxci, citing year-book evidence.

3 *Magna Carta*, c.4.

4 1 *SR* 48.

5 CP 40/300, m.113 (1335) (damages but no recovery, perhaps because the wardship had ended); CP 40/398, m.203d (1359) (recovers 30 marks, but not certain whether this was single or triple damages); JUST 1/1090, m.[14d] (1292-3) order for a second jury to determine the damages.

6 CP 40/141, m.112 (1302). The fact that the wardship had six years to run was taken into account in fixing the damages at 5 marks. CP 40/26, m.49d (1278) states that the remaining term was not equal to the damage in the wardship, and a further jury was ordered to determine recompense.

7 E.g.: JUST 1/367, m.11 (1278-9) (mentions the statute, but does not say 'triple'); CP 40/138, m.161 (1301); CP 40/181, m.236d (1310); CP 40/244, m.74d (1322).

part of juries, manifestly contrary to the statute, were simply copied from the inquest on to the plea rolls without amendment by the court is perhaps a sign of the large role which the jury played in the settlement of suits. These awards of triple damages in cases of wardship were, however, very often overturned on a writ of error brought by the defendant: as in an Irish case which came to the King's Bench in 1303, where the Dublin decision was not upheld for this very reason.[1] Another instance in which triple damages were inappropriately awarded in a wardship case was in one of the cases which William Butler, a former royal ward, was allowed to bring on the authority of his so-called 'statute', for waste done in the time of his ancestor.[2] Later the courts generally held that William Butler's remedy was a special favour for a royal ward, and that heirs could not normally sue for waste done in the time of an ancestor.[3] There are a few cases where no subsequent reversal of the original award has been found,[4] but these may have been against royal officers who were punished by statutes more severely than non-official wasters.[5]

By the late thirteenth century, especially after prohibition in waste

---

1 KB 27/174, m.75 (1303). This case is discussed on the basis of Irish records in G.J. Hand, *English Law in Ireland 1290-1324* (Cambridge, 1967), 163-4, 168-9, 150 n.3.

2 The plea rolls for 19 Edward I (1291-2) contain several pleas initiated by William Butler ('Boteler' of Wemme) for waste made in the time of his ancestor, his brother Gawain Butler. In one entry (KB 27/128, m.8d) he was awarded triple damages for waste in wardship. The case was before the king's council the next Easter term: KB 27/131, m.6 ('loquela'). The question was not whether triple damages were applicable to waste in wardship, but whether remedy could be had for waste done in the time of an ancestor. The matter was referred to Parliament, and resulted in the so-called Statute *De Vasto* or the Statute of William Butler (1 *RP* 79:6; 1 *SR* 109), which provided that heirs might indeed have an action for waste done in the time of their ancestor. The 'statute' ordered Gilbert of Thornton and his fellow justices to see justice done to William; but we do not know whether William Butler himself ever profited from the parliamentary directive.

3 According to the year books, the courts later denied the validity of the 'statute': e.g. Pas. 8 Edw. 2 (41 *SS*, 1925), 116, pl. 10, with comment on pp.xiii-xvi; Pas. 7 Edw. 2 (39 *SS*, 1922), 126, pl. 12, at 127, *per* Inge J.

4 In CP 40/153, m.104d (1305), for waste in wardship, the ward is given triple damages according to the statute; the final annotation says the successful plaintiff is already in seisin of the land, so there is no need for recovery.

5 *Articuli super Cartas* (1300), 28 Edw. 1, c.18 [1 *SR* 140] (remedy against escheators who make waste in wardships); 14 Edw. 3, stat. 1, c.13 [1 *SR* 285] (against escheators making waste in wardships, and providing that the next friends of wards whose lands were wasted should have the wardship). It was not easy to reform escheators: 36 Edw. 3, stat. 1, c.13 [1 *SR* 374] deprived them of what might formerly have been considered reasonable estovers; moreover escheators convicted of waste were to be punished with a fine to the king and triple damages to the heir on his own suit.

was abolished in 1285,[1] evidence becomes more ample, allowing procedure to be followed more closely and the role of the jury in the determination of waste cases to be seen more clearly. Although wager of law was available in many actions, few defendants in waste offered to clear themselves by recourse to compurgation.[2] In the *Casus Placitorum*, wager of law is described as inappropriate in waste because in any event the view must be taken to determine the waste made.[3] Persons injured by wasting tenants, if not aided by royal administrative surveillance,[4] secured a writ of waste from the Chancery. It was possible to complain by bill or plaint, but this was done only infrequently.[5]

There was considerable flexibility in the wording of writs of waste. The year books sometimes referred to waste as a personal trespass,[6] but terms of a transgressory sort were rarely used in the writ or on the plea rolls.[7] It was customary to use a formula such as 'waste, sale and exile' in 'houses, gardens, woods and men'.[8] Fitzherbert, much later, remarked

1 Even after 1285 a few cases mention prohibition: CP 40/42, m.126; CP 40/59, m.28, 24d (1285); CP 52/1, 14 Edw. 1 (county obscured, but after Surrey); CP 52/1, Pas. 15 Edw. 1 (Surrey); CP 40/121, m.339d (1297); CP 40/240, m.368 (1321). Whether the possibility of any injunctive use of prohibition (dear to Holdsworth and Plucknett) was prevented by the statutory clarification of 1285 remains an open but perhaps insoluble question.

2 In *Brevia Placitata,*cxli, a widow denied making waste after the prohibition and waged her law. See also Bracton, iii, 410 (f. 315); 2 *BNB* 681: 880 (1232); KB 26/126, m.45d (1259); 8 *CRR* 338 (1220) finally goes to a jury.

3 *Casus Placitorum and Reports of Cases in the King's Courts 1272-8* (69 *SS*, 1950), 81-2. Professor John Beckerman has suggested to me that wager of law was uncommon because if the defendant went to compurgation and lost he could not then get the damages taxed, but had to pay the entire amount claimed.

4 The eyre and hundred rolls furnish examples of the Crown's desire not only to enforce its rights but also its obligation to keep wards' estates in proper condition. See, e.g., *Rotuli Hundredorum*, i, 90, 148, 162, 172, 217, 409; 3 *CIM* 113: 331 (1357-9); 4 *CIM* 34: 50 (1377), 74: 123 (1380). The Memoranda Rolls show regular internal administrative surveillance of royal custodians or recipients of royal wardships: e.g. E 367/87, m.214; E 159/37, m.28d; E 159/38, m.9v, 13; E 159/40, m.21d. The relatively few cases found in the central courts which touch waste in royal wardships testify to the effectiveness of this system: KB 26/151, m.25 (1253-4); KB 26/201, m.20 (1271); KB 26/205, m.20; KB 27/87, m.1 (1284); KB 27/99, m.3 (1286); KB 27/119, m.1d (1289); KB 27/123, m.36 (1290); KB 27/145, m.2d (1295). In several of these cases 'contempt of the king' was alleged as well as the waste.

5 *Select Cases of Procedure without Writ under Henry III*, ed. H.G. Richardson and G.O. Sayles (60 *SS*, 1941), lxxix, 57, 64, 90-1, 98.

6 A writ of waste is called a writ of trespass in Pas. 32 Edw. 1 (*RS*, 1864), 180-3; Pas. 3 Edw. 2 (20 *SS*, 1905), 89-91, pl. 13; Hil. 11 Edw. 2 (61 *SS*, 1942), 152-62, pl. 1 esp. at 153; Pas. 12 Edw. 2 (70 *SS*, 1950), 107-9, pl. 4.

7 An exception is in JUST 1/699, m.22 (1246-7), where the jury uses it.

8 *Early Registers of Writs*, ed. E. de Haas and G.D.G. Hall (87 *SS*, 1970), 16: HIB 51; 53-4: CC 64-8; 72: CC 129-129c; 149-52: R 162-176. KB 26/136,

that one should include 'exile of men' only if this were indeed true;[1] the writs so far examined did not mention 'exile' and 'men' unless villeins were claimed as wasted.[2] What could be comprised within the standard formula can be seen from the following list, drawn from the plea rolls: plough-teams,[3] forges for making armour,[4] fortified dwellings with chapels and halls above the gates,[5] halls and chambers with 'solars',[6] military chambers,[7] kitchens,[8] brewhouses,[9] mills,[10] parts of mills,[11] and the ovens of manorial privilege.[12] Habitations for animals are

m.15d (1259); CP 40/8, mm.9, 58d (1275); CP 40/59, mm.6, 32 (1285); CP 52/1, Pas. 15 Edw. 1 (Oxon); CP 52/1, Hil. 29 Edw. 1 (Rutl, Warw, and Linc).

1 Fitz. N.B. 55C. Cf. *Early Registers of Writs*, ed. de Haas and Hall, 149: R 162 ('Rule. The word "exile" should not be used except in a case where there is waste of men'). This was not the terminology used by Bracton, or in the plea rolls of Henry III, where 'exile' is often used without allegation of waste of men: e.g. KB 26/136, mm.2d, 6d, 26d (1249); KB 26/141, m.2d (1250); KB 26/205, m.20 (1272).

2 E.g. CP 52/1, Hil. 10 Edw. 1 (Staffs) (waste, etc. 'in terris domibus boscis et gardinis' demised); CP 52/1, Hil. 10 Edw. 1 (Oxon) (woods only, in wardship).

3 *The Earliest Lincolnshire Assize Rolls 1202-9*, ed. D.M. Stenton (22 Lincolnshire Record Soc., 1924), 228: 1281.

4 KB 27/119, m.1, continued in KB 27/123, m.36 (1290) includes damage to the armour itself; CP 52/1, Trin. 27 Edw. 1 (Glos) (forge); CP 40/95, m.95 (1292) (house with forge); *Rotulorum Originalium in Curia Scaccarii Abbreviatio*, ed. H. Playford and J. Caley (London, 1805-10), i, 224 (waste of war-engines).

5 CP 40/145, m.309 (1303) (chamber over gate); m.374 (chapel and hall); CP 40/138, m.35d (1301); CP 40/215, m.200 (1316); 3 *CIM* 113: 331 (chapel in gatehouse).

6 JUST 1/382, m.44d (1312-3); JUST 1/932, m.2 (1287-8); CP 40/138, m.35d (1301); CP 40/139, m.152 (1301) (damages also awarded for waste in a 'bower'); CP 40/69, m.39d (1287) (hall and chamber); CP 40/59, m.42 (1285) (hall and solar); CP 40/148, m.73d (1303) (solar); CP 52/1, Trin. 10 Edw. 1 (Kent) (solar dependent on a hall); CP 40/145, m.309 (1303) (cloister with walls).

7 CP 40/95, m.77 (1272); CP 40/148, m.73d (1303) (loopholes for arrows).

8 CP 40/138, m.35d (1301) (kitchens); JUST 1/932, m.2 (1287-8) (and a timber room); CP 40/193, m.8d (1312); CP 40/371, m.68 (1352); JUST 1/932, m.2 (1287-8) (and a timber room); JUST 1/382, m.71 (1312-3); CP 40/141, m.112 (1302) (one amount given for a kitchen, cow-shed, grange, stable and sheep-fold).

9 CP 40/26, m.49d (1278); CP 40/132, m.131d (1300); CP 40/138, m.35d (1301).

10 CP 40/26, m.49d (1278) (mill sold); CP 40/95, m.95 (1272) (several mills referred to as being in the tenure of various millers); CP 40/145, mm.329, 374 (1303) (grinding mill); CP 40/425, m.50 (water-mill), m.447 (various mills) (1366).

11 CP 40/132, m.131d (1300) (mill-arm); JUST 1/382, m.44d (1312-3) (mill-wheel).

12 JUST 1/382, m.71 (1312-3); CP 40/125, m.148d (1298); KB 27/174, m.75 (1303); 12 *CRR* 473: 2360 (1226); 3 *CIM* 125: 353 (1358-9); CP 40/122, m.7d (1298).

frequently mentioned: granges,[1] sheep-folds,[2] cow-sheds,[3] stables,[4] falcon-houses,[5] and dove-cotes.[6] One may also read of fish-ponds[7] and gardens,[8] orchards and woods with their oak, elm, hawthorn, pear, apple and cherry trees,[9] gates and fencing,[10] houses of stone[11] and houses so portable that they were carried off and sold[12] − in one case the plaintiff claimed that a stone-mason had been hired by the defendant to dismantle and 'asport' the stone fortification.[13] There are larders,[14] kilns,[15] weaving-rooms,[16] and a 'hospicium' for strangers (or perhaps undesirables such as lepers).[17]

---

1 CP 40/139, m.6d (damages awarded for several of different values; another on m.46d); CP 40/132, m.131d.

2 CP 40/60, m.70d (1285); CP 40/121, m.23; JUST 1/323, m.14d (1277-9); CP 40/132, m.131d (1300); JUST 1/383, m.86 (1312-3); CP 40/13, m.40 (1276); CP 40/26, m.49d; CP 40/139, m.46d (1301).

3 CP 40/32, m.52d (1280); KB 27/128, m.8d (1291); CP 40/121, m.23 (1297); CP 40/139, m.152; CP 40/153, m.104d (1305); CP 40/215, m.200 (1316).

4 KB 27/128, m.8d (1291); CP 40/132, m.131d (1300); CP 40/145, m.329 (1303); KB 27/174, m.75 (1303); JUST 1/382, m.86 (1312-3); CP 40/371, m.68 (1352); CP 40/425, m.367 (1366).

5 CP 40/95, m.77 (1292); CP 40/125, m.148d (one worth 6s. 8d.).

6 CP 40/138, m.35d (1301).

7 KB 26/205, m.24 (1272); CP 40/8, m.9 (1275); CP 40/14, m.120 (1276); CP 40/27, m.159 (1278); CP 40/28, m.21 (1279); CP 40/68, m.64 (1287); CP 40/131, m.302 (1300); CP 52/1, Hil. 19 Edw. 1 (Bucks).

8 CP 40/198, m.116d (1313); KB 27/99, m.39 (1286); JUST 1/932, m.2 (1287-8); JUST 1/924, m.25d (1287-8); CP 40/278, m.40 (1329).

9 CP 40/26, m.49d (1278); JUST 1/367, m.11; JUST 1/918, m.32d (1278-9); CP 40/145, m.374 (1303) (where the jury agreed with the defendant that the trees were used for repair and improvement); CP 52/1, 15 Edw. 1 (Beds) (damages shown); KB 27/74, m.2d (1283); CP 40/193, m.8d (1311); CP 40/198, m.116d (1313); CP 40/215, m.200 (1316) (damage found in many named woods); CP 40/131, m.302 (1300).

10 KB 27/145, m.2d (1295); KB 27/147, m.2 (1296); CP 40/193, m.8d (1311). In *Somerset Pleas,* i, ed. Healey, 209: 668, an inquisition revealed that 'the cattle go out at their pleasure and wander about the country and are destroyed because of the fencing'. CP 40/148, m. 73d (1303) (hedges around the court).

11 KB 27/99, m.3 (1286).

12 KB 27/45, m.2d (1295) (house worth £40. 10s.); CP 40/371, m.68 (hall sold); 12 *CRR* 46: 262, 121: 607 (1225) (some sold, some burned, some ruined); CP 40/14, m.30 (1276) (hall, chamber, chapel, kitchen, bake-house, grange, cow-shed, and all other houses, 'asported and sold').

13 CP 40/95, m.72 (1292): 'amovendo cooperturnam lapideam unius camere militum'.

14 CP 40/138, m.35d (1301); CP 40/145, m.309 (1303).

15 CP 40/138, m.35d (1301).

16 CP 40/132, m.131d (1300) (above room for brewing).

17 CP 40/132, m.131d (1300) (worth 4s.); CP 40/30, m.21 (1279) ('hostia'); CP 40/148, m.73d (timber 'hostia' with other items, 5 marks).

Custom determined what was fair usage of an estate. In areas of limited forest, certain trees and bushes were considered timber, whereas in other areas they would be simply undergrowth of little value.[1] To fail to repair a building, to tear it down, or sell it separately from the land (without replacing it by a new building), were regarded as waste. Sometimes juries were very circumstantial in stating in the inquest the precise nature of the waste, while at other times they would merely state 'a dove-cote worth so much'. Peasants could be held wasted or 'exiled' if their services were lost to their lord through the actions of the defendant.[2] McKechnie argued that this meant the enfranchisement of villeins;[3] but Round pointed out that waste of men also occurred when oppressive tallage drove the villeins to abandon their holdings.[4] There were in fact four ways in which the loss of men could be treated as waste: excessive tallage,[5] manumission or the sale of their freedom to villeins,[6] allowing a female villein to marry a freeman,[7] and allowing the houses to decay so that the inhabitants left. While the records do not say so explicitly, it may be that 'exile of men' really meant that the property was wasted because the men had gone away. There may have been other instances which involved simple flight, but none has been found in which flight was pleaded by the defendant.[8] A defendant in 1307 claimed that he was not culpable for the exile of the villeins because the men's homes were in such ruinous condition when he received the estate that the villeins had fled.[9] If this can be taken to imply that villeins had a right to a minimal standard of housing, or that

1 E. Coke, *First Part of the Institutes* (London, 1628), 53 (and many year-book citations in the margin).

2 2 *BNB* 381: 485 [14 *CRR* 217: 1059] 466: 607 [14 *CRR* 382: 1785]; CP 40/283, m.487 (1330); CP 40/371, m.62 (1352); CP 52/1, Mich. 27 & 28 Edw. 1 (Linc) (exile of villeins alone).

3 W.S. McKechnie, *Magna Carta: a Commentary on the Great Charter of King John* (Glasgow, 1905), 245 and notes.

4 *Rotuli Dominibus et Pueris et Puellis* (35 *PRS*, 1913), xxix.

5 CP 40/95, m.77 (plaintiff recovers 10s. for men wasted, multiplied by three according to the statute); KB 27/145, m.2d (1295) (damages £40. 7s. for waste of men 'per extorsionem'); KB 27/99, m.3 (1286); CP 40/281, m.167 (1330). A plaintiff in KB 27/181, m.6d, claimed exile of burghers as well as villeins, but lost: CP 40/425, m.447 (1366).

6 CP 40/70, m.65d (1288) (judgment for the plaintiff in respect of waste of men as well as things); CP 40/95, m.99d (1295) (names each exiled villein, with his or her value).

7 CP 40/141, m.112 (5 marks awarded for the waste made by allowing daughters of named villeins to marry named freemen).

8 It might be possible to gain some insight into this through pleas of naifty. I have nowhere seen it suggested that proper care of an estate demanded pursuit of fleeing peasants.

9 CP 40/164, m.136 (1307); Pas. 32 Edw. 1 (*RS* 1864), 112-4.

they had a right to refuse to pay heavy tallage, nevertheless from the point of view of the law they were listed along with chattels. Actions could be brought for the asportation of manorial denizens as for chattels.[1] An action of trespass charging the asportation of chattels was used when a whole family of villeins was carried off:[2] perhaps the family had been coerced to move to another manor, but the record does not explain the circumstances. In a Middlesex case the jury awarded damages of 30s. for taking a villein (who was named) and three cows, but no distinction was made between man and beast.[3] This case also suggests that in certain conditions, such as in a loss because of improper fencing, waste could be claimed for farm animals.

Procedure in waste began with the purchase of the writ and, as the Bench writ-files show, the taking of security from the plaintiff.[4] Some cases ran the whole gamut of summons, attachment, distraint and *habeas corpus* to compel the defendant to appear, before the order was made to the sheriff to view the property claimed as wasted and to give judgment in default of the defendant's appearance.[5] Other cases followed the formula outlined in Westminster II, that if the defendant did not appear after the distress the sheriff was to go himself with a jury of twelve to view the place wasted; after the inquest was returned, the court could proceed to judgment.[6] In a number of cases the authority of the statute is specifically claimed for expediting the view.[7] There are many examples of cases of waste brought to a rapid conclusion with an award to the plaintiff when the defendant defaulted,[8] while others followed the long process involved in compelling the defendant to answer the complainant. The use of the longer procedure on occasion is understandable, as can be seen in three cases where the

1 KB 26/141, m.2d.

2 KB 27/395, m.81 (1359).

3 CP 40/145, m.309 (1303).

4 E.g. CP 52/1, Pas. 6 Edw. 1 (Essex), Hil. 17 Edw. 1 (Norf), Hil. 19 Edw. 1 (Bucks), Pas. 27 Edw. 1 (Wilts, Dev, Northants). In a Northampton waste in wardship case, in the last file, pledges are given for both parties and there is an interesting annotation regarding the clerical plaintiff and his pledges.

5 For all stages save judgment, see CP 52/1, Pas. 6 Edw. 1 (Oxon); CP 40/58, m.21d (1285); CP 40/215, m.200 (1316). For distraint, mainprise, and then the view, see CP 40/154, m.42 (1305).

6 1 *SR* 81, c.14.

7 CP 40/145, m.46 (1305); CP 40/153, mm.93, 287 (1305); CP 52/1, Trin. 27 Edw. 1 (Glos); and many of the cases in the next note.

8 CP 40/121, m.152 (1297); CP 40/138, m.35d (1301); CP 40/148, m.73d (1303); CP 40/154, m.41 (1305); CP 40/193, m.86 (1311); CP 40/220, m.329 (1317); CP 40/328, mm.21d, 123 (1341); CP 40/391, m.178d (1357); CP 40/392, mm.194d, 449d (1357); CP 40/398, m.203d (1359).

defendants had nothing to distrain in the county.[1] Where possible, distraint and other modes of placing the defendant's valuables within the jurisdiction of the court facilitated the payment of damages to a successful complainant: as in a Hereford case where the plea roll states that the goods and chattels of the defendant were turned over to the plaintiff as recompense for the waste made; or in the writ-files, where there are endorsements to the like effect.[2]

Cases settled by the defendant's default are naturally less interesting than those in which the defendant appeared, especially if the defendant went on to offer an explanation of his deeds.[3] Defendants who answered the summons, or one of its re-issues, would appear in person or by attorney and could choose a variety of answers. The most obvious response was a simple denial, and a request for a jury to decide the matter.[4] The many instances in which the defendant's explanations were given,[5] especially when combined with a result, are more useful in attempting to define actionable waste and to understand the methods of compensation. Some defendants made different denials to the different kinds of waste alleged, all of these denials aiming, of course, to prove that they were 'not culpable'. A common defence was that the estate was in ruinous condition when received; this would explain some delapidation and justify the cutting of trees 'to emend and ameliorate' the estate.[6] Because tenants were entitled by custom, which varied in different parts of the country, to the use of a certain amount of wood, thorns and brush for repair and firewood, the jury often had to decide whether the defendant had exceeded such reasonable estovers.[7] This must have been difficult: many of these

---

1 JUST 1/382, m.86 (1312-3); CP 52/1, Hil. 17 Edw. 1 (Midd), Pas. 27 Edw. 1 (Essex).

2 CP 40/16, m.1 (1276); CP 52/1, Trin. 19 Edw. 1 (Beds).

3 CP 40/293, m.80 (1333) (split verdict, by which defendant found guilty of waste in some tenements and not in others); CP 40/132, m.51d (1300) (absent defendant went *sine die* and plaintiff amerced for false claim as to the waste).

4 Successful defendants: KB 26/171, m.40 (1261); CP 40/283, mm.135, 142 (1330); CP 40/286, m.179 (1356). Unsuccessful: CP 40/59, m.36d (1288); JUST 1/406, m.66d (1291-2); CP 40/184, m.297 (1311); JUST 1/382, m.44d (1312-3); CP 40/220, m.252d (1317); CP 40/253, m.184 (1324); CP 40/277, m.42. No result: CP 40/122, m.7d (1298).

5 JUST 1/408, m.66 (1291-2); CP 40/220, m.236 (1317); CP 40/281, m.64d (1330); CP 40/302, m.136 (1335). The last three defendants all claimed trees were cut for repair and improvement.

6 CP 40/181, m.99d (1310); KB 27/395, m.18 (1359).

7 CP 40/26, m.25d, continued in CP 40/27, m.31d (reasonable estovers claimed); CP 40/37, m.249 (1290); CP 40/39, m.22 (1281); CP 40/181, m.99d (estate claimed to be in ruins); KB 27/395, m.18 (defendant claims to have needed more to sustain and mend the estate).

cases, in which defendants pleaded that they had taken no more than reasonable estovers, ended in concords.[1] It was, however, waste to exceed reasonable estovers, and defendants were punished for it.[2]

Again and again inquests would say that such an item was wasted by 'defective sustenance'.[3] Failure to repair constituted actionable waste. Usually the tearing down of something old to replace it with something new was not termed waste, nor was cutting trees called waste if 'improvement' resulted, such as new houses or gates.[4] The views examined are never to the effect that, for instance, £10 worth of timber was misused in building a £5 shed; nor do they comment on appropriateness of style. Defendants were not generally held responsible for such accidental disasters as inundation by the sea, unless they were responsible for failure to repair the sea-walls.[5] A number of defendants in a fourteenth-century case sought to excuse damage on the grounds of earthquake.[6] Accidental fires, as Bracton had observed, were not waste unless unusual carelessness was involved. Manuals such as that of Walter of Henley abound in suggestions for caution with the use of candles in out-buildings and so forth,[7] though we do not know whether jurors applied these sound principles to their determinations. The year books contain many arguments to the effect that fire not caused by bad custody was not waste.[8] A Surrey defendant, a tenant for years,

1 JUST 1/560, mm.11-12 (1249-50); KB 26/165, m.26 (1260); CP 40/69, m.39d. The latter case has an interesting fire, discussed below.

2 As in CP 40/121, m.23 (1297) (dowager claimed to have taken only reasonable estovers; but waste found in many buildings, and she had exceeded reasonable estovers in woods in the amount named; damages and recovery for the plaintiff).

3 CP 40/32, m.52 (1280) (40s. damages for waste in a chamber and a cow-shed 'which deteriorated through want of sustenance'); CP 40/145, mm.309, 360 (1303); CP 40/152, m.11d (1304).

4 CP 40/145, m.374 (1303) (all manner of detail regarding repairs and improvements in such buildings as stables and the building of new houses, one of which was termed 'sumptuous'; no damages assigned for items damaged by fire); CP 40/27, m.110d (defendant claims to have improved state of mill; no result recorded).

5 Mich. 31 Edw. 1 (RS, 1863), 480-1 (if post and timbers carried away by flooding, the defendant shall not answer for waste). See S.F.C. Milsom, 'Trespass from Henry III to Edward III', 74 LQR (1958), 213-5, 586-7. In CP 40/37, m.201, the defendant says houses were burned but he made no waste or sale; there is no result.

6 In CP 40/446, m.59, the defendant pleads that the damage was caused 'per tempestatem terremotus', and the plaintiff replies that the waste was committed long before the earthquake. Similar cases appear in CP 40/474, m.382; CP 40/480, m.218. I am grateful to Professor Morris Arnold for these references, which come from rolls just later than those which I have examined.

7 D. Oschinsky, Walter of Henley (Oxford, 1971).

8 E.g. 20 Edw. 1 (RS, 1866), 28-31; Mich. 9 Edw. 2 (45 SS, 1929), 76-8, pl. 32.

pleaded among other things that when the 'aula et camera' burned, he lost goods of his own worth 100 marks: the case ended by a concord, whereby the defendant returned the estate in question to the prior and the defendant received 100 marks to be paid in instalments over the next few years.[1] This is a curious ending, because if the fire had been the tenant's fault (which was not established) the fact of his own losses was no excuse; but compromises reflect the wishes of the parties.

A few of the defendants in waste cases claimed that the damage had been done while they were disseised.[2] Some of the cases found ended in judgment, but presumably the disseisees would have been punished, for they could in turn sue their disseisor. Novel disseisin gave damages for waste committed, and there are examples of such cases.[3] Some defendants sought to fix the blame for the waste on their tenants by demise. Two fourteenth-century cases indicate that responsibility was placed upon the lessor:[4] who could, of course, sue the real waster by a writ of waste. In some cases in which defendants pleaded a demise, the jury found for the defendants, but the verdicts may merely have been to the effect that no waste had been made:[5] the enrolled verdicts do not give particulars. In the settlement of many common-law actions in the fourteenth century there seems to be a variance between the issue raised in pleading and the issue which the verdict shows to have been put to the jury.

In the fourteenth century, recourse to concords seems to be much less than in the preceding century; yet sometimes it was still used, so that one finds the terms of a concord instead of a judgment.[6] But, like other actions, pleas of waste could fail because of non-prosecution,[7] or

1 CP 40/69, m.39d (1287) (more is perhaps involved here than a compromise in a waste case).

2 CP 40/61, m.24 (1286) (plaintiff replied that waste made during the term and not while defendant was disseised; no result found).

3 D.W. Sutherland, *The Assize of Novel Disseisin* (Oxford, 1973), 86, 97, 119 (attempt to halt waste by what becomes a disseisin). The use of self-help in waste was rare. Britton writes about waste in the context of novel disseisin: *Britton*, ed. F.M. Nichols (Oxford, 1865), ii, 22. For waste claimed in novel disseisin, see e.g. KB 26/141, m.6 (1250) (jury found for the defendant).

4 CP 40/371, m.136 (1332) (damages and recovery against a dowager, who never appeared, for waste in various tenements which she had demised to various named millers); CP 40/391, m.180d (1357).

5 CP 40/316, m.201 (1338); CP 40/340, m.62 (1344). No result known: CP 40/228, m.17 (1319); CP 40/240, m.292d (1321); CP 40/318, m.242d (1339).

6 *Staffordshire Record Society*, xiii, 55 and note; Hil. 7 Edw. 2 (39 *SS*, 1922), 36-43, pl. 6. For 13th-century concords, see above, p. 189, n. 1.

7 E.g. JUST 1/483, m.22d (1271-2) (particularly unfortunate, as it contains an interesting reference to prohibition); CP 40/417, m.53 (1364).

could be settled on the basis of some issue other than whether or not the defendant had committed certain kinds of waste: so that what might have been interesting judgments in waste would not be given. A defendant could succeed in a claim that the tenure alleged in the writ was mistakenly described; for example, a woman described as a dowager successfully claimed to have been a tenant by demise,[1] and in a plea of wardship the defendant claimed to hold nothing in wardship.[2] Such objections were sometimes overlooked: as when defendants claimed to have been tenants at will, not tenants by demise, and yet waste in fish-ponds was found; damages were awarded, but no recovery was ordered, perhaps because none was needed to oust tenants at will.[3] If it could be proved that because of his bastardy a plaintiff was not entitled to bring a suit as heir, the defendant would go quit.[4] A defendant was successful when the jury supported his claim that he had received permission to cut the trees and also when he claimed to have received a grant without impeachment of waste.[5] If a plaintiff had already lost a previous suit, the defendant would be quit, because a second trial of the same facts was not permitted.[6] On the other hand, some of the explanations proffered by defendants might be rejected by the jury, as in a Suffolk case where the defendants denied liability for waste because they were minors.[7] There are occasions, with minors who had lost their suits and were in mercy for false claim, where the roll would note that nothing had yet been detained since the plaintiffs were within age.[8]

Although a few requests for wager of law have been noted from the

---

1 CP 40/164, m.142 (1307); CP 40/281, m.167 (1330); CP 40/294, m.130 (1333); CP 40/371, m.68 (1332) (no result noted; but question finally put to jury after much interlining).

2 JUST 1/932, m.2 (1287-8) (waste in wardship; plaintiff lost by reason of tenurial considerations); JUST 1/932, m.2 (1287-8); JUST 1/487, m.61d (1280-1); CP 40/324, m.547 (1340) (land claimed as dower, not in wardship); CP 40/233, m.150 (land claimed as dower, not leased for years).

3 CP 40/27, m.159 (1278); CP 40/28, m.21 (1279) (same plaintiffs against different defendants; same result, and no order to recover the land).

4 CP 40/335, m.39 (1320).

5 CP 40/281, m.124 (1330). Other examples: CP 40/198, m.116d (1313); CP 40/352, mm.140d, 332d (1347); Pas. 13 Edw. 3 (RS, 1885), 166-9, pl. 1. The defendant in CP 40/148, m.22d, makes reference to a quit-claim from the plaintiff for waste made and says he made no waste since the quit-claim; he goes *sine die.*

6 CP 40/194, m.22 (1312); CP 40/281, m.124 (1330).

7 CP 40/138, m.149 (1301) (damages assigned).

8 CP 40/103, m.56 (1294); JUST 1/1046, m.35 (1250-2); JUST 1/1089, m.25d (1291-2).

early thirteenth century, and even one from the mid-fourteenth century,[1] the action of waste turned upon the extensive use of the jury. Often it took not just one jury, but several, to determine what waste had been made. The Bench writ-files for Easter term 1287 contain a writ to the sheriff of Nottingham and Derby to go with a jury of twelve men to the four manors held by one Avelina as her dower. A view from each of the manors is attached to the writ; the jurors named in each of these panels are different for each manor.[2] Avelina had made some waste in each manor, but another step was needed to make an 'extent' of those tenements to decide which parts should be returned to the successful plaintiff. The four juries, which had been called to decide the waste in the case, assigned the amount for each kind of waste they had found — the normal procedure for juries in waste cases.[3] On occasion, however, it was necessary to call another jury to say just how much damage was caused by, say, the destruction of three cottages and forty trees and the exile of one villein.[4] The working out of the total sum, then multiplying it by three according to the Statute of Gloucester, often required separate sheets and marginal enumeration.[5]

The discrimination of medieval juries in settling complex pleas, based upon their knowledge of local custom and the particular facts in issue, deserves some comment. The efficacy of the common-law remedy for waste depended upon the care they took in their deliberations. The process was expeditious, which meant that cases ended in time to have the *postea* clauses inserted in their proper place in the plea-roll entry, so that 'Dampna' is splashed down the left side of the membrane a gratifying number of times. The jury seemed able to decide not only that an estate sustained £50 damage by a certain kind of ill-usage, but also to determine that certain parts of the estate were wasted before the defendant entered and other things were wasted afterwards — the defendant, of course, being liable only for the damage done during his tenure.[6] The procedure was flexible enough to permit a last-minute

---

1 CP 40/335, m.39 (1343): This eventually goes to a jury after the swearing of many oaths; perhaps the jury is to assess damages, but this is unclear. See also notes 2 and 3 on p. 192, above.

2 CP 52/1, Pas. 12 Edw. 1 (Notts and Derb).

3 Ibid.

4 Examples of second juries to assess damages: CP 40/31, m.[98] (1279); JUST 1/1090, m.14d (1292-3); CP 40/154, m.41 (1305).

5 CP 40/125, m.148d (1298) (marginal calculations with totals); CP 52/1, 10 Edw. 1 (Kent) (the total of £123. 6s. 8d. does not seem correct, but it is very difficult to read).

6 CP 52/1, Hil. 15 Edw. 1 (Beds): in a copy of the proceedings before the justices itinerant, in addition to determining what damage was made both before and

adjustment of the findings of the jury. After the jury in a case of Trinity term 1301 had found waste and assigned damages, and an extent had been made of lands to be recovered by the plaintiff, the record notes that the inquisition declared that in place of the cow-shed alleged to have been wasted the defendant had built a new and better one, so that it should not be counted as waste; and the houses in the same messuage were not wasted. A day was set for a hearing in Michaelmas term.[1] It was a complicated process; the record does not say who noted the variance between the view and the extent. An Essex case for waste in gardens, fish-ponds and woods ended with a final note of damages for the additional waste made while the plea was pending, thereby seemingly saving the litigants the trouble of a separate suit for this estrepement.[2]

The amount of damages claimed and the amount which the jury awarded were usually at variance. Plaintiffs did not have to put a price-tag on each item, and many gave a total amount claimed as damages.[3] This portion of the suit often drops out of the plea-roll entry before the conclusion of the case, so that one has to look back to compare the amount demanded with the amount awarded. Over-claims were common, and were not penalised.[4] If, however, waste was claimed in a brew-house and stables, but was found in only one of them, the plaintiff was amerced for his false claim regarding the other. Such 'split verdicts' are recorded in many cases where waste was found in some parts of the estate but not in others.[5] This affected the recovery

after the demise, the jury gave the defendants credit for improvements and repairs to offset the damages.

1 CP 40/139, m.46d (1301).

2 CP 40/141, m.302 (1302). This case gives much detail as to the kinds of fish (pickerel, perch, roach and bream) wasted in destroying a stew ('lupus aquaticus'). A separate suit for estrepement could have been brought in accordance with the Statute of Gloucester (1278), c.13 (1 SR 50), which provided a remedy for waste committed while a suit was pending.

3 CP 40/59, m.36d (100s. claimed; triple damages of 30 marks awarded); CP 40/125, m.148d (total of £40 claimed; damages £6. 17s. 6d. multiplied by three); CP 40/37, m.200 (all items claimed given a value); CP 40/95, m.77 (1292) (long, detailed claim, with villeins exiled in a variety of ways, to a total amount of £100); CP 40/122, m.7d (1298) (before the total of £10 damages the items are grouped together and priced: e.g. an oven and a hall worth 6 marks).

4 E.g. CP 40/28, m.21 (1279) (£100 claimed, 100s. awarded: too early to be trebled under the statute); CP 40/70, m.65d (1288) (£70 claimed, damages of 120s. multiplied by three); CP 40/125, m.148d (1298) (£40 claimed, damages of £6. 17s. 6d. multiplied by three); CP 40/139, m.46d (£100 claimed, with details of each item wasted and the individual amounts, and an annotation that one cow-shed had been replaced).

5 E.g. CP 40/69, m.82 (1287); CP 40/95, m.33 (1292); CP 40/253, mm.191, 357 (1324); CP 40/281, m.161d (1330); CP 40/293, m.80 (1333); CP 40/308, m.491d (1336); CP 40/340, m.472 (1344); CP 40/352, m.385d (1347); CP 40/371, m.136 (1352); CP 40/379, m.283d (1354); CP 40/392, m.344d (1357); CP 40/

of property as well as damages, since those parts of the estate in which no waste was found remained in the defendant's hands.

The estates under consideration in pleas of waste appear to have been considered separable not merely into manors but further into principal and secondary messuages and other tenements. Waste committed in one manor would not cause the forfeiture of other manors held from the plaintiff by the same wasting tenant; waste in a secondary messuage would not cause the forfeiture of the principal messuage; waste in one house would not cause the forfeiture of others; and so on. The year books are filled with discussions about whether waste in a hedge would cause the forfeiture of a messuage: but, of course, it would not.[1] Medieval law was reluctant to shirk the complex and difficult question of which portions of the property should be recovered, by making waste merely a suit to recover money.

The plea rolls are not consistent in the way they record the findings of juries. Some entries contain an itemized list of waste made in trees, houses, and so forth, with an amount for each category, as though copied directly and completely from the inquest which the sheriff had returned.[2] Other entries give only the total amount of damages awarded. An entry 'taxed at triple' meant that the actual amount of the damages had been multiplied by three to give the amount written on the roll. Many entries are heavily abbreviated.[3] But the Bench writ-files contain more information than the original inquisitions, some showing abstracts with the sums totted up.[4]

The successful plaintiff usually received his damages from the sale of the defendant's chattels.[5] Sometimes *postea* clauses recorded the

398, m.144d (1359); CP 40/425, m.144 (1366).

1 E.g. Mich. 5 Edw. 2 (63 *SS*, 1944), 247, pl. 52, and 274, pl. 96 (note by Bereford C.J.); Pas. 8 Edw. 2 (41 *SS*, 1924), 89, pl. 2; Mich. 9 Edw. 2 (45 *SS*, 1929), 76-8, pl.32; Mich. 10 Edw. 2 (52 *SS*, 1934), 158, pl.65-7.

2 E.g. JUST 1/922, m.26 (1278-9); CP 40/95, m.95 (1292); CP 40/139, m.152 (1301); CP 40/141, m.112 (1302), CP 40/153, mm.180d, 392d (1305); CP 40/198, m.116d (1313); CP 40/187, m.133 (1311) (with amount for each in margin).

3 They state the total taxed at triple and the amount: JUST 1/36, m.11 (1278-9); CP 40/183, mm.168, 405d (1310); CP 40/187, m.90 (1311); CP 40/220, m.381 (1317); CP 40/253, m.379d (1324); CP 40/281, m.169 (1330); CP 40/283, m.114d (1330); CP 40/316, m.257 (1338); CP 40/391, m.283 (1357).

4 E.g. CP 52/1, Trin. 10 Edw. 1 (Kent) (summary sheet shaped like a writ, referring to the statute); CP 52/1, Trin. 27 Edw. 1 (Glos, Kent); CP 40/125, m.148 (1298) (multiplication in the margin); JUST 1/922, m.26 (1278-9).

5 CP 40/138, m.149 (1301) (the roll notes that those dower lands which had been wasted have been received by the plaintiff, together with the triple

complaint that the victor had not received his goods.[1] Most of these references disclose that damages were often received in kind. This conversion of cash damages to recovery in kind was presumably by agreement. Generally, the defendant's chattels were sold to raise the cash. Some rolls note that the defendant came into court and paid the damages, presumably in full,[2] or that so much was paid and that such an amount was still owing.[3] But a few entries simply noted that the defendant had not yet made satisfaction for the damages,[4] while others ordered a *scire facias* to determine why the damages had not been received.[5] One defaulting defendant, against whom waste was found in a term of years, proved to be a cleric not holding a lay fee; the Bishop of Bath and Wells was therefore obliged to give his licence for the cleric's goods and chattels to be distrained to raise the damages.[6] The Bishop of Durham in 1329 received a judgment in waste, in respect of land demised for a term of years, against the Perucci of Florence, which entitled the bishop to the recovery of the land wasted and £461. 6s; the *postea* records an imparlance between the attorneys.[7]

The success of common-law justice depended in part on distraining enough chattels and lands to compensate a successful plaintiff, even where the defendant defaulted. The goods and chattels might not be sufficient, however, to cover the damages awarded to the plaintiff. In one case a *fieri facias* was issued to the sheriff so that a portion of the lands could be used to raise the amount.[8] After Westminster II,[9] the same result could be achieved by granting a writ of *elegit*, which put the successful plaintiff in possession of a portion of the defendant's

---

damages); CP 40/302, m.107d (1335); CP 40/335, m.72d (1343) (orders the goods and chattels to be used); CP 40/398, m.94d (1359) (records that the chattels were turned over to the defendant).

1 E.g. CP 40/194, m.12 (1312); CP 40/308, m.161 (1336).

2 JUST 1/167, m.45 (1330-1).

3 CP 40/145, m.309 (1303): here too the arithmetic seems wrong, and the final amount said to be outstanding reflects an adjustment.

4 E.g. JUST 1/167, m.45 (1330-1); CP 40/283, mm.193, 301d (1330); CP 40/308, m.491d (1336).

5 CP 40/33, m.65d (1280); CP 40/198, m.116 (1313) (*fieri facias*).

6 JUST 1/382, m.86 (1312-3) (clerical defendants in the jurisdiction of Coventry and Lichfield); CP 52/1, Mich. 27 & 28 Edw. 1 (*mandamus* concerning the goods of clerics, to pay the triple damages). In CP 52/1, Hil. 17 Edw. 1 (Oxon), lands were in the Honour of Wallingford.

7 CP 40/278, m.167d (1329).

8 CP 40/135, m.157d (1300); CP 40/152, m.9d (1304).

9 1 *SR* 82. See T.F.T. Plucknett, *Concise History of the Common Law* (5th ed., London, 1956), 390-1, 608-9. See also Hil. 17 Edw. 3 (*RS*, 1901), 84-5 (defendant has nothing).

lands.¹ An award of damages did not always mean immediate recompense, but the law did provide successive stages in pursuit of this end.

The findings of the jury in waste, as in other actions, could subsequently be questioned. Among the grounds were technical defects in the return of the enquiry by the sheriff. A year-book case of 1307 is illuminating here. The fact that the sheriff was not personally present at the inquest was overlooked by the unexpected phrase 'we forgive you that'; but the return was defective in saying 'cut turf' when it meant 'waste in woods' and 'turf houses'. Moreover, the return said 'fifty turves' in one place, and 'ten oaks' in another. A new inquest was ordered.² In a waste case in the Court of Common Pleas in 1293 the *postea* records that the inquisition was defective because the sheriff did not go in his own person: he was again ordered to do it, and the findings were entered on the roll.³ Less technical but more serious were allegations that a jury was biased in favour of the plaintiff. In a year-book case it was charged that no notice had been given of the inquest, that the sheriff was an ally of the plaintiff, and that one of the plaintiff's men was on the jury, which in any event had failed to hold the inquest at the correct place: the verdict of the sheriff's inquest, finding waste, was accepted and the defendant was told he could sue a writ of deceit against the sheriff; but the outcome is not known.⁴ The Bench writ-files contain an example of the empanelling of fifty-six jurors (each named, with two pledges) to determine the matter of attaint in a case of waste, but again the result is not known.⁵

The documents do not clarify every question in the history of the action of waste. One must also recognise that certain aspects of the law of waste were still in an uncertain condition in the fourteenth century. What is especially striking is the role of the jury. The judge had an important part to play in the joining of issue, and in submitting

---

1 CP 40/148, m.153d (1303) (makes specific references to the statute concerning *elegit*); KB 27/126, m.29 (1291); CP 40/193, m.8d (1311); CP 40/316, m.236 (1338); CP 40/340, m.231 (1344). The last two are instances in which wasted tenements had been recovered, but *elegit* was required for the satisfaction of damages. In CP 40/283, m.95 (1330); CP 40/330, m.327 (1342); and CP 40/371, m.78 (1352), there is a *scire facias*, seemingly to find out why the *elegit* did not satisfy the plaintiff. See also CP 40/425, m.144.

2 Trin. 35 Edw. 1 (*RS*, 1879), 542-3 (new inquest ordered). See also Pas. 12 Edw. 2 (81 *SS*, 1964), 21, pl. 35.

3 CP 40/102, m.175d.

4 Hil. 33 Edw. 1 (*RS*, 1864), 356-9.

5 CP 52/1, Pas. 27 Edw. 1 (Lincs) (entry in two parts: first the order for the jury, and second the jurors' names and their mainpernors).

answerable questions to the jury of neighbours for their verdict, but seems to have played little or no part in giving judgment. When the inquests on the writs are compared with the 'judgment' enrolled in the plea rolls, one usually finds that the jury's verdict has been merely copied onto the roll. It is a matter of comment in the plea rolls when there is a variance between the roll and the inquest. It is the activity of the juries which made the action of waste efficient. Juries on the whole appear to have had a grasp of the value of depredations and an ability, based on their personal knowledge, to locate the blame for them. This rested in part on their fixing the time when the waste had been made — for instance, the mill was in ruins before the ward's father died, or it worked well until the land was let by the doweress to the tenant for years. If this suggests more of fact-finding than of law-finding, it was done within the framework of customary rules concerning waste.

INDEX

208
Atts, John, labourer *or* ostler, 63
audience, episcopal court of, 90, 140-9; appellate causes, 142, 146-7; correction causes, 141, 144-5; instance causes, 142, 145; sessions outside diocese, 148
Avelina . . . , her dower, 201

Bacon, Sir Francis, Viscount St Alban's, 45, 46
Bacon family, 70
Baga *see under* King's Bench (files)
bail (in civil actions), 104, 110-1; bail pieces, 110
Ballia Communia files *see under* King's Bench (files)
Balsall (Temple), Warw, preceptor of, 34 n.7
Bangor, diocese, 90
Bankes, John, Att.-Gen., 169, 181
bar: size of (17th cent.), 25-6; practice in country, 26-7; *see also* counsel; serjeants at law
Bard, Thomas, of Gray's Inn, 15
Barkway, Herts, 63
Barlee, William, attorney, 58
Barnes, William, labourer *or* yeoman, 62
Barnwell, Cambs, prior of, 35 n.4
Barnwell, Thomas, filazer, 136
barristers *see* bar; counsel
Basoche, William de la, 30
Bastard, William, filazer, 137
bastardy, plea of, 200
Bath and Wells, bishop of, 204
Bawtree, Leonard, serjeant at law, 26
Bedford, Thomas, filazer, 137
Bedfordshire, filazers for, 137
Beell, John, filazer, 134
Bench *see* Common Pleas
Bench, King's, *see* King's Bench
benefices, 90, 146; *see also* quare impedit; tithes
Benn, Sir Anthony, recorder of London, 57
Bennington, Herts, 62
Berkeley, George, Lord Berkeley, 50, 51
Berkshire, filazers for, 136-7
Best, Thomas, of Inner Temple, 15
Beston, Thomas, filazer, 135
Betley, William, filazer, 137
Beverley, Yorks, commissary court of Salisbury at, 148
Bicknoll, Oxon, 15
bill procedure *see under* King's Bench

Jarrett *see* Gerrard
Jebbe, John, filazer, 135
Jenkins, David, barrister, 26
Jenkinson, Sir Hilary, 116
John, king of England, 31
John XXII, pope, 148
Jones, Mr ... (1584), 44 n.2
Jonson, Ben, 56
judges: autograph signatures, 111; chambers practice, 109; clemency, 75-6; influence on jury, 72, 74, 75-6, 206; order drawing of indictment, 68-9
judgment by default, 196-7
judgments, entries of: low proportion in rolls, 87
jury, grand, 71-2, 153
jury in civil cases: charged with perjury, 20 n.4; role in actions of waste, 192, 201-6; *see also* attaint; embracery; verdict
jury in criminal cases: difficulty of procuring, 78; influence of trial judge, 72, 74, 75-6; mitigation of harshness of penal system, 71-3; *see also* embracery; verdict
justices of peace: absenteeism at assizes, 70-1, 78; role as prosecutors, 69-70

Keeler, Alice, burglar, 75
keepers of peace, files of, 99
Kemp, George, secondary of K.B., 127 n.1
Kenilworth, Warw, prior of, 30
Kent, filazers for, 134
Keswick, Cumb, 169
king, litigation by, 4, 9, 84-6, 95
King's Bench, court of:
  actions in, 4, 12, 23 n.1
  attorneys become clerks of chief clerk, 55
  bill procedure, 4-5, 100, 105-10
  business, 43, 86-8
  chief clerks: attorneys for city of London, 112; gain business from filazers, 4-5, 102, 107, 110, 131-2; list, 131-3
  chief justices *see* Billyng; Coke; Crewe; Fortescue; Hale; Hyde; Markham; Popham; Shareshill
  clerks of crown, 132
  crown business, 98-100, 103, 126-7
  custos brevium, 130, 131
  error from Ireland, 191
  filazers: as attorneys, 129; list, 133-9; names in records, 102, 106, 110, 128-9; number, 102, 129, 130-1; records of appointment,

substitution, alienation by, 29
Suffolk, filazers for, 133
Surrey, filazers for, 130, 134-5
Sussex, filazers for, 130, 134-5
Sutton, John, common informer, 14 n.1
Sutton, Oliver, bishop of Lincoln, 147, 149
Swinfield, Richard de, bishop of Hereford, 149
Swyllyngton, . . . , filazer, 137
Swyneford, Elizabeth, 92-3
Symcott, George, filazer, 134

tallage, excessive, 195
Tarent, John, 143
Taughton, Joan, 17
Tawton, Edward, 17
Templars, Order of: master, 35 n.4, 36
Temple Balsall *see* Balsall
tenant at will, 200
tenant for years, waste by, 186, 188-9
testaments, 88, 90; *see also* probate
Thames, river, 68
Thaxted, Essex, 67
Thelwall, Sir Euble, counsel, 180
Thelwall, [? Simon] , master in chancery, 19 n.1
Thornton, Thomas, bencher of Lincoln's Inn, 170, 172, 173, 174, 182, 183
Thurkleby, Roger de, justice, 151, 153
Thwaytes, Thomas, filazer, 133, 134
tithes, 18, 23 n.1, 88, 90, 144, 146
Tofft, Henry, promoter, 85
topographical analysis of litigation, 10-11
Topsall, William, 63
Totnes, Dev, borough, 168, 179
Towcester, Northants, 62
Townshend, . . . , counsel, 180 *bis*
tradesmen as litigants, 47
trailbaston proceedings, 103, 105, 114
trees, waste in, 194, 195
trespass, waste treated as, 192
trespass, actions of: decline, 50-1; for criminal offences, 87; for ravishment, 159; for taking villeins, 196; numerous in K.B., 86
triple damages *see* damages
Trye, John, filazer, 97 n.1, 102, 131-2
Turge, . . . , filazer, 136